Imagining the Unimaginable

Imagining the Unimaginable

Speculative Fiction and the Holocaust

Glyn Morgan

BLOOMSBURY ACADEMIC
NEW YORK • LONDON • OXFORD • NEW DELHI • SYDNEY

BLOOMSBURY ACADEMIC
Bloomsbury Publishing Inc
1385 Broadway, New York, NY 10018, USA
50 Bedford Square, London, WC1B 3DP, UK
29 Earlsfort Terrace, Dublin 2, Ireland

BLOOMSBURY, BLOOMSBURY ACADEMIC and the Diana logo
are trademarks of Bloomsbury Publishing Plc

First published in the United States of America 2020
This paperback edition published in 2021

Copyright © Glyn Morgan, 2020

Cover design by Eleanor Rose | Cover images © Alamy

All rights reserved. No part of this publication may be reproduced or
transmitted in any form or by any means, electronic or mechanical,
including photocopying, recording, or any information storage or retrieval
system, without prior permission in writing from the publishers.

Bloomsbury Publishing Inc does not have any control over, or responsibility for,
any third-party websites referred to or in this book. All internet addresses given
in this book were correct at the time of going to press. The author and publisher regret
any inconvenience caused if addresses have changed or sites have ceased to exist,
but can accept no responsibility for any such changes.

Library of Congress Cataloging-in-Publication Data
Names: Morgan, Glyn, author.
Title: Imagining the unimaginable: speculative fiction and the Holocaust /
Glyn Morgan.
Description: New York: Bloomsbury Academic, 2020. | Includes
bibliographical references and index.
Identifiers: LCCN 2019026048 (print) | LCCN 2019026049 (ebook) |
ISBN 9781501350542 (hardback) | ISBN 9781501350559 (eBook) |
ISBN 9781501350566 (ePDF)
Subjects: LCSH: Holocaust, Jewish (1939–1945), in literature. |
Speculative fiction, American–20th century–History and criticism. |
Speculative fiction, English–20th century–History and criticism. |
Speculative fiction, American–21st century–History and criticism. |
Speculative fiction, English–21st century–History and criticism.
Classification: LCC PS374.H56 M67 2020 (print) | LCC PS374.H56 (ebook) |
DDC 813/.009358405318–dc23
LC record available at https://lccn.loc.gov/2019026048
LC ebook record available at https://lccn.loc.gov/2019026049

ISBN: HB: 978-1-5013-5054-2
PB: 978-1-5013-7315-2
ePDF: 978-1-5013-5056-6
eBook: 978-1-5013-5055-9

Typeset by Deanta Global Publishing Services, Chennai, India

To find out more about our authors and books visit www.bloomsbury.com
and sign up for our newsletters.

Dedicated to all victims of fascism

Contents

Acknowledgements	viii
Introduction: Fictionalizing the Holocaust	1
1 Precursors and Early Texts: *Swastika Night* (1937) and the Myth of Silence	19
2 Problematizing History: *The Man in the High Castle* (1962), *Fatherland* (1992) and *Making History* (1996)	41
3 The Damned and the Saved: *The Boys from Brazil* (1976), *The Portage to San Cristobal of A.H.* (1981), *Hope: A Tragedy* (2012) and *The Yiddish Policeman's Union* (2007)	71
4 Reimagining Horror: *The Plot Against America* (2004), *Farthing* (2006), *A Man Lies Dreaming* (2014) and *J* (2014)	101
Epilogue: Further Fabulation	147
Notes	163
Bibliography	195
Index	210

Acknowledgements

This book would not exist without the support and contributions of a wide range of people, more than I could possibly list. However I'd like to pay particular tribute and thanks to my peers, mentors and friends who have lifted my spirits when this project seemed endless and overwhelming, enriched my research through their recommendations and conversations, listened patiently to research papers and lectures and asked searching and thought-provoking questions, or have just been there for me when it all felt too hard.

So thank you to my University of Liverpool PhD cohort and departmental staff, the many *many* amazing new scholars who have come through CRSF over the years, the SFRA and BSFA communities, the LSRFC crew, my Prestatyn posse, my Hay Festival family, my Waterstones warriors, and the amazing team at the Science Museum who have been the most recent to welcome me so warmly. Thank you too to Katherine De Chant and everyone at Bloomsbury for supporting this book.

Huge thanks to Katherine Bishop, Mark Bould, Andrew M. Butler, Amy Butt, Amy and Tom Carroll, Molly Cobb, Cate Cowton, Nick Davis (we miss you Nick), Sarah Dillon, Robert Eaglestone, Neil Easterbrook, Caroline Edwards, Alice Felstead, Andrew Ferguson, Pawel Frelik, Leimar Garcia-Siino, Francis Gene-Rowe, Natalie Hannah, Emma Hayward, David Hering, Nicola Hill, Matthew Hitchcock, Stephen Hoggarth, Edward James, Sing Yun Lee, Roger Luckhurst, Anna McFarlane, David McWilliam, Farah Mendlesohn, Keren Omry, Danny O'Connor, Matthew O'Donoghue, Chris Pak, Grace Redstead, Deryn Rees-Jones, Adam Roberts, Bethan Roberts, Andy Sawyer, David Seed, Will Slocombe, Katie Stone, Rhys Williams, Peter Wright, Michelle Yost. There's part of you all in here somewhere, but it goes without saying any errors and shortcomings are mine alone.

I am grateful to the Wiener Library for the Study of the Holocaust and Genocide and the staff of Humanities 1 at the British Library for their extensive resources and for allowing me the regular use of their excellent reading rooms.

Finally of course, my family, in particular my parents Tony and Wendy Morgan whose support has been invaluable, and Anna Garnett who held me together even when I was extremely difficult.

Introduction: Fictionalizing the Holocaust

This book developed from my dual interests in representations of atrocity and trauma, and the manner in which alternate history manipulates historical narrative. In particular, over the course of my research it soon became evident that the critical dialogue surrounding the Holocaust, and its representation in fiction and art, provide a unique friction against the limitless possibilities of science fiction, fantasy and alternate history – genres which we can group, however loosely, under the label speculative fiction (SF). Yet the fictional texts which occupy this niche have received an uneven critical reception, with a few high-profile texts overshadowing what is in fact a broad selection dating back to the Second World War and continuing to attract new fictions today, ranging from science fiction pulp to literary fiction via bestselling popular thrillers.

The Holocaust occupies a unique position in Western cultural thought: there is no other event in the common history of humanity which is so heavily studied and written about and simultaneously coded as uninterpretable and unapproachable. Nonetheless, attempts to interpret, approach and understand are legion, not least through the medium of fiction. It could be that these texts persist as an artistic development of Freud's concept of *durcharbeiten*, or 'working through', an expression of Anglo-American readers' continued fascination with not only the Second World War and the Nazis, but with the greatest crime of that conflict.

Yet, the sheer weight of numbers removes none of the problems or controversies surrounding representation. Many representations of the Holocaust in fiction draw upon the implicit assumption that its traumatic experience cannot, and perhaps should not, be conveyed through art. This is a situation perhaps true of other traumatic and significant events both personal and societal, but in this as in many other things the Holocaust supersedes them. For example, in an influential and relatively early survey of the field of Holocaust literature, Alvin H. Rosenfeld wrote that the Holocaust 'occupies another sphere of study' compared to other topical literatures about 'the family, of slavery, of the environment, of World War I or World War II', continuing that Holocaust literature 'force[s] us to contemplate what may be fundamental changes in our modes of perception and expression'.[1]

The Holocaust has been consistently rendered as Other by scholars, as an earthquake, another planet, another universe, a rupture, a void, as being beyond language, or else having its own incomprehensible tongue. It should not, therefore, be surprising that such an event has attracted the attention of literature which routinely engages the Other, the uncanny, the grotesque and the inhuman. From Katharine Burdekin's prophetic *Swastika Night* (1937) to Lavie Tidhar's revolutionary *A Man Lies Dreaming* (2014), these non-realist responses to Nazi Germany's persecution and attempted extermination of the Jews are as continuous a presence as any realist fiction or historical essay. And yet, the Holocaust has also been said to be totally beyond art, to the extent that survivor Elie Wiesel wrote of the impossibility of the 'Holocaust as Literary Inspiration'.[2]

Often presented as an event on the cusp of modernity and postmodernity, the Holocaust has been suggested as being perhaps even the source of postmodernity through the responses of Emmanuel Levinas, Jacques Derrida, Walter Benjamin and others, leading to the opinion 'that postmodernism – understood as poststructuralism ... – begins with the Holocaust'.[3] Science fiction, and SF criticism, is often more interested in the ideas of postmodernity than in being demonstrably postmodern, preferring 'to pride itself on its status as a paraliterary phenomenon'.[4] While this is by no means an irrevocable truth, there is nonetheless a noteworthy disconnect between a representation of the Holocaust and an SF novel written in a style more akin to a nineteenth-century scientific romance than a late-twentieth-century piece of postmodern trauma fiction such as D. M. Thomas's *The White Hotel* (1981). Similarly, there is tension between the unapproachability of the Holocaust which, if it must be represented, seems to insist upon 'high art' (whatever that is), and the 'low' popular genres of SF.

These tensions between postmodern unrepresentability and popular fiction, traumatic caesura and SF storytelling, high subject and low art, are key discussion points which will be explored in the coming chapters. However, there is another motivation behind a study such as this. I am not Jewish nor, to the best of my knowledge, do I have a personal connection to anyone who was a victim of Nazi atrocity in any manner atypical for a British citizen of the time. However, as is reflected by many (though by no means all) of the authors in this book having a similar relationship to my own, the experience of the Holocaust has become entwined within the Anglo-American historical consciousness and in doing so has become a crucial thread in the history of humanity. Yet, those individuals who experienced the atrocity first-hand (whether survivor, participant, or even bystander) are now mostly gone, a fact made all the more obvious by the recent death of one of the most vocal survivors of the Holocaust, Elie Wiesel, in 2016.

We are entering a new phase in our relationship with the Holocaust, that of the post-survivor era. In this unprecedented time, it is crucial that we bolster all our resources and efforts to re-learning the horrors of war and genocide, the outcomes of intolerance, fascism and hatred. Now, perhaps more than any time since 1945, as the far-right makes inroads across the map of Western democracy, we need to look at the Holocaust, and atrocities like it, through every lens at our disposal, and analyse it with every tool in our kit. SF, and non-mimetic fiction more broadly, is one such tool, and an underutilized one with regard to Holocaust studies.

This book examines some of the key works of SF which try to represent the Holocaust and attempt to say something meaningful about the pre-eminent genocide in human history. To offer this study some cohesiveness, rather than select from across the full and diverse spectrum of SF, I have largely selected works which can be attributed to the two most frequently drawn upon sub-genres or movements in the field: the alternate history and the dystopia. Given the subject matter these are often one and the same, though some texts lean more strongly in one direction than the other.

In addition to being groupable by their genre, the texts I examine here also emerge from a common Anglo-American locus. Culturally, the Anglo-American experience of the Second World War, and especially the Holocaust, is different from that of other European nations that experienced either occupation or collaboration. One of the questions which drove Peter Novick to write his book *The Holocaust and Collective Memory* was the puzzle of 'why here?':

> The Holocaust took place thousands of miles from America's shores. Holocaust survivors or their descendants are a small fraction of 1 percent of the American population, and a small fraction of American Jewry as well. Only a handful of perpetrators managed to make it to the United States after the war. Americans, including many American Jews, were largely unaware of what we now call the Holocaust while it was going on; the nation was preoccupied with defeating the Axis. The United States was simply not connected to the Holocaust in the ways in which these other countries [Germany and Israel, particularly] are.[5]

Similarly, Caroline Sharples and Olaf Jensen raise a similar point with regard to the United Kingdom:

> One might immediately question why the Holocaust *should* become a central part of British memory culture. ... Mainland Britain, of course, was geographically removed from the killing sites, unencumbered by occupying Nazi forces and neither perpetrator nor collaborator in the crimes of the Third Reich. As a result, the nation has not had to endure the same painful, soul-searching questions as Germany, Austria or the former occupied territories. In many ways the Holocaust was, and remains, a distant event for the British population.[6]

Nonetheless Sharples and Jensen and Novick present the truth that despite this dislocation of geography, experience and culture, the Holocaust *has* become a prominent part of Anglo-American cultural identity. Thus, the writers I have called upon in this book are writing from a culturally unique position, both disconnected and yet also connected; voyeurs to a genocide which happened in a distant land. Some of these writers have a more visceral connection, they are the children or grandchildren of those affected by the Holocaust, but the narratives which they have produced are nonetheless tempered by, and marketed to, a culture which has a very different relationship to the Holocaust than any other in Europe.[7]

Fictionalizing the Holocaust

The Holocaust, albeit by other names, has been a subject of literary exploration even before Germany invaded Poland in 1939. Yet, despite a long chronology of texts, and a selection of authors who encompass the geography of the Western world, many critics hesitate to define exactly what is meant by Holocaust literature. Even while compiling and editing a collection of critical essays on the subject, Harold Bloom confessed that he '[does] not know exactly what "Holocaust literature" is'.[8] Alvin H. Rosenfeld, in his aforementioned study, is similarly cautious (despite his certainty that the topic is in a new sphere of study), beginning his book with the question 'Just what is Holocaust literature?'. Whatever it is, he asserts 'the need to see Holocaust literature against the history that has produced it, a history that reduces the expressive powers of language almost to silence'.[9]

The invocation of silence is paradoxically one of the most common apparatuses with which to discuss the Holocaust, especially with regard to literature or art.

Among the greatest champions of the requirements of silence was Holocaust survivor, writer and Nobel Peace Prize recipient Elie Wiesel. Indeed, Wiesel himself embodied the paradox of articulation, referring to himself as an author who arrived at writing not through worship, or anger, or love, but 'through silence'.[10] The historian Saul Friedländer has argued that in some ways the silence is even older than the Holocaust itself; it can be found in the responses to pervasive and powerful anti-Semitism which was commonplace across Europe at the beginning of the twentieth century, but is also *a presence in the absence* of direct, traceable orders linking the genocide to Hitler himself:

> Eight months before the war began, Hitler told the Reichstag: 'If Jews are responsible for a new war ... the result will be the extermination of the Jews.' Once again words; at the time only words. No decision seems to have been taken. For another two years the threats delivered in the Reichstag are not yet policy. Then comes the decision, in *silence*; the setting in motion of the machine of destruction, in *silence*; the end, in *silence*. Not even words written in an order, nothing. Not even the direct evidence of an oral order. ... Sinister hints, horrifying in what is left unsaid, what is left to the imagination. ... Brief passages in a speech, no more than the muted accompaniment of *silence*.[11]

The most famous call for silence after the Holocaust is surely found in the words of Theodor Adorno's essay 'Culture Criticism and Society' (1951): '*nach Auschwitz ein Gedicht zu schreiben ist barbarisch*', conventionally translated (notably, out of context) as 'to write poetry after Auschwitz is barbaric'.[12] Cynthia Ozick once remarked that she agreed with 'Adorno's famous dictum', and that she was 'not in favour of making fiction out of the data [of the Holocaust], or of mythologizing or poeticising it'.[13] Yet she would later publish her best-known work, *The Shawl* (1980), a novella fictionalizing the march of three women to their internment in a Nazi concentration camp.

While Wiesel and Ozick are both proponents of silence, they are both also prolific writers about the Holocaust, including of fictionalized versions. They might, nonetheless, be remaining true to Adorno's dictum; Ruth Franklin suggests that the importance of *ein* Gedicht has been overlooked, translating it not as 'poetry' but as 'a poem'; 'it would be horrific to write only one poem about Auschwitz', she writes, 'because it would take an infinite number of works of literature to represent the vast multiplicity of voices and experiences that constitute the Holocaust'.[14] Adorno himself partially retracted and modified his own statement in his later work,[15] but at this point his intended meaning is almost irrelevant, so great has the weight of critical work become which conscripts his words to its cause.

Ironically, it is precisely poetry which Bloom suggests might be the best example of a representation of the Holocaust 'in imaginative literature', specifically the 'the stunningly oblique poems of Paul Celan'.[16] Celan too recognized the importance of silence and the incapacity of language to overlay meaning onto the Holocaust, yet he suggests that rather than being an obstacle it was part of a process:

> Only one thing remained reachable, close and secure amid all losses: language. Yes, language. In spite of everything, it remained secure against loss. But it had to go through its own lack of answers, through terrifying silence, through the thousand darknesses of murderous speech. It went through. It gave me no words for what was happening, but went through it. Went through and could resurface, 'enriched' by it all.[17]

Jean-François Lyotard conceived of the Holocaust as something new to history, saying that from it 'a différend is born from a wrong and is signalled by a silence'.[18] He presented the difficulties in discussing the Holocaust, and the traumatic implications for survivors and those attempting to understand them, as a force of nature, an 'earthquake' which 'destroys not only lives, buildings, objects but also the instruments used to measure the earthquakes directly and indirectly. The impossibility of quantitatively measuring it does not prohibit, but rather inspires in the mind of the survivors the idea of a great seismic force'.[19]

Lyotard's earthquake evokes the Lisbon earthquake of 1755, and just as that cataclysm triggered a crisis of morality and ethics among European writers and philosophers of the eighteenth century such as Voltaire, Rousseau and Kant, so too has the Holocaust generated crises among twentieth-century and twenty-first-century thinkers. The events of Lisbon's earthquake, and the tsunami it triggered, caused Voltaire to question the nature of evil, yet these were natural events; as a completely man-made event, the Holocaust raises problems and issues of a whole new magnitude. Hence, George Steiner's contemplation about whether we who 'come after' can cope with a world where we 'know now that a man can read Goethe or Rilke in the evening, that he can play Bach and Schubert, and go to his day's work at Auschwitz in the morning'.[20]

The earthquake of the Holocaust caused a fundamental shift in our understanding of human nature and it has forever altered our language. On the most basic level it introduced a raft of new terms and sets of imagery into popular consciousness, including the word genocide itself to describe an act once labelled the 'crime without a name' by Winston Churchill.[21] Genocide – from the Greek *genos*, race or tribe, and the Latin *-cidium*, a killing – was coined by Polish Jew Raphael Lemkin, spurred by his reading of the suffering of Christians in pagan Rome, the fates of the Aztecs and Incas, the Ottoman destruction of Armenian Christians, and the pogroms against his fellow Jews. It was the Holocaust itself, and the slaughter of the Second World War more broadly, which led to the formal acceptance of Lemkin's terminology, its use in the Nuremberg Trials, and in particular its enshrining in international law in 1948 with the adoption of the Convention on the Prevention and Punishment of the Crime of Genocide by the General Assembly of the United Nations.[22]

Yet, while injunctions against its writing and statements about the impossibility of expression are easy to find, the Holocaust continues to be a source of literary inspiration. Thus, Berel Lang justified Holocaust fiction as an ethical necessity, writing that 'the Holocaust *is* speakable, *has* been spoken, *will* be spoken ... and, most of all, *ought* to be'.[23] Elsewhere Lang wrote that 'one could concede the possibility of this failure and *still* hold that such writing is justified – because of the menace of the alternative; that is, the silence into which the Holocaust would otherwise disappear'.[24] Similarly, Raul Hilberg concedes that the inexpressibility of the Holocaust is equally true of other massive traumatic events:

> 'If you were not there, you cannot imagine what it was like.' These words were said to me in Düsseldorf some years ago by a one-legged veteran of the German army who had been trapped in the Demyansk pocket on the Russian front at the end of 1941. The man had been wounded six times. One cannot deny that he had a valid point.[25]

This idea directly contradicts attitudes such as Rosenfeld's which place the Holocaust in its own traumatic realm aside from other 'topical literature', but Saul Friedländer argues that 'if there is an inadequacy ... between language and certain events', it is one that 'began well before Auschwitz, perhaps with the First World War, only to reach its culmination with Auschwitz'.[26] Indeed, there are moral concerns that the urge to insist upon the Holocaust's primacy among genocides and travesties of humanity has led to a sense of exceptionalism which rather than protect the memory of the Holocaust has undermined it by presenting a situation with damaging implications for the empathic reception of other atrocities. Peter Novick provides a powerful example in his work on the Holocaust in American culture:

> That the experience of Holocaust victims is uniquely unrepresentable carries with it a corollary, doubtless often unintended by those who make the claim: whereas the terror and horror of Tutsi mother seeing her child hacked to pieces with machetes is representable, that of a Jewish mother in analogous circumstances is not.[27]

The ethical problems which Novick highlights are powerful and undeniable and raise serious questions about the manner in which we talk about genocide and the Eurocentric models of trauma and remembrance which often accompany them. Yet these issues are also found within the study of the Holocaust itself. By default the Holocaust is often taken by commentators, politicians and subsequently by the general public to refer exclusively to the extermination of approximately six million Jews at the hands of Nazis and their supporters and collaborators, and this view is deliberately buttressed by scholars such as Steven T. Katz, for example, who deny the remaining millions access to the term Holocaust and in some cases even genocide, demoting them instead to instances of mass murder or mass death.[28] Yet at least eleven million people were exterminated, people who were deemed no longer worthy of life because they were homosexual, Slavs, communists, Jehovah's Witnesses, handicapped or infirm and more. Particularly striking in relation to the Jewish experience of the Holocaust are the Romani and Sinti peoples whose experience is known in Romani as the *Porajmos* (the destruction or devouring). Like the Jews, these peoples (labelled as Gypsies) were targeted for complete destruction and indeed by most reckonings their numbers, while far lower than the six million Jews removed from the face of the earth, were a higher percentage of the total population in Europe and indeed globally.[29] At the same time, the mass murder of Roma and Sinti was not referenced at the Nuremberg Trials, as Isabel Fonseca notes in her landmark history of the gypsy experience: 'to this day, just one Nazi ... has received a sentence specifically for crimes against Gypsies'.[30] While the texts I study here, and those in the field more widely, are inevitably funnelled down the popular perception of the Holocaust as a tragedy of six million deaths, it is important to remember those additional millions. Cultural memory shouldn't be treated as a finite resource and just as using 'Auschwitz' as a metonym for the Holocaust (a common linguistic shortcut in Holocaust studies) risks the cultural erasure of Belzec, Chelmno, Majdanek, Sobibor,

Treblinka, the ghetto, the gas vans, Babi Yar, Rumbala, Ponary and more, so too the idea that certain mass exterminations are more 'worthy' than others of remembrance risks an eclipsing of memory vital for combatting future persecution; it also imposes a hierarchy of suffering which is at best dubious and at worst morally repugnant.

While it is unavoidable that the Holocaust has been conceived of as a Jewish catastrophe by much of the commentary and fiction cited in this book, it remains also a human atrocity, increasingly central to Western cultural identity.[31] The Holocaust is intrinsically tied into a long history of anti-Semitic thought in Europe, but the dangers of a second Holocaust-like event need not come from the same place. Timothy Snyder asserts that one of the things that made the Holocaust possible was the belief among some that 'the Jews were understood as the makers and enforcers of a corrupt planetary order'. On the possibility of a second Holocaust Snyder continues, remarking that 'Jews can again be seen as a universal threat, as indeed they already are by increasingly important political formations in Europe, Russia, and the Middle East'. However, Snyder also sees a universal danger, pointing out that 'so might Muslims, gays, or other groups that can be associated with changes on a worldwide scale'.[32] Thus a Holocaust-type calamity could happen again to Jews, but also to other groups. History has already shown with depressing regularity that genocide can and will happen again; however, Snyder's assertion that a genocide of the scale and industrial nature of the Holocaust could be repeated is truly disturbing.

Such comments, combined with our entry into a post-survivor era, only add urgency to the drive to learn something from the Holocaust. Yet, fictionalized accounts of the genocide are increasingly recognizable for their adherence to a fixed set of tropes (ghettos, camps, fences and watchtowers, skeletal prisoners, the SS and so forth); the Holocaust has become a genre. Without survivors to offer fresh insights and reinvigorate debates with personal insight, alternate methods of transmitting must be located. Texts from outside of the 'realist' novel fill a vital position in our continued study of, and attempt at understanding, the Holocaust. While we may never truly relate to the Otherness of genocide, and indeed should never want to for to do so might necessitate calling down such a trauma upon ourselves, alternate narratives such as graphic novels and speculative fictions like dystopian and alternate history texts can engage with the Other and at least bring us closer to an empathic understanding.

Dystopian and alternate history narratives answer the same call as the texts which Michael Rothberg identified as 'traumatic realism', 'a realism in which the scars that mark the relationship of discourse to the real are not fetishistically denied, but exposed; a realism in which the claims of reference live on, but so does the traumatic extremity that disables realist representations as usual'.[33] Similarly, Slavoj Žižek writes that 'the point is *not* to remember the past trauma as exactly as possible: such "documentation" is a priori false, it transforms the trauma into a neutral, objective fact, whereas the essence of the trauma is precisely that it is too horrible to be remembered, to be integrated into our symbolic universe'.[34] Dystopian and alternate history texts perform this delicate balance, remembering while not remembering too precisely, talking about the Holocaust without talking about it, tracing the edges of the trauma to give us some indication of its shape even if none of the details.[35] Speculative fictions such as the dystopian and alternate history novel have the potential to be deliberately situated within the paradoxical contradiction Giorgio Agamben refers to when he labels Holocaust fiction as the 'aporia of Auschwitz indeed the very aporia of historical knowledge', yet they also have the potential to emerge relatively unscathed while still respecting the legacy of the genocide.[36]

After all, Rothberg describes his traumatic realism as being necessary to represent the 'concentrationary universe'.[37] This is an echo of the language of Elie Wiesel's description of the Holocaust as a 'universe outside the universe', itself an echo of David Rousset's coining of the phrase *L'Univers Concentrationnaire*.[38] Rousset, a non-Jew, was writing shortly after returning to Paris of the camp he survived, Buchenwald (although over his sixteen-month imprisonment he was also held in three other camps); this was a camp focused on imprisonment and concentration rather than the extermination machines of the East, yet he still recorded horrors:

> The next morning, they battered bodies in the ditches. At Wöbbelin, guards, armed with clubs, will have to be posted over the dead to kill those who eat the scrawny, fetid flesh of the cadavers. Amazing skeletons with empty eyes trample blindly over heaps of stinking corruption. They lean against the beam, heads sunken on their chests, and stand motionless and mute, one hour, two hours. After a while, the body has crumpled to the ground. A living corpse has become a dead one.[39]

Emphasizing the realist nature of his experience, Rousset couches his powerful descriptions in the language of the uncanny and the Other while also drawing on metatextual terms describing how the 'inmates of the camp belong to a world of Céline with overtones of Kafka' and how '[Alfred Jarry's] Ubu and Kafka cease to be fantasies and become component elements of the living world'.⁴⁰ In a world in which the boundaries between fantasy and reality are permeable, where Kafka and Jarry can be realism, where the living and the dead are indistinguishable, literature which goes beyond conventional realism is surely essential.⁴¹ We are routinely confronted by language which tells us that the Holocaust is Other as an environment of death, survivors and victims are Other in their suffering, and perpetrators are Other in their evil. What is called for, therefore, is a literature intimately associated with describing the Other.

Dystopian Fiction and Alternate History

The argument of this book is that non-realist, speculative fiction texts bring valuable contributions to Holocaust studies by accessing areas of the imagination out of bounds for realism, dismissing the idea that there is something innately literary about realism or quasi-realist texts which better qualify them for discussing such difficult topics. I'm using dystopian fiction and alternate history as the key examples of this, though my argument could also encompass speculative fiction genres like fantasy and the gothic more broadly. In his survey of science fiction, with the suitably chthonic title *New Maps of Hell* (1961), Kingsley Amis identifies that apocalyptic and dystopian fiction presents 'one possibility of science fiction as a literary mode: as a forum, if not a podium, for the discussion of topics as what happens when our society breaks down'.⁴²

In his *Metamorphoses of Science Fiction* (1979) Darko Suvin describes science fiction as a 'literature of cognitive estrangement',⁴³ a concept which he says owes a debt to a technique of estrangement which Bertolt Brecht called *Verfremdungeffekt*, itself rooted in the Russian Formalist device of making strange or *ostranenie*. Brecht describes the effect of images which employ this technique: 'A representation that alienates is one which allows us to recognize its subject, but at the same time makes it seem unfamiliar'. He continues that they are 'designed to free socially-conditioned phenomena from that stamp of familiarity which protects them against our grasp today'.⁴⁴ Speculative fiction is thus able to employ such devices to take the expected images of fascism, Nazism, anti-Semitism and the Holocaust and re-transcribe them in a manner which pays tribute to the dialogue of Otherness while still conveying a digestible narrative with the capacity to say something meaningful about the Holocaust and our relation to it. Gerry Canavan alludes to this capacity when he describes SF as operating 'in the paradox of the realistic dream, the dream that is or might be (or could yet become) real'.[45]

The science fiction author Ray Bradbury writes that 'science fiction is, after all, the fiction of ideas, the fiction where philosophy can be tinkered with, torn apart, and put back together again, it is the fiction of sociology and psychology and history compounded and squared by time. It is the fiction where you may set up and knock down your own political and religious and moral states'.[46] This admirable intellectual aim seems to be incompatible with the Holocaust for some: the arguments for its exceptionality as a historical event double as arguments for its exceptionality from rational thought, sealing it away in an inaccessible bubble. By arguing for the exceptionalism and unrepresentability of the Holocaust, commentators are effectively stifling artistic impulses, attempts at understanding a historic event, and the production of tools to generate empathy. Rather than undermine the Holocaust, speculative fictions (broadening out Bradbury's terminology) enfold it within wider disciplines of sociology, psychology and philosophy not to lessen our understanding or appreciation of the horrors involved but to support new ways of thinking about genocide and encourage us to think about and identify the reasons behind such hatred.

I am comfortable in asserting that Bradbury's claims for science fiction are equally true for SF more widely. Indeed, much about the claims of Canavan and Suvin cited above are similarly applicable to other SF genres such as horror or fantasy. One of the appeals of the label 'speculative fiction' or SF is that it can act as 'synecdoche for the sum of so-called non-mimetic genres'.[47] Dystopian and alternate history fiction, the topics which are the focus of this book, are close bedfellows with science fiction but not completely interchangeable. Dystopian fiction is intimately connected with utopian fiction, a worst-case scenario to mirror the latter's ideal world, and thus has a long and literary heritage distinct from and yet sympathetic towards science fiction texts. Alternate history is a genre with similar roots: with precursors and precedents which can be traced at least as far back as the Roman writer Livy, the first alternate history novel in Western literature is Louis-Napoléon Geoffroy-Château's *Napoléon et la conquête du monde*, published in France in 1836. This novel began a new genre in French literature, that of the *uchronie*, a utopia which trusts not in finding the perfect society in a new or changed geographic locale (a *topos*), but in a changed time period. Upon its transfer across the language barrier into English, alternate history fiction has become less utopian and optimistic; indeed alternate history forms a perfect partner with dystopian novels in this book because many (though by no means all) of the texts fall into both categories, becoming what we might call *dyschronia*.[48]

Alternate History and dystopian fiction share Suvin's sense of cognitive estrangement with science fiction; they also share the other key component of his theorization of the genre – the *novum*. He writes that 'SF is distinguished by the narrative dominance or hegemony of a fiction "novum" (novelty, innovation) validated by cognitive logic', and this application of cognitive logic to a newly defined society altered by a change in historical causality (alternate history) or a thought experiment based on sociopolitical extrapolations of worst-case scenarios (a dystopia) is equally valid.[49] The novum is also where these concepts of the non-mimetic, SF, alternate history and dystopia are most capable of tapping into the fictive representation of the Holocaust. Exceptionalists and relativists alike acknowledge that the Holocaust represents something new in the history of genocide and marks the beginning of a new chapter in how we think about human rights, war crimes, and the ideology of the state: 'the *novum* that is the *Endlösung* [Final Solution] reveals the dark eccentric *essence* of Nazism'.[50] Indeed, given the desire to remember and understand, which accompanies the Holocaust into fiction, a more accurate formulation with regard to Suvin is that speculative fiction of the Holocaust is estrangement seeking cognition. The ultimate achievement of SF Holocaust fiction is to allow us to learn something about the Holocaust, to come closer to understanding it, while maintaining the Otherness (estrangement) which the topic insists upon. A side effect of this is that through estrangement, SF can push back against 'the homogenization of Holocaust comprehension that eschews difficult testimony or stories that fall outside of accepted narratives', which Zoë Vania Waxman among others recognizes as a side effect of 'the collectivization of Holocaust memory'.[51]

Through their techniques of cognitive estrangement, alternate history and dystopian texts can look sideways into *l'universe concentrationnaire*; as forms of non-realist or anti-realist fiction, these SF genres are intrinsically well-suited for engaging with difficult concepts of the Other or using representations of strange places to show us something of our world without depicting it. If we are to continue to engage with '*un autre monde*', 'another world', 'a distorted mirror', as the Holocaust survivor and composer Szymon Laks referred to Auschwitz, incorporating texts of this type into our discussion of the Holocaust is an essential step moving forward into the post-survivor era.[52] These texts are not intended to supersede mimetic trauma fiction, many excellent examples of which are rightly lauded and studied already, but to supplement them. The rise to prominence of SF of the Holocaust, and the dawning of the post-survivor era, is not a harbinger of the end of the Holocaust, some form of a Hegelian end of history. On the contrary, by redirecting the Holocaust's narratives through non-realist impulses, SF can revitalize the historical narrative, keeping it visceral, living, and reminding us of its continuing contemporary relevance. Alongside the work of historians to uncover and share alternative narratives from the genocide such as those of women and from outside of the extermination camps, the role of this type of fiction may be the most important contribution to our continued relationship to the Holocaust.

Key Texts

The first key text I examine is Katharine Burdekin's *Swastika Night* (1937), written under the *nom de guerre* Murray Constantine. That a far-future dystopian novel could exist, predicting the ferocity and hunger for conquest of the Nazi regime, two years before the outbreak of war becomes less surprising when we note that the novel was published as part of the Left Book Club, under the auspices of publisher Victor Gollancz, grandson to a German-immigrant rabbi, and appropriate given that the publishing house that bears his name later became synonymous with UK science fiction publishing. Writing in the 1930s, Burdekin cannot have been expected to articulate the full horrors of the Holocaust, yet the novel is chillingly prescient. Somewhat more reflective are post-war narratives which draw upon Nazi imagery and racial ideology to convey something of the horror of the conflict and the genocide which accompanied it. C. S. Forester (better known for his *Hornblower* Napoleonic adventure novels) wrote a disturbing short story, 'The Wandering Gentile' (1954), which plays on anti-Semitic tradition to weave a supernatural tale, while William L. Shirer wrote an alternate history in an essay format (described as 'an historical fantasy') which weaves historical commentary with fictional journalism to describe a dystopian United States in the eponymous situation of 'If Hitler Had Won World War II' (1961). The most striking of these early post-war efforts, however, is *The Sound of His Horn* (1952) by British diplomat John William Wall, writing as Sarban. This novel highlights the intrinsic fetishism of Nazi fascism, creating a highly sexualized novel and a fascinating if disturbing SF counterpoint to the pornographic *stalag* novels circulating in

Israel at the time, as well as pre-empting the Nazisploitation genre of work which frequently blurs its boundaries with SF.[53] Though far outnumbered by their post-Eichmann Trial successors, the variety and power of these early texts is notable for the fact that they emerge before Anglo-American popular consciousness has formed a stable set of Holocaust tropes (the camp, skeletal survivors, death's head SS, etc.) and are thus unique in their approach and represent important evidence that for SF, as for other responses, the myth of silence is precisely that – a myth.

For the subsequent chapters of this book I have broken the texts into broad themes. Chapter 2 addresses texts which problematize history, either through the primary focus of their plots or as a by-product of their manipulation of history's narrative. To some extent all alternate history fiction draws the construction of historical narrative into question – although many retain the notion of a causal linearity (albeit one springing from a timeline diverged from our own) – but the texts of this chapter take the literary trope to another level. Philip K. Dick's *The Man in the High Castle* (1962), for example, is not explicitly a Holocaust fiction yet the genocide is conspicuous by its absence, existing in the cracks of the dystopian society. The looming presence of Nazi Germany is an ominous one, inherently evil and unstable, a threat to the entire world, yet Dick also uses the mechanics of the alternate history and the metatextual presence of his novel-within-a-novel, 'The Grasshopper Lies Heavy', to cast doubt on the solidity of history, and to problematize notions of authenticity and historical narrative. In doing so, he implicitly calls into question the narrative of the Second World War and as a result the Holocaust. He also explicitly compares the Holocaust through references to other, even more atrocious, crimes committed by the victorious Germans within the fictional world of the novel.

Narratologically, Robert Harris's *Fatherland* (1992) has a much simpler and linear plot: it lacks the metanarrative fracturing that makes *The Man in the High Castle* so intriguing, yet it too demonstrates how dystopian novels can disrupt historiography. Harris cleverly subverts the detective format by having his protagonist uncovering a conspiracy of which he cannot conceive, putting the reader ahead of the detective as we begin to recognize the Holocaust before him. *Fatherland* too questions our notions of validity and historical truth, directly contrasting the notion of the Holocaust as an unimaginable event with the fictional reality of its secret completion, as well as with historical truth through Harris's careful research and meticulous dedication to genuine historic documents in plotting the novel.

Stephen Fry's *Making History* (1996) draws more heavily on the science fiction tradition, crafting an alternate history through a time-travel experiment gone wrong. Like Dick and Harris, Fry problematizes the notion of historical narrative, this time through a protagonist who is a historian. His adapted time-travel trope creates an alternate world without Hitler but with a more effective genocide and Nazi military dominion. In doing so Fry undermines the Carlylian notion of 'great men' of history, subscribing instead to something closer to Daniel Jonah Goldhagen's then freshly-published theory, presented in *Hitler's Willing Executioners* (1996), of a collective responsibility for the Holocaust. Fry, like Harris, foregrounds the Holocaust in his narrative, comparing it with not only an even more lethal version of itself but, in Fry's case, comparing the suffering of the Jews with the suffering of other groups, specifically the homosexual community. However, *Making History*'s power comes not from descriptions of terrors, or imaginative spaces opened up by the language of the author, but from its effect of the relativization of Adolf Hitler. Removing Hitler from reality, and yet creating a history which is even worse, particularly for the long-term survival of the Jewish people, shifts some of the blame from the man to the environment. The significance of this is striking for our contemporary era (in which it feels like the politically far-right are in resurgence) as it suggests that, in contrast to the writings of scholars such as Wiesel, the circumstances of the Holocaust were not unique and may in fact be horrifically replicable.

Chapter 3 develops from Fry's supposition of the Holocaust as an inevitability. The texts discussed here explore alternate histories not where the Holocaust is prevented, or dystopias in which it is made worse, but instead present scenarios in which some people (but not all) are able to be saved. The tradition of Nazis surviving the Second World War, normally living in hiding ready to strike again, finds its basis in infamous historical examples of Germans who fled through 'ratlines', such as Adolf Eichmann and Josef Mengele, producing works of fiction like Ira Levin's *The Boys from Brazil* (1979) or George Steiner's *The Portage to San Cristobal of A.H.* (1981). More recently, works of speculative fiction have emerged which act as fascinating counterpoints to this sort of narrative: *The Yiddish Policemen's Union* (2007), by PulitzerPrize winner Michael Chabon, depicts an alternate history in which the Holocaust's death toll is limited to two million, the majority of European Jews having escaped to settle in a specially designated reserve in Alaska. Like Harris's *Fatherland*, Chabon's novel merges the genre of detective fiction with the alternate history; yet while Harris's novel is very much directed at British and European sensibilities, Chabon's use of the hard-boiled style of Raymond Chandler or Dashiell Hammett, combined with the thoroughly unique and engaging setting of 'Jewlaska', creates a fundamentally American interpretation of the Holocaust's role in contemporary society. Particularly fascinating is Chabon's use of the Alaskan Native American population, in this case the Tlingit people, whose juxtaposition with the Jewish refugees invites serious questions about America's role in genocide.

While Chabon's novel imagines a hypothetical homeland for millions of Jews who would otherwise perish in the Holocaust, Shalom Auslander's novel *Hope: A Tragedy* (2012) imagines saving just one additional individual. However, that individual is the single person most synonymous with the Holocaust in Western (and probably global) imagination, and certainly the most synonymous Jew: Anne Frank. A shocking novel, Auslander portrays Frank as having survived the Holocaust, somehow making her way to the United States and spending the best part of the last sixty years living in an attic in New England, becoming a foul-mouthed geriatric who eats dead birds and the neighbour's cat to survive. Though very different in style and subject to Chabon's novel, *Hope: A Tragedy* is, like *The Yiddish Policeman's Union*, a darkly comic novel, which automatically invites us to examine the Holocaust through a less familiar lens. Ultimately, as we shall see, re-contextualizing Anne Frank allows Auslander to re-contextualize the Holocaust as a whole and, through a colourful cast of supporting characters, re-examine its relevance to young Jews in the United States in the twenty-first century.

Chapter 4 retains the contemporary concerns of Chapter 3 to examine novels which are very much conscious of their status as twenty-first-century fiction, and as much products of that environment as they are responses to the Holocaust. This is most clearly evident in Philip Roth's *The Plot Against America* (2004) and Jo Walton's *Farthing* (2006), which I examine as a pair. Written in the aftermath of the 11 September terrorist attacks in the United States, both authors use the Holocaust to criticize the shifting Overton window for acceptable political dialogue, rising intolerance, and development of a surveillance state in the United States and United Kingdom respectively. While Roth (though he denies it in various interviews) and Walton respond to their recent past using the more distant history of the Holocaust to create alternate history dystopias, Howard Jacobson and Lavie Tidhar respond to their contemporary environment to warn of near-future horrors. Writing a decade after Roth, Tidhar's *A Man Lies Dreaming* (2014) and Jacobson's *J.* (2014) are dystopian novels which respond to the rise of the far-right, anti-Semitism and right-wing politics in general. Tidhar and Jacobson tap contemporary concerns about these political shifts, two years before the Brexit vote and the presidency of Donald Trump. Of all the novels in this book, these are the starkest reminders of the specific roots of the Holocaust and the most powerful warning that our reactions to its trauma may be masking a renewed blooming of a similar monstrosity.

The texts I've referenced in this book are a concentrated case study which embrace the dystopian power of the Holocaust, utilizing it to craft a non-mimetic narrative. They encourage us to analyse the historic evils of both Nazism and the Holocaust, but also to carefully consider contemporary concerns. They challenge us to think again about easily accepted historical narratives, especially those which portray our own history in a completely positive light. My selection of texts is far from comprehensive, and numerous equally fascinating and important texts have had to be reluctantly placed by the wayside. This wealth of potential material however does justify the validity of this study: that fiction has already been asking the questions that cultural theorists are only relatively recently beginning to ask, the implications of *imagining the unimaginable*.

1

Precursors and Early Texts: *Swastika Night* (1937) and the Myth of Silence

The majority of fictional works referenced in this book are modern near-contemporary works; almost all date to after the emergence of so-called Holocaust consciousness in the United States and United Kingdom in the 1960s. While it is these texts and the cultural phenomenon they represent which is the crux of my study, it is important to understand that they did not simply emerge from a text-less void, writing in ways that had never been seen before about things that had never been written about. Just as the Holocaust did not suddenly appear fully-formed as a genocidal *novum*, instead emerging from a long history of anti-Semitism and as the final development of a system of discrimination and persecution, so too the speculative fiction of the late-twentieth and early-twenty-first centuries which engages with the Holocaust emerges from a body of texts which engage with the Second World War and genocide through speculative fiction.

Before the Holocaust was Auschwitz and the extermination camps, before it was *gaswagen* and mass executions, even before it was *Kristallnacht* and the discriminatory Nuremberg Laws, the Nazi's answer to the so-called Jewish Question existed, however partially formed, in doctrine and imagination. The most infamous of the literary expressions of these impulses, and certainly the best known in the English-speaking world before 1939, was Hitler's own exercise in autobiographical myth-making, *Mein Kampf*. The future Führer analyses Germany's mistakes of the past and implicitly and explicitly lays out a plan for the future. The Jews, he writes, are like parasites, adopting the manners and languages of their 'host' in order to appear better integrated when in fact they are undermining all that is good for the host nation for their own benefits and in accordance with *The Protocols of the Elders of Zion*.[1] Possibly one of the most dangerous forgeries ever created, Hitler insisted that the very fact that the Jews deny the authenticity of the *Protocols* is 'the surest proof they are genuine'.[2] This is an argument that strikes a worryingly familiar chord in today's political climate with wide-ranging distrust of sources and testimony, and David Aaronovitch points out that it is an 'undefeatable' argument:

> The Protocols confirm what I believe and what I see around me, therefore they are true in the most important sense, even if they themselves are forgeries. Furthermore, whether they are forgeries or not does not matter; because they confirm what we see around us, they will help people better understand what is going on.[3]

Reading *Mein Kampf* now one may be surprised by how brazenly open Hitler is about many of his views and aspirations. A German reader of Primo Levi wrote to the Holocaust survivor apologizing for Hitler's influence on his nation by writing that 'all his beautiful words were falsehood and betrayal we did not understand at the beginning'.[4] Levi responded:

> That dread man was not a traitor, he was a coherent fanatic whose ideas were extremely clear: he never changed them and never concealed them. Those who voted for him certainly voted for his ideas. Nothing is lacking in [*Mein Kampf*]: the blood and the land, the living space, the Jew as the eternal enemy, the Germans who embody 'the highest form of humanity on earth', the other countries openly regarded as the instruments of German domination. These are not 'beautiful words'; perhaps Hitler also uttered other words, but he never retracted these.[5]

In the context of this book, a modern reader may also be struck by the predictions Hitler makes about the conflict to come and the relationships between Germany and other nations, some of which – such as his assertions that England was the only possible European ally for Germany – read like pages from a strange alternate history:

> ... the English nation will have to be considered the most valuable ally in the world as long as its leadership and the spirit of its broad masses justify us in expecting that brutality and perseverance which is determined to fight a battle once begun to a victorious end, with every means and without consideration of time and sacrifices ...[6]

Swastika Night (1937), Katharine Burdekin

Of course, the disturbing fact is that *Mein Kampf* is not a work of fiction and the Hitler who wrote it was not a product of an alternate world like those we will encounter throughout this book but a historical reality whose ideologies ripped apart the fabric of society in Europe and beyond and led to the slaughter of millions of lives.

Knowing this as we do, the views of Hitler in *Mein Kampf* and of Nazism more generally with regard to women are overshadowed by our knowledge of the importance of the views on politics and race. For some feminists in the 1930s, however, they were worryingly prominent. Published in 1937, two years before hostilities would erupt in Europe, the novel *Swastika Night* describes a future world carved up between two massive global empires: Imperial Japan and the German Reich. Written by Katharine Burdekin, under the *nom-de-plum* Murray Constantine, the novel focuses particularly on the role of women in Nazi society. Burdekin envisions a German Empire, 700 years after the conclusion of a twenty-year global war, centred around a feudal society with German 'Knights' at the top followed by a larger group of Nazi Germans; this in turn is followed by the servant peoples of the empire such as the British; they are themselves ranked above Christians who live a wild existence in remote areas, and women who have been debased and reduced to an animalistic state. There is, of course, no reference to the Holocaust by name but Germany has 'killed all the Jews off' and deified Hitler and persecuted anyone who does not recognize him as an instrument of the Teutonic 'Thunderer'.[7]

Hitler himself is preserved in popular memory as having 'colossal height, long thick golden hair, a great manly golden beard spreading over his chest, deep sea-blue eyes, the noble rugged brow – and all the rest'. In short, as an Aryan Superman.[8] While there are obvious parodic elements to this description, ones which become relevant to the plot when a photograph of the real Hitler is located, the reinvention of Hitler's identity is an extension of what Hitler himself was trying to achieve in publishing *Mein Kampf*, as James J. Barnes explains:

> Hitler needed to build a legend, not only about himself, but about the Nazi movement. He had to show the world how he had struggled as a youth against adversity, how he had come through the war creditably, and how he had gradually come to be the leader of a new party. ... In *Mein Kampf* he would set forth the future directions of a potentially great movement with an appeal to all Germans, and a defiant warning to Germany's enemies.[9]

All evidence to contradict these legends, and indeed all knowledge and literature that was not approved by the knights centuries earlier, has been destroyed and the evidence of its very existence also expunged from the face of the earth, creating a new Dark Age, the historical/cultural phenomenon from which many of our own myths and legends developed. The sole exception is a photo of Hitler and Eva Braun, and a book of lost knowledge, both passed down through the von Hess line of knights whose distant ancestor wrote the book in remote seclusion while all others were being burnt around the globe. This book connects our version of history with this futuristic yet medieval-feudal society, a society which is otherwise estranged by its ignorance of its own past.

Swastika Night is a development of future war stories in the tradition of George Tomkyn's *The Battle of Dorking* (1871), anticipating war with Germany as was increasingly commonplace in the 1930s.[10] However, Burdekin's novel remains unique among other pre-war predictions due to its vast scale and uncompromising depiction of the implications of Nazi rule imposed over Europe and the world. She posits that the Nazi vision of a 'Thousand Year Reich' would be a disaster not just for civilization, or the status of women, but for humanity in its broadest terms. The Germans 'have made women be what they cannot with all their good will go on being – not for centuries on end – the lowest common denominator, a pure animal – and the race is coming to extinction... women... are not being born'.[11] After centuries of being told women are worthless, 'nothing but birds' nests', of being conditioned to believe such an idea to be a divine truth, being encouraged to breed strong male children, less and less girls are being born and the population imbalance is becoming critical.[12]

Burdekin highlights the futility and destructive repercussions of a society which is not only hierarchically class-based, but which also sees gender as a contributory factor towards an individual's standing within that hierarchy. Daphne Patai remarks that 'if this is satire, it is also an accurate representation of Nazi ideology and only a slight exaggeration of a masculine gender identity considered normal in many parts of the world'.[13] This only emphasizes *Swastika Night*'s importance as Western society grapples with both a resurgent right-wing politics sympathetic to much ideology found in Nazism and an (often related) increasingly toxic culture of masculinity which revels in debasement, degradation and violence towards women.

One of the many startling features of Burdekin's portrayal of women in *Swastika Night* is how closely it foreshadows the historical treatment of Holocaust victims. In the novel women have been stripped of all rights and regarded as inhuman or Other. They have been deposed as subjects of love and affection by fervent passion for the Nazi cause and, when pleasures of the flesh are required, by young boys. They have their heads shaved and wear uniform rags, living in women-only compounds under constant guard and surrounded by fences:

> To love a woman, to the German mind, would be equal to loving a worm, or a Christian. Women like these. Hairless, with naked shaven scalps, the wretched ill-balance of their feminine forms outlined by their tight bifurcated clothes – that horrible meek bowed way they had of walking and standing, head low, stomach out, buttocks bulging behind – no grace, no beauty, no uprightness, all those were male qualities.[14]

This 'Reduction of Women' is both physical and spiritual, as the Knight von Hess remarks: 'Women will always be exactly what men want them to be. They have no will, no character, and no souls.'[15] While Burdekin was writing in reaction to actual and dangerous gender imbalance that she perceived in the Nazi ideology that had risen in Germany, she was also continuing the themes of her previous feminist novel *Proud Man* (1934). Gavriel D. Rosenfeld suggests that because of her feminist ideology Burdekin fails to expose the true horrors of a Nazi-ruled world, ending the novel on a vaguely optimistic tone which distinguishes the novel from most post-war narratives: her 'feminist agenda partly explains the oversight' of placing women and Christians above Jews on the Nazis' list of sworn enemies.[16] This strikes me as an unfair criticism of the novel given how closely it mirrors many of the dehumanizing tactics employed in the Holocaust, especially as it predates the camps themselves. That Burdekin chooses women as the subject for this dehumanization rather than the Jews does of course serve the point she wants to make about gender roles but, as already noted above, by the time of the novel in c.2650 the Jews had already been extinct for approximately 700 years leaving Christians and women as the most reviled of the surviving population.[17]

Women live in 'a large cage about a mile square at the north end of the town. The women were not allowed to come out of it without special permission, which was very rarely granted. They had a hospital inside it, and their house of corrections, where they were sent if they injured each other or failed in perfect humility.'[18] Again this description is striking when compared to accounts of the Holocaust's camps:

> our Lager is a square of about six hundred yards in length, surrounded by two fences of barbed wire, the inner one carrying a high tension current. It consists of sixty wooden huts, which are called Blocks ... certain Blocks are reserved for

specific purposes. First of all, a group of eight, at the extreme end of the camp, form the infirmary and clinic.[19]

One critical difference is worth noting, however, in that the camps Burdekin imagines while terrible do not match the brutality of the Holocaust's, partly because of the unprecedented nature of those specific experiences, but also because the women camps are not extermination camps like Auschwitz, rather they are concentration camps based on an older (notably, British) model, intended for the residence and control of a specific population.[20]

While the world *Swastika Night* predicts did not come to pass, the novel remains an important piece of the picture of representation of the Holocaust in speculative fiction. It transcends its contemporaneous environments and continues to remain relevant not as a future war novel but as an alternate history (or more accurately, alternate future). Perhaps this is because as Robert Crossley succinctly points out, 'the important utopian fictions of the late 1930s never seem entirely at home in their own decade',[21] or perhaps it is because more than any other Anglo-German war novel its imagery and narrative can be found reverberating through post-1945 literature in the works of a wide range of authors of dystopian fiction and alternate history.

Most obvious of these echoes is the one found within Orwell's *Nineteen Eighty-Four* (1949). This in itself is significant due to the linchpin-like nature of Orwell's novel among the dystopian fiction that would follow. While it is difficult to find direct evidence that Orwell read *Swastika Night*, it is worth noting he was an 'inveterate borrower' and that the novel was first published as part of Gollancz's Left Book Club, a list of authors and books of which Orwell was also a part, *The Road to Wigan Pier* appearing among the titles in 1937.[22] We also know that Orwell read many of the pre-war and interwar anti-fascist novels and pamphlets, and wrote reviews on some such as *I, James Blunt* (1942) by H. V. Morton which he described as 'a good flesh creeper, founded on the justified assumption that the mass of the English people haven't yet heard of Fascism'.[23] Such circumstantial evidence aside, there are also numerous textual similarities between *Swastika Night* and *Nineteen Eighty-Four*. Both novels have protagonists named after English heroes: Alfred [the Great] and Winston [Churchill] respectively. Both novels contain long-established totalitarian states who maintain their control by limiting the knowledge and education of the general population, Burdekin's by destroying all records, Orwell's by altering them beyond recognition.[24] Finally, both contain a book of 'truth' entrusted to the protagonist, a book which claims to detail how the world came to be the way it is and offers enlightenment: the von Hess book in *Swastika Night* and Emanuel Goldstein's heavy black volume '*The Theory and Practice of Oligarchical Collectivism*' in *Nineteen Eighty-Four*. It is worth noting however that the presence of a book of 'truth' is also symptomatic of the age in which both Burdekin and Orwell were writing; political, philosophical and ideological pamphlets were extremely common and some, from the *Communist Manifesto* to the *Protocols of the Elders of Zion*, proved to be world changing in their significance. Nonetheless, should all of these elements prove to be an unlikely coincidence and proof emerge that Orwell had never read, nor even heard about, *Swastika Night* it would still not diminish the novel's status as 'undoubtedly the most sophisticated and original of all the many anti-fascist dystopias of the late 1930s and 1940s'.[25]

1940–1960: The Myth of Silence

Swastika Night was not the only pre-1945 work of speculative fiction to imagine a Second World War with Germany, nor the only text to imagine a scenario where Germany was victorious in that conflict. Indeed, there is a significant body of literature from the period 1939–45 itself, from both the United States and the United Kingdom, which is remarkable in a way given that rationing in the United Kingdom extended to paper supplies.[26] One of the reasons for these publications succeeding into print was likely of course because of their value as propaganda. *Loss of Eden* by Douglas Brown and Christopher Serpell was published in 1940 and reissued in 1941 with the less poetic but more direct title *If Hitler Comes: A Cautionary Tale*. It is an interesting novel not only for its description of British life under German rule, but also because of the framing device deployed by the authors. The novel opens with an undated 'extract from the records of the New Zealand Society of Pre-Cataclysmic Research…' which posits the rest of the novel as a document found by archaeologists of the future and mentions other events and texts which would make fitting accompaniments. These include:

> the admirable volume of drawings recently published by Mr. Rota-iki-pa-wei, after his return from the Society's expedition to the site of the ancient city of London. His sketch of the ruins of St. Paul's Cathedral drawn from a precarious perch on a broken arch of London Bridge … is a fine example of how even the dry bones of antiquity can be revived by the artist's visionary eye.[27]

By employing a post-apocalyptic framing narrative, Brown and Serpell are unambiguously underlining the severity of the threat of Nazi Germany to the fabric of European society and culture. The bleak image of St. Paul's cathedral in ruins, and repeated references to a cataclysm, anticipate the apocalyptic language of the Holocaust while acting as a counterbalance to any interpretation of the novel's ending as a positive one with hints at an organized resistance to the Nazis. Of the novel itself, Brown and Serpell remark in the foreword that 'this is no fanciful picture. It is painted from life … it is not intended to cause despondency or alarm, but to confirm and justify that resolution with which we are now fighting. If such a tale is to have a dedication it can only be to THOSE WHO WILL NOT LET THIS HAPPEN'.[28]

While the United Kingdom begins as a client state for Germany, akin to Vichy France, Germany's influence in Britain grows to the point at which, after an assassination attempt on Adolf Hitler during his visit to Lord's Cricket Ground, Germany annexes the United Kingdom. The novel continues with the protagonist Charles Fenton, a UK correspondent from a New Zealand newspaper, describing the dangerous existence of Londoners under direct Nazi rule. As an effective neutral, being of New Zealand citizenship, he is at times horrified by what he encounters yet also surprisingly pragmatic. He rarely, if ever, condemns those who cooperate with the new regime, largely because he too is forced to work alongside them on more than one occasion:

> If you have lived in London under the Captivity, if you have seen a friend after the Gestapo have had him, if you yourself have been threatened with the concentration camp and have had to reach a decision such as mine in the presence of your wife – then you have the right to judge me. … I do not for one moment blame those who now accepted minor office under the Nazis. I do not blame them for saluting the Swastika flag, or even for taking an enforced oath of loyalty to Adolf Hitler. A sanitary inspector, after all, has as great a responsibility to a conquered as to a free people.[29]

It is interesting that Brown and Serpell, through Fenton, specifically defend collaborators from criticism (although given that the apocalyptic framing narrative shows an end to Western civilization it is equally possible to read a condemnation of collaboration from the authors themselves); this is especially interesting given post-war British culture's overwhelming disdain for collaborators and its peddling of the idea of moral superiority versus the conquered nations of Europe.[30]

There is a fleeting but notable reference to the Holocaust in the earliest work of Second World War alternate history to have been written after the war had concluded: the play *Peace in Our Time* (1946) by Noël Coward. Set in 1940s England under German occupation, the play was written in a flurry of productivity in 1946, Coward having been inspired to write it after visiting Paris early in the same year. It was his first return to the city since its occupation by German forces; previously Coward had occupied an apartment in the city while working for the British Secret Service setting up propaganda radio stations. He found that his apartment had been vandalized by Nazi occupiers as they had withdrawn, but more crucially he found that several of his French friends and fellow artists including Sacha Guitry, Arletty and Maurice Chevalier were now facing charges of collaboration of varying degrees. Enquiring about these and other friends was a task which Coward soon gave up on after receiving too many contradictory, self-exculpatory versions of the same stories; in his diary Coward wrote that the experience of returning to Paris 'confirmed my belief that worse things than bombardments can happen to civilians in wartime'.[31]

The question of who in London would have collaborated with the enemy and who would have been a hero or a heroine of resistance was a source of fascination for Coward. Although Michael Billington asserts that the play was as much rooted in Coward's own political leanings, writing that 'Coward, still smarting from the 1945 election, wrote the toxic *Peace in Our Time* implying that a Nazi victory might have taught us all a jolly good lesson'.[32] According to his secretary, long-time confidante and biographer Cole Lesley, Coward also drew inspiration from Saki's story 'When William Came', which imagined a German invasion of England; although Lesley incorrectly remembers the story as an alternate history set during the First World War, when actually published in 1913 it is an anticipatory future-war narrative. Originally titled *Might Have Been* (another of his secretaries, Lorna Loraine, is credited with suggesting the title which references Chamberlain's ill-fated promise), *Peace in Our Time* is a play of eight scenes spread over two acts with the entirety of the action taking place in a small London pub called 'The Shy Gazelle' somewhere between Knightsbridge and Sloane Square.

The relevant reference comes during a conversation between a senior Nazi official in the area, Albrecht Richter, the pub landlord Fred, and two of his regulars George and Chorley:

> Albrecht: The Fuhrer believes that the spirit of this country is indestructible. He
> believes ... Great Britain will become reconciled to the inevitable, not through

> any weakening of her spirit but through the strengthening of her innate wisdom and common sense. As soon as that innate wisdom and common sense reasserts itself, as soon as you are willing to renounce your imperialistic convictions and cut your losses sensibly and courageously, then we can stand firmly together – your country and mine who have so much in common – and combine to drive the evil forces of Jewry and Communism from the face of the earth.
>
> George: That was a very excellent speech, Mr. Richter.
> Fred: Do you believe it, Mr. Bourne?
> George: The important point is, Fred, that Mr. Richter believes it.
> Chorely: It's rather a shock, isn't it, Fred, to be made to realise that we in England haven't got the monopoly of ideals?
> Fred: Do you think that what the gentleman said just now represented an ideal?
> Chorely: It's an intelligent and consistent policy for the future of civilisation.
> Fred: There are lots of Jews in England, Mr. Richter, and lots of Communists too – what's going to happen to them?
> Albrecht (sharply): The former will be liquidated or deported. The latter will change their views.
> Fred: Liquidated?
> Albrecht: A certain amount of ruthlessness is unavoidable when the end justifies the means.[33]

The euphemism of liquidation would be as obvious to a 1946 audience as it would be today and while this is the lone direct reference to the fate of Jews in occupied Britain, like the references to Churchill's execution, the Royal Family's internment in Windsor Castle, and the construction of a concentration camp on the Isle of Wight, it contributes to a very dark depiction of the world beyond the walls of The Shy Gazelle.

Indeed, the play was not a success and among the many factors for this was the rapidity with which it followed the war. With some reviews more enthusiastic than others, W. A. Darlington of *The Daily Telegraph* wrote: 'This play cannot possibly fail. It is too moving, too exciting, too deft – and too timely. We need to be reminded, just now, that we are people of spirit.'[34] However when Coward read the first scene to his friend Natasha Wilson, her response was that 'it was too horrible to put England in such a position, especially now, when everyone is so down'.[35] Coward himself seemed to become aware of this as the show began to underperform; in a letter to one of his secretaries he remarked: 'I'm fairly depressed about *Peace In Our Time* not being the smasheroo we thought it was. ... I suppose the public really don't feel like seeing anything serious at the moment and I must say I can't blame the poor sods. All the same it's disheartening.'³⁶ As Philip Hoare remarks: 'Crucially, for a man of exquisite timing, he had misjudged his moment. The British public did not want to be reminded of years of deprivation and war; the depressing picture of a defeated people undergoing shortages and domination was all too close to the truth, since Britain was still suffering from austerity and rationing. His audiences expected the escapism of his later war films, *Brief Encounter* and *Blithe Spirit* ... he had not delivered the goods.'³⁷

Contrasts are commonly drawn between the level of Holocaust consciousness we now possess in Europe and America versus that in the more immediate aftermath of the war. Levi and Rothberg describe a near consensus among scholars who describe 'an interval that many think of as a kind of "latency period" but which might also be thought of in terms of what Marxist cultural theory describes as the inevitable "cultural lag" between the emergence of the new and the development of a vocabulary – be it conceptual or artistic – to describe it'.³⁸ The absence of critical attention given to non-mimetic fiction with regard to the Holocaust is an example of a conceptual lag which, I would argue, has not been in step with the artistic developments of the genre. This latency period between the event of the Holocaust and its emergence into popular consciousness should not, as Levi and Rothberg go on to write, be confused with another form of silence.

The notion of a lag has also been attractive to scholars and commentators because it echoes the language of trauma and the concept of *Nachträgichkeit* or 'afterwardsness' of trauma linked to memories which were initially repressed after the initial traumatic event, as described by Freud. While the memory of trauma could indeed have been a factor in some survivors contributing their accounts after a number of decades had passed, it is also worth bearing in mind that many were beginning new lives in countries that had welcomed them after the war (such as the United States and United Kingdom) and desired a clean start without the responsibilities of victimhood or being a survivor. At the same time, as is hinted at by the reception of Coward's *Peace in Our Time*, there was a sense that revisiting the events of the war wouldn't do anyone any good and so there was an unwillingness to listen among those nations who may be considered bystanders or, even worse, collaborators. The first edition of Primo Levi's masterpiece of Holocaust testimony, *If This Is a Man*, was rejected in his native Italy for being written too soon and in danger of reopening old wounds. It eventually received a limited publication in 1947 from Franco Antonicelli's small publishing house Francsco de Silva with a print run of 2,500. Despite generally positive reviews and being hailed by Italo Calvino as a masterpiece, sales were poor and within five years the book was out of print.[39] Similarly, Italian journalist, school teacher and partisan Liana Millu, who was in the women's camp at the same time Levi was in the men's, published her account *Il fumo di Birkenau* in 1947 but it remained an obscure text until its award-winning translation into English almost fifty years later.[40] Examples such as these, of which there are ample to choose from, all feed what has become known as the 'myth of silence'.

A speculative fiction novel which defies the notion of silence in the early post-war era is *The Sound of His Horn* (1952) by Sarban, the authorial pseudonym of John William Wall, a senior British diplomat. The novel harnesses what is implicit or veiled in Burdekin's *Swastika Night* and lays it out in all its naked brutality. In this alternate world German officers hunt what they believe to be sub-men, *Untermensch*, through the woods in the same way they might a stag or a fox. The novel is set 102 years after the Nazis win the Second World War and the protagonist is a British naval lieutenant, Alan Querdillon, who becomes a prisoner of war during the Battle of Crete. After escaping and fleeing through a forest until he collapses from exhaustion, he wakes up in a future nightmarish world, in 'the hundred and second year of the First German Millennium as fixed by our First Fuehrer and Immortal Spirit of Germanism, Adolf Hitler'.[41] The inexplicable transportation through time and space of a (temporarily, in this instance) defeated soldier to an alien and otherly world has overtones of Edgar Rice Burroughs's *A Princess of Mars* (1917), but *The Sound of His Horn* is very much a successor to *Swastika Night*; the regression of society into a semi-medieval state, despite a futuristic setting, mirrors Burdekin's feelings that Nazism is an anti-modern movement. There are no German resistors in *The Sound of His Horn*, no positive characters; the society is irredeemably bloodthirsty and vicious. By portraying the Germans in this way Sarban is conforming to the cultural stigma that somehow German culture is innately warlike and as such Britain was justified in going to war with her. It removes moral ambiguities and suggests that all necessary measures to win were justified because Germany had no redeeming features. Interestingly this is something that Sarban didn't take from Burdekin, who emphasizes nurture over nature as the problem with society.

In 1954 John Wyndham highlighted the significance of Sarban's novel, alongside *Swastika Night*, in an essay called 'Roar of Rockets!'; the two texts receive high praise as the best kind of SF, 'the implicatory story'.[42] The topic must have been pressing for Wyndham as he himself had tried to publish a novel about Nazis in the 1950s. It was written around the same time as his classic *The Day of the Triffids* (1951) but declared unpublishable by numerous editors. Collier's for example 'objected to the Nazi content' while Tim Seldes of Doubleday wrote to Wyndham that 'my problem was that I couldn't become interested in either the multiplication of human beings or the recrudescent Nazism'.[43] It more recently saw the light of day after being rescued from the Wyndham Archives in the Science Fiction Foundation Collection and reassembled and published by David Ketterer and Andy Sawyer. Titled *Plan for Chaos*, it is a post-war tale of a resurgent Nazi threat in the form of identical clones raised in the Nazi doctrine and preparing to trigger a new war between the West and the Soviet Union and claim the ashes of the world for a New Germany. It is not Wyndham's strongest book, and yet it was not the quality of the work which blocked its publication but its subject matter.

Of course, Sarban wouldn't have known about Wyndham's book and there's no evidence he was aware of Burdekin's either, nor other forerunners such as *Loss of Eden*, but the books nonetheless share many thematic links. Mark Valentine, in his survey of Sarban's works, credits the author with being 'perhaps the first to isolate and recreate the Nazi's use of Teutonic mythology and the interest of some of their leaders in occult principles and powers (now, but not then, quite a commonplace theme of conspiracy and alternate history books)'.[44]

The medieval-eque woodland setting of *The Sound of His Horn* is a far cry from the wasteland-like descriptions of huts and earth described in survivor testimonies of the Holocaust; however, beneath the superficial differences similarities lurk. The woodland is itself a giant prison camp, surrounded by deadly fences powered by 'Bohlen Rays', a form of radiation emitted by the wires which is normally fatal in close proximity. After offending Count Johann von Hackelnberg, the Reich master Forester, Alan is cut free from the hospitality of Doctor Eichbrunn. He is re-clothed in the uniform of the 'prey' and let loose in the forest. He quickly realizes that 'the forest of Hackelnberg was most effectively fenced; to be free in it was only to be in a wider prison'.[45] The emphasis on uniforms and the role they play in dehumanizing the prey echoes the Otherness induced by the near-ritualized induction of inmates into concentration camps. However, the language used to describe the uniforms and the materials used in their makeup echo the fetishistic nature inherent to the uniforms of the Nazis' particular brand of fascism. For example, among the sport conducted in the forest is the hunting of women who are forced to dress as birds; Alan encounters one such woman who has survived against the odds thus far:

> As Kit crouched there on all fours with her head bent low to the water and her face hidden, with the moonlight glinting on that strange, glossy dark coat which clothed her uniformly from head to toe, she looked like a lithe and sleek wild beast that had slipped out from the darkness of the woods to drink. For a second she seemed utterly strange to me, and with a shock of fright I felt the net of sorcery fall round us once again and saw von Hackelnberg's red lips laughing wickedly as he put a term to our brief holiday as human beings.[46]

This late description captures the dehumanizing effect von Hackelnberg's hunt has on its prey, the implication being that Kit has been hunted for so long that she has started to become more animal than human. The blurring of boundaries between animal and human are further seen in the savage feline cat people used in the hunts, and the oxen-like passive slaves on the estate who Doctor Eichbrunn describes as 'Slavs I suppose. I've never really gone into their breeding. They seem to me very much just lumps of undifferentiated Under-Race. They are breeding them extensively in the South Russian Glau nowadays.'[47] The transformation of these humans into animals represents a literalization of fascist policies of dehumanization, practised by the Nazi government in its depiction of Jews as rats, vermin, bacterium, a rot or a plague, placing them within a conceptual framework which makes them less-than-human and thus easier to exterminate.[48] In this way euphemism and metaphor form a lexicon of death which helps to obscure the implications of actions for the perpetrators and bystanders, but which also compounds difficulties of comprehension in modern readers. It is this lexicon, and the difficulties of comprehension attached to it, which Art Spiegelman channels in his essential work *Maus*, and can be seen in a more primitive state in Edmond-François Calvo's *La Bete est Morte!* or *The Beast is Dead*, published in Paris in 1944.[49]

The animal–human relationship in *The Sound of His Horn* also allows Sarban to focus on the sexual proclivities of the Nazis in the novel, bringing an additional element of forbidden bestiality to their already violent and abusive sexuality. For example, the women who are hunted while dressed as birds are trussed and presented to the hunter at an evening banquet:

> Exposed on the dish then in front of each guest was the 'bird' he had bagged at the end of the morning's drive, plucked of her feathers now, all but her beaked

mask, and trussed tightly, knees to chin, wrists to ankles. The forester officers deftly moved away the chairs behind the guests, and with a gesture or two indicated where the 'bird's' bonds might be slit with the knife; then discreetly nodded towards the convenient alcoves behind.[50]

Like Burdekin, Sarban is drawing special attention to the underlying sexual fetishism evident in Nazism but where *Swastika Night* focuses on the homoerotic and explicit hatred of women, *The Sound of His Horn* is the red-blooded hetero power fantasy taken to its extreme end, a BDSM rape fantasy wrapped in bestial carnality and a quasi-medieval sense of manhood.

The Sound of His Horn is perhaps the most prominent speculative fiction novel which engages with the Holocaust in the 1945–1960 period, which is to say not very prominent at all, but this does not endorse the fallacy of a silent response; rather there were a large number of responses to the Holocaust from all over Europe and further afield but their impact was at a lower register than the texts which would become standards from the 1960s onwards. Many further examples can be found in short fiction published in this time, of which two stories in particular stand out: 'The Wandering Gentile' (1954) by C. S. Forester and 'Two Dooms' (1958) by Cyril M. Kornbluth.

Originally published as the final story in a collection of realist short stories about the Third Reich called *The Nightmare* (1954), 'The Wandering Gentile' is exceptional in the context of the collection as Forester himself acknowledges in the introduction where he observes that 'not one of the incidents herein tells of an actual happening, but all of them, except the last, easily could have'.[51]

'The Wandering Gentile' is a play on the figure of the Wandering Jew, a character rooted in medieval legend, described in the Oxford English Dictionary as '[a] legendary personage who (according to a popular belief first mentioned in the thirteenth century, and widely current at least until the sixteenth century), for having insulted Jesus on his way to the Cross, was condemned to wander over the earth without rest until the Day of Judgement'.[52] The Wandering Jew features in works of English literature from Chaucer ('The Pardoner's Tale') to Diana Wynne Jones (*The Homeward Bounders*, 1981), and is even more prolific in European literature from France, Germany, Poland, Russia, Italy and more. As a late addition to *Lyrical Ballads*, Wordsworth used him as a device to tour a globe of natural wonders (as well as a counterpoint to Coleridge's Ancient

Mariner, a fellow cursed traveller) from the frozen Alps to ocean caves, sea cliffs to desert sands:

> Day and night my toils redouble,
> Never nearer to the goal;
> Night and day, I feel the trouble
> Of the Wanderer in my soul.[53]

While Wordsworth's character toils endlessly, it is relatively clean of the anti-Semitic overtones that figure in most, particularly early Christian, representations. Indeed, until Wordsworth's final stanza we might envy the wanderer the sights of nature he witnesses but, as Alberto Manguel writes, the true implications of the legend are far less romantic and indeed it characterizes a history of expulsion and punishment that comes to typify not only the diasporic Jewish people after the destruction of the Temple of Jerusalem but other individuals too: 'Pogroms, expulsions, ethnic cleansings, genocides regardless of nationality or creed are the abominable extensions of this reading of the legend.'[54]

By inverting the legend and reversing the Jew–Gentile dichotomy, Forster curses Adolf Hitler to face the fate of wandering the world for all eternity. Thus, as the original wanderer received divine punishment for forsaking Jesus Christ, so too Hitler receives a punishment which defies his original intent to cheat justice via suicide. Joseph Gaer writes that 'as the legend began to lose its mystic character and to be reinterpreted in literature, the Wanderer gradually reverted to his universal role as the symbol of the Man in search of his Soul'.[55] So, the story would then appear to continue the presentation of Hitler – found in texts such as Michael Young's *The Trial of Adolf Hitler* (1944) – as the Führer as a godless man, guilty of 'high treason against the dignity of God and man'.[56] He is not, however, cursed to wander alone; he is accompanied by Eva Braun, she apparently damned by association, and together they are cursed for eternity as they were together in death in Berlin.

> by shifting my position in the driver's seat I could get a glimpse of their faces in the mirror, or rather of the man's face ... It was with surprise that I noticed what charming blue eyes he had – the deepest blue. Adonis eyes, fantastically out of place in that unhealthy face. I thought he must in his youth have been a man of mark. Then I realized he was speaking German, and I remembered the dragging leg and the twitching face; we all know what happened in the concentration camps in Germany. He must have been one of the few lucky ones who survived the horrible things that happened there (yet was he lucky to have survived?) and

must have had the supreme good fortune of being admitted to the United States after the war.⁵⁷

It is a twisted irony that leads Hitler to be mistaken for a concentration camp survivor, but it creates a crucial juxtaposition between the unimaginable reality of the camps and the imaginable uncanny of the supernatural. It also makes clear that these are among the crimes for which Hitler is deserving of punishment, not merely crimes associated with Germany's military belligerence. At the same time, by dressing him in the metaphoric clothes of a survivor, Hitler gains an air of tragedy in his portrayal. By being stripped of the trappings of power which he enjoyed at his most dangerous, Forster has exposed the paranoid, delusionary ranting old man beneath. The narrator quickly becomes convinced that 'the old man was a little touched in the head – as was likely to be the case with anybody who had escaped from Hitler's Germany'.⁵⁸ Adolf is determined to reach Washington but whether, as the narrator suspects, to protect him from the implications of arriving at the American capital with his hostile opinions, or whether as a condition – perhaps even the means – of his endless wandering, Eva 'was keeping him travelling around the United States, hitching, eternally hitching, always on the promise that they were on the way to Washington'.⁵⁹

Rosenfeld argues that 'Hitler's fate represent[s] a form of divine justice. It is not humanity, after all, that has compelled him to wander, but an otherworldly power, possibly God himself. Unlike later narratives, in which Hitler would be charged by the entire civilized world with crimes against humanity, Hitler in Forester's tale remains unrecognized by postwar society'.⁶⁰ Such a reading fits with Rosenfeld's model of Second World War alternate histories (which to a certain extent relies upon the myth of silence, or at least a weakened version of it), however, it also puts aside the narrators frequent references to the horrors he assumes his unidentified passenger has experienced at the hands of Hitler's regime and specifically within concentration camps. The camps are referenced a second time, in addition to the above, as the narrator begins to think his passenger might have been incarcerated as a political prisoner:

> I was curious to know who he was. He might have been someone prominent in pre-war German politics, perhaps even the leader of one of the innumerable German parties; in that case he would have undoubtedly gone into a concentration camp if he had been foolish enough to stay in the country after Hitler's accession to power, and that would account for his insanity – no other explanation was necessary.⁶¹

The irony of these references only works with the assumed familiarity of both Hitler and the concentration camps. Forester even makes references to other facts about the former Führer, some relatively obscure, such as his twitch, 'his memory of a dog named Blondi ... his wife named Eva, his general named Wenck who had failed to relieve Berlin'.[62] The narrator realizes his passengers' apparent identities just as they leave him and hitchhike a ride in a new vehicle. Forester emphasizes the supernatural element of the story at its end, taking on the tone of campfire ghost story:

> I have seen that pitying look on the faces of the one or two other people I have told about this incident, too. That is why I am telling this story as fiction. Pure fiction. Or perhaps that was not a man to whom I gave a hitch. It may have been a spirit, a wraith, doomed to eternal wandering.[63]

Forester's tale speaks to a desire to see Hitler punished for his crimes as both the commander-in-chief of a conquering Nazi Germany and as the architect of the Holocaust. Transposing him (and indeed the Wandering Jew motif itself) from a European setting to the United States, however, puts him into a category of supernatural horror tales to frighten waders on the road, evocative of the Wendigo, The Headless Horseman of Sleepy Hollow or Michael Myers.

C. M. Kornbluth's 'Two Dooms' first appeared in the July 1958 issue of *Venture Science Fiction* magazine, and later in the same year in an anthology of collected Kornbluth stories called *A Mile Beyond the Moon*. Very much a Cold War nuclear-anxiety story, 'Two Dooms' features an atomic physicist, Edward Royland, who has an encounter with a Hopi Native American and undergoes a drug-induced hallucination. He is transported to an alternate world in which the United States has lost the Second World War and been conquered by the Japanese Empire and Nazi Germany, the two powers now in control of the globe and dividing the North American continent between them in a manner which pre-empts similar treatment in *The Man in the High Castle* (1962) by Philip K. Dick.

Royland is one of the scientists working on the Manhattan Project under Robert Oppenheimer and he is struggling to reconcile the progress of the project with his conscience:

> Oppie and the rest of them were going to break the sky, kick humanity right in the crotch, and unleash a prowling monster that would go up and down by night and day peering in all the windows of the world, leaving no sane man unterrified for his life and the lives of his kin.[64]

The vision transports him to a universe where his worst fears are never realized; the United States never successfully manufactures an atomic weapon. The consequences of this involve the Americans having to wage a costly amphibious invasion of mainland Japan; they are forced to strip occupying forces for Europe and, even then, are unable to successfully invade, but this allows Germany to rise again and quickly rearm and reconquer the territory it had been pushed back from, and more. The version of history delivered to Royland comes from German forces in the United States who, like in Burdekin's and Sarban's novels, know only a corrupted mythology of the relevant events.

Royland is told that the Second World War (or 'The War of Triumph, 1940–1955') began when Germany was 'simultaneously and treacherously invaded by the misguided French, the subhuman Slavs, and the perfidious British. The attack, for which the shocked Germans coined the name *Blitzkrieg*, was timed to coincide with an internal eruption of sabotage, well-poisoning, and assassination by the *Zigeunerjuden*, or Jewpsies, of whom little is now known; there seem to be none left'.[65] Germany is a defeated and occupied power but the American failure to force the Japanese into surrender gives Germany a chance to rise again, under the leadership of Goebbels who is the leader idealized in the history of this new world rather than Hitler who is a forgotten footnote, considered by some to be a traitor for losing the war in the first place.

The primary message of 'Two Dooms' is centred on nuclear arms. It is part of a reassessment of both guilt about the bombing of Hiroshima and Nagasaki, and of anxiety about the developing arms race and Cold War stand-off with the Soviet Union. Things are bad, Kornbluth's story seems to suggest, but they could have been far worse. The use of alternate history narratives to present our lived-in history as the best of possible options is one of the most venerable uses of alternate history there is, dating back to Gottfried Leibniz's ideas of philosophical optimism expressed in his *Theodicy* (1710). Leibniz's theories of a benevolent God guiding us through events which may seem terrible in the short term but which result in a better long-term destiny for humanity is a product of a Western-centric view of history of linear progression upwards; it was difficult enough to reconcile in the face of natural disaster – such as the Lisbon earthquake of 1755 which caused Voltaire to explicitly criticize Leibnizian interpretations – but becomes truly problematic in the face of mass slaughter like the First World War or the Holocaust.

Nonetheless, Leibnizian alternate history remains not uncommon and Kornbluth's interpretation of possible greater evils being visited upon humanity is an implicit undertone of most dystopian alternate history, although few are as certain in their resolve as Royland when, upon eventually returning to his original timeline, he returns to working on the Manhattan Project with renewed zeal and sense of purpose, absolved of his guilt and doubt about the morality of the project.

David Cesarani was a key figure in the challenging of the myth of silence, noting that towards the end of the 1940s there was actually a wealth of material recording and discussing the Holocaust in most of the languages of Europe, including English. Having produced such material to minimal impact, however, the early years of the 1950s did experience a recession of interest in the story of the Jewish suffering and struggle suggesting that 'quite simply, enough was enough. However, this regression should not be equated with "silence" or lack of awareness'.[66] Nonetheless, it cannot be denied that though testimony and fiction had begun to appear in the first decades it was not until later that it became part of a wider cultural identity.[67]

That identity emerges in the late 1950s and early 1960s as a result of a number of factors, as Holocaust memory began to transition from what David Roskies and Naomi Diamant identify as the second of its four phases, 'communal memory', into the third, 'provisional memory'.[68] Chronologically the first of the triggers for this change is the Berlin crisis of 1958, culminating in the construction of the Berlin Wall, which some scholars such as Gavriel D. Rosenfeld credit with refocusing the West's attention on Germany's recent history.[69] More concretely, in 1960 William L. Shirer, a CBS correspondent in Berlin during Hitler's rise to power, published *The Rise and Fall of the Third Reich*. The book is monumental in its influence, with authors throughout this study, from Philip K. Dick to Stephen Fry, citing its significance in their acknowledgements. It became an international multi-million bestseller garnering effusive reviews from the mainstream press, such as the *New York Times* who proclaimed it 'one of the most important works of history of our time'.[70] It sold over a million copies in its first year alone, and upon being condensed and serialized in *Reader's Digest*, became one of the bestselling history books of all time.[71] Far less commonly known is the fact that in 1961 Shirer would also go on to write a counterfactual history essay, 'If Hitler Had Won World War II', described as 'an historical fantasy'.[72] The essay imagines the behaviours of Nazi forces occupying the United States by extrapolating from real-world events during the European occupation. Pre-empting the non-mimetic fiction to come, Shirer's essay features a

United States divided between Japan and Germany, with the Japanese the comparatively benevolent rulers. Meanwhile, the Germans impose an iron rule, culminating in the razing of Washington DC and the importing of the Holocaust to American shores:

> Here in America, no Jews have been included in the first transports to Germany. ... Later, we learned why. Hitler and SS chief Heinrich Himmler ... have decided that the Jews are to be liquidated in the United States. It is more economical. ... A few gas chambers and ovens are still functioning at Auschwitz. Eichmann has been overheard to say that the Führer, in his next New Year's proclamation, will proudly announce that Europe has at last been made *Judenfrei* – free of Jews.[73]

The essay switches frequently between Shirer's contemporary commentary ('Such an account of what might have happened is not as fanciful as it sounds. I have seen Hitler's secret plans for his regime of terror in Great Britain.'[74]) and the writings of his alternate self, living in this nightmarish America:

> The figures for those gassed at the great extermination camp in New Jersey have never been published. Eichmann, who was in charge of the grisly business, recently boasted ... that they amounted to nearly five million. ... After the Jews in the United States, it was the turn of the Negroes.[75]

While far from the first alternate history narrative to feature a United States conquered by its Second World War foes (indeed, works such as Fred Allhoff's *Lightning in the Night* (1940) were being produced even during the war), it is no coincidence that the publication of both Shirer's historical magnum opus and his alternate history essay coincided with a growing closeness both culturally and strategically between the United States and West Germany, which became a member of NATO in 1955.[76] It can also not be written off as coincidence that these events and publications all occur immediately prior to the boom in Holocaust interest in the West.

The most significant factor in the Holocaust's 'rediscovery' however seems to be the 1960 capture in Argentina of Adolf Eichmann. His trial in Jerusalem pushed consciousness of the Holocaust to unprecedented levels and caused a new generation of historians and commentators to consider the mechanisms behind genocide in greater depth than ever. However, while this process is traceable, and seems to have developed significant consensus, it is worth pointing out the abnormal route into memory the Holocaust has taken. Peter Novick highlights the peculiarity of this in the introduction to his seminal study of the Holocaust's role in American culture:

> Generally speaking, historical events are most talked about shortly after their occurrence, then they gradually move into the margin of consciousness. ... The most-viewed films and the best-selling books about the Vietnam War almost all appeared within five or ten years of the end of the conflict, as did the Vietnam Veterans Memorial in Washington. With the Holocaust the rhythm has been very different: hardly talked about for the first twenty years or so after World War II; then, from the 1970s on, becoming ever more central in American public discourse – particularly, of course, among Jews, but also in the culture at large.[77]

Returning to the theme of silence, S. Lillian Kremer writes of the trial's literary impact that the 'post-Eichmann transformation from Holocaust silence to expression in Israeli literature was paralleled in American writing'.[78] This move away from silence as an adequate mode of expression was not without controversy, however. Leslie Epstein was in the process of researching and writing his Warsaw ghetto tragicomic novel *King of the Jews* (1979) when he wrote that he had 'come, finally and reluctantly, to the conclusion that almost any honest eye-witness testimony of the Holocaust is more moving and more successful at creating a sense of what it must have been like in the ghettos and the camps than *almost* any fictional account of the same events'.[79] Nor was this seemingly contradictory position of proclaiming the ineffectiveness of writing about the Holocaust while writing about it limited to Epstein or Wiesel himself.

2

Problematizing History: *The Man in the High Castle* (1962), *Fatherland* (1992) and *Making History* (1996)

The Holocaust forced a confrontation with the notion of evil upon White Western Europe and the United States unlike any which had previously surfaced. That organized mass slaughter could be perpetrated on such a scale, amid the bloodiest of wars, was horrifying in itself but that such actions should be undertaken within the boundaries of twentieth-century continental Europe, ensnaring most of its nations in some level of cooperation, either willing or coerced, was unthinkable. Rather than happening on a distant shore in a misrepresented colony, it happened in the heart of the 'old country' and its victims and perpetrators were often regular people who may previously have been thought of as safe, integrated, productive members of society. Genocide was nothing new to Europe or the United States; what was shocking about the Holocaust was its proximity at least as much as its methods and its scale.[1]

The nature of evil was no longer an issue of moral philosophy or theology, it became a political, social, even personal question for the leaders of European-style democracies and for the people they governed. The Holocaust assumed a position as the ultimate manifestation of humanity's potential for evil, and thus its designers and instigators were the ultimate agents of that evil. For some commentators this status was not simply an expression of *extreme* evil but rather *absolute* evil. Thus, following this line of thinking, the Holocaust is humanity's most evil action not on a scale of morality which includes other genocides and wars, but rather in a category of its own: separate and unapproachable.

The novels I analyse in this chapter use speculative fiction to reassess that thought process. By hypothesizing other possible outcomes to the Second World War these texts problematize the notion of absolute evil. The effect of this repositioning allows the authors to critique contemporary issues, calling attention to compromises made in rituals of remembrance, specifically the mantra of 'learning lessons from the past'. *The Man in the High Castle* (1962) by Philip K. Dick is a science fiction classic which unravels the readers' assumptions about what is (and is not) real, the nature of truth and history, and our assumptions about moral superiority whether between individuals, nations, or in the present looking back at the past. One of the fascinating features of alternate history as a sub-genre of speculative fiction is the variety of writers who engage in it; this is particularly apparent when we examine texts which cluster around similar historical nexus points. The Second World War attracts authors of alternate history who are best known as science fiction writers, such as Dick, but there are also numerous novels written by historians and journalists such as Robert Harris. *Fatherland* (1992) is so far Harris's only sustained work of speculative fiction, an alternate history novel set in 1964.[2] Unusually for alternate history novels about the Second World War, especially those by British and American authors, it is set in Germany rather than one of the occupied or puppet states. A detective novel about history set in a timeline which never existed, *Fatherland* exposes the artificiality of historical narrative, as Walter Benjamin wrote: 'Once one asks the question, with whom does the historical writer of historicism actually empathise. The answer is irrefutably with the victor.'[3] *Making History* (1996) is the third novel of the three which form the spine of this chapter. Written by Stephen Fry, who is best known as a comic wit and TV personality, as well as a popular writer, the novel uses a time-travel mechanic to ask questions of our notion of totality and absolutes. If we discuss events like the Holocaust in terms of absolutes, Fry seems to ask, then what does it mean if we are confronted with an atrocity and a world which is even worse?

All three novels challenge our ideas about history and about the Holocaust; they undermine faith in the notion of an absolute evil and call into question issues of historicity, morality and a hierarchy of suffering. They do not necessarily provide answers, instead they find new ways of asking important questions, keeping them in the forefront of our minds and in so doing problematizing history in a manner which feels increasingly vital.

The Man in the High Castle (1962), Philip K. Dick

The Man in the High Castle is probably the best-known Second World War alternate history novel from within the science fiction genre; it played a major role in popularizing that genre within Anglo-American SF fandom (winning the Hugo Award for Best Novel in 1963) and is 'paradigmatic of alternate histories'.[4] Within the novel, Nazi Germany and Imperial Japan have carved the world into two vast territories and their associated spheres of influence, preserving a few minor neutral states such as Sweden. Emblematic of this division of the world, a distorted mirror of Soviet-Western division, is the rendering of the United States into three portions: a Nazi-occupied East, a Japanese-administered West and a neutral buffer-state along the Rocky Mountains.

As Katharine Burdekin's *Swastika Night* has already shown, part of the terror of a dystopia based on Nazi Germany is the worry that its combination of ruthless violence, leader cult, careful control of information, and nationalism could render manifest Hitler's promised *Tausendjähriges Reich* [Thousand-Year Reich]. The anxiety of an inescapably stable totalitarian dystopia is famously expressed in Orwell's *Nineteen Eighty-Four* which offers a 'picture of the future' as 'a boot stamping on a human face – forever'.[5] Yet the world of *The Man in the High Castle* is far from stable. It is indeed a world long conquered by the Axis powers, set in an alternate 1972, and the resistance to their rule has apparently long faded away. This illusion of stability, the Thousand-Year Reich, rests on a knife edge: Hitler is an aging madman, riddled with syphilis, and the true power in the Reich is Martin Bormann. On Bormann's death, early in the novel, the power struggle to succeed him threatens nuclear war and global annihilation. This political instability is only one of the fractures in the novel which expose the fragility of attempting to live a passive existence.

A key theme of the novel is that of authenticity and duplication. This is best expressed by Wyndham-Mason, a supplier in artefacts from pre-war, independent America. He compares two antique cigarette lighters with regard to their historical importance, and thus their value to collectors:

> One of those two Zippo lighters was in Franklin D. Roosevelt's pocket when he was assassinated. And one wasn't. One has historicity, a hell of a lot of it. As much as any object ever had. And one has nothing. ... You can't tell which is which. There's no 'mystical plasmic presence', no 'aura' around it. ... It's all a big racket ... I mean, a gun goes through a famous battle, like the Meuse-Argonne, and it's the same as if it hadn't, *unless you know*. It's ... In the mind, not the gun.[6]

'Historicity' is a socially agreed-upon construct, assigned to an item by consensus of a seller and a buyer; in this regard it is similar to the representation of history itself as an agreed-upon narrative between historian and reader. This takes on particular resonance, and is given a particular irony, when it is revealed that many of the antiques Wyndham-Mason sells are fakes, manufactured to order. Dick further highlights the fragility of history by including within *The Man in the High Castle* a novel written by the reclusive writer Hawthorne Abendsen called 'The Grasshopper Lies Heavy'. Rather than acting as a simple mirror so that the characters can look back on our world, 'Grasshopper' acts instead as a window into yet another reality, another history. Or perhaps a better analogy would be to think of it as a funhouse mirror, looking back at the readers. Japan is defeated but there was no attack on Pearl Harbour; the United Kingdom has defeated Germany in Europe helped by a crucial victory in North Africa, but finished the war as an industrial-military superpower and is able to maintain control of the empire; post-war the United States becomes a more peaceful and tolerant society, eliminating racism by the 1950s. Ultimately, this world is just as alien to our timeline as the world of *The Man in the High Castle*. Thus, 'Grasshopper' allows us to reassess the Axis victory timeline of Dick's novel; we are put in the bizarre situation of considering it a more plausible world than one in which the Axis lost the war. This effect is aided by the initially incredulous responses of characters who read 'Grasshopper' ('Japan would have won anyhow. Even if there had been no Pearl Harbour'[7]), as well as what Pamela Sargent refers to as the unnerving realization that a California ruled by the Japanese Empire, as Dick presents it, is not that dissimilar to the actual California of the 1960s.[8]

The Japanese rule over the Western portion of the former United States is presented as benign relative to the Nazi rule over not just the Eastern portion but of Europe and the wider world. 'Grasshopper' is, for example, 'one of those Banned-in-Boston' books yet is read widely in the Rocky Mountains, the West and even on Japan's home islands.[9] References are made throughout the novel to the 'Nazi experiment' in Africa, 'that huge empty ruin'.[10] One character, Robert Childan, reflects on it in relation to the Holocaust:

> and after all, they had been successful with the Jews and Gypsies and Bible Students. And the Slavs had been rolled back two thousand years' worth, to their heartland in Asia. Out of Europe entirely, to everyone's relief, back to riding yaks and hunting with bow and arrow. ... But Africa. They had simply let their enthusiasm get the better of them there, and you had to admire that.[11]

The evocative language of 'the ghosts of dead tribes. Wiped out to make a land of … automatons, building and toiling away', 'the billion chemical heaps in Africa that were now not even corpses' evokes the enslavement, deconstruction and destruction of Israel's tribes.¹² The imagery is as horrifying as it is mysterious and powerful, sufficiently so to provide other authors with their jumping-off point: Guy Saville, for example, cites these passages as being a major influence on his novels *The Afrika Reich* (2011) and *The Madagaskar Plan* (2015).¹³ Saville's novels are the first two books in an as-yet-incomplete trilogy depicting a reality in which the Holocaust is avoided through the successful deportation of the Jewish population of Europe to Madagascar. Following Dunkirk, the United Kingdom reaches armistice with Germany under the terms of which Africa is carved up between the two powers: the United Kingdom retaining its colonies and protectorates and the French and Belgian empires largely transferring to German control. The result gives new meaning to the old colonial label of Africa as a Dark Continent.

While Saville avoids the Jewish Holocaust, he remains true to the spirit of Dick's initial horrifying images. *The Afrika Reich* is a fast-paced thriller which tours the dark recesses of 1950s German Africa; most vivid is the description of the SS base at Schädelplatz, a fictitious location north of Stanleystadt in Deutsch Kongo (or Kisangani, formerly Stanleyville, now in Democratic Republic of the Congo). The German name has the somewhat melodramatic meaning of 'shadow place', although such a name does evoke a sense of liminal Otherness appropriate to the sense of being outside time and space which the Holocaust conventionally requires. Besides, the melodrama seems apt when the base is first seen by the novel's protagonist Burton Cole:

> There were guard towers in each of the corners; a patrol stalking the perimeter with a Doberman. Enough barbed wire for a concentration camp. But it was the ground that most caught Burton's attention. Searchlights dived and soared over it. For a second he stood dumbfounded at the sheer scale of it. The sheer barbarity. His father would have wept at its sight.
> Then his stomach curdled.
> … 'Twenty thousand nigger skulls.'
> Burton looked back at the quadrangle and its gruesomely cobbled square. … Inside him something screamed. He saw children torn from parents, husbands from wives. Families left watching the horizon for loved ones who would never return home to smile and bicker and gather round the fire. Every skull was one more reason to kill Hochburg.¹⁴

Afrika Reich's alternate history presents readers with a single inescapable dystopian reality; Dick's novel however offers a more complex tableau. There are three realities in *The Man in the High Castle*: the reality of the novel, the reality of 'Grasshopper', and our reality. The Japanese character Mr Tagomi is temporarily transported to our reality when he handles a piece of jewellery, notable for having been designed and manufactured by Frank Frink and Ed McCarthy while living in California, yet not based on Japanese or German styles but on something new, an unheard-of artistic decision. Tagomi recognizes in the pieces of jewellery that 'there is something new which animates these ... The Law of Tao is borne out, here; when yin lies everywhere, the first stirring of light is suddenly alive in the darkest depths'.[15]

The Law of Tao, of a small space for light even when surrounded by dark, is both representative of the secretly Jewish Frink making a positive cultural contribution while living in the darkest of times for Jews and is also borne out in the narrative. Upon purchasing some of the jewellery, a small silver triangle, and interrogating it for its secrets, Tagomi is dazzled for a moment by the sunlight reflecting on it; he finds himself in a San Francisco which is strange to him, full of 'white barbarian[s]', unfamiliar landmarks such as the Embarcadero Freeway, with no pedecabs upon it, instead with cars 'like brutal big crushers, all unfamiliar in shape'.[16] Bewildered, he seeks respite in a diner:

> Ahead, a dingy lunch counter. Only whites within, all supping. Mr Tagomi pushed open the wooden swinging doors. Smell of coffee. Grotesque jukebox in the corner blaring out; he winced and made his way to the counter. All stools taken by whites. Mr Tagomi exclaimed. Several whites looked up. *But none departed their places. None yielded their stools to him. They merely resumed supping.*
>
> 'I insist!' Mr Tagomi said loudly to the first white; he shouted in the man's ear.
>
> The man put down his coffee mug and said, 'Watch it, Tojo.'
>
> Mr Tagomi looked to the other whites; all watched with hostile expressions. And none stirred.[17]

The racial slur identifies this as an America other than that of 'Grasshopper', but Dick explicitly identifies it as our real world in an excerpt printed in *Exegesis* (2011). He writes that the section is emblematic of Taoism's yin-yang dialectic, the whole is contained in the part, thus:

> Our universe (world) is a scene in *TMITHC* [*The Man in the High Castle*]. A place where Mr. Tagomi goes.
>
> Mr. Tagomi is a fictional person in a work of fiction produced in our universe.

... Our world contains *TMITHC* which contains our world which contains *TMITHC* which contains our world which contains *TMITHC* which contains.[18]

By embedding our world within *The Man in the High Castle* (and vice versa), and by making the world of 'Grasshopper' as strange to us as it is to the characters living in *The Man in the High Castle* timeline, Dick simultaneously highlights the symbiosis of the two worlds even while Mr Tagomi is undergoing severe estrangement. Thus, the novel itself ratifies Pamela Sargent's unnerving realization about the similarities of our two worlds.

The racist jibe directed towards Tagomi is a challenge to any sense of moral superiority, an 'it can't happen here' attitude and, while there is a difference between racist verbal abuse and genocide in extermination camps, the location and context of this scene is crucial: in California in the 1960s the rounding up of Japanese immigrants and Japanese-American citizens and forcing them into concentration camps during the war was still a very recent stain on the American moral character. It is hard to disagree with Howard Zinn's assessment that through this policy 'the United States came close to direct duplication of Fascism' or with Hugh Brogan when he notes that the seizure of Japanese-Americans' land bears a 'strong resemblance to Indian removal and the Trail of Tears', linking the episode both to the Holocaust and the genocide and persecution of Native Americans.[19]

Tellingly, Mr Tagomi perceives our world as a 'dull, smoky, tomb-world', the negative imagery further undermining our sense of historical superiority over his reality. Howard Canaan notes that Dick also references the 'tomb-world' in other novels such as *The Three Stigmata of Palmer Eldritch* (1965), *Do Androids Dream of Electric Sheep* (1968) and *Ubik* (1969), and that the image is a reference of a 'Gnostic myth that Dick explores in endless variations in his fiction … a condition of spiritual sleep or illusion from which characters must struggle to come alive, to reach the light (in Platonic terms) that has become occluded from them'.[20] That Tagomi perceives our world as the unreal dream from which he must awake rather than his own shakes the prejudice inherent in the reader that our world is the primary world and that the fictive world of the character is a secondary, lesser reality.

Late in the novel it is revealed that 'Grasshopper' was not written by Hawthorne Abendsen, or at least not composed by him, but was written based on the interpretations of an oracle, the *I Ching*, a Chinese divination text also known in English as the *Book of Changes*. When Julia Frink comes to ask the oracle, in the presence of Abendsen, why it wrote the novel the oracle replies with the symbol Chung Fu, or Inner Truth, meaning that the text is true and that Germany and Japan actually lost the war.[21] The revelation collapses the three realities thus far presented into a single whole, opening the possibility that the oracle was actually accessing our reality but being misinterpreted by Abendsen, while keeping open the possibility of a third 'Grasshopper' reality equally as true, or fictitious, as either our own or that of *The Man in the High Castle*.

The lines between real and fiction, history and fantasy are confused both within the novel and as a result of it. Dick said in interviews that he had written *The Man in the High Castle* itself with the aid of the *I Ching*, casting hexagrams at the same moments as his characters and assigning actions to them based on the results, thus assuming the role of Abendsen in our own world.[22] Dick further blurs these lines in a piece he wrote in 1974, 'Biographical Material on Hawthorne Abendsen', in which he appeared to have experienced a shift in reverse to Mr Tagomi's and is writing from within the *High Castle* reality:

> I am, of course, one of Mr. Abendsen's admirers; my own works, such as they are, have been influenced strongly by his, in particular my novel *Man in the High Castle*. ... It goes without saying that *The Grasshopper Lies Heavy* (its German title, *Schwer Liegt die Heuschrecke* [München: Konig Verlag, 1974] is perhaps more familiar to us) has become Hawthorne Abendsen's most renowned book, although 'underground' both in printing and distribution, due to its political and religious nature.[23]

Dick himself relates to Tagomi, specifically Tagomi's incapacitating horror at the personality traits of the most likely contenders to replace Martin Bormann as German Führer.[24] Compounded by the persistent theme of false reality ubiquitous in Dick's fiction, and the theme of authenticity and historicity in *The Man in the High Castle*, Dick calls into question the boundaries between realities, and indeed the historical narrative of our own time and place as much as that of his novel, or his meta-novel. Just as Dick's character Julia reads 'Grasshopper' and comes to the realization that, although an alternate history novel, it is actually 'about our own world', we too reach the same point with *High Castle*.[25] Indeed, so important is this realization that for John Rieder the novel is most usefully seen 'not as an alternative history ... but rather as a complex set of metafictional possibilities concretized by objects and texts within the novel'.[26]

Of prime concern here, given the collapsing of realities presented by Dick, is the issue of relative morality. If our world and that of the triumphant Nazis are so interchangeable as to become indistinct, then what does that say about the human capacity for genocide or evil? Dick writes that 'simple, clear "answers" to this question ("Why the Nazis did what they did, and will we do it, and are we also guilty?") defy us; they cannot be had'.[27] Indeed in the seven years he spent preparing to write *High Castle*, Dick read many and varied sources on the Second World War and galvanized a hatred of fascism:

> The writing wasn't torturous. Writing was a catharsis for me. It was the research that was so tough. I thought I hated those guys before I did the research. After I did the research then I had created for myself an enemy that I would hate the rest of my life. Fascism. Wherever it appears. Whether it's in Germany, the United States, Soviet Union or anywhere. Fascism, wherever it appears, it is the enemy. … Fascism and Germany are not that intimately linked. Fascism is a world wide phenomena. It can hit a bunch of baboons swinging in the trees in Polynesia. They can all suddenly put on iron helmets and march around. Fascism is very much with us today, boys and girls. And it's still an enemy.[28]

The tone of Dick's statement here, in an interview on Californian radio in 1976, reasserts what the novel already proposes to be true: just as the Nazis did not win the Second World War in *The Man in the High Castle*, in our world we did not win the war either, not if the aim was the destruction of fascism. Karen Hellekson contends that *High Castle* tells the careful reader that 'truth (and history) is created inside the individual' and that this is the 'Inner Truth' the *I Ching* is referring to.[29] The assertion by Dick – both within the novel and in other venues such as the above interview – that within every individual, or at least every group, there is still the capacity for fascistic behaviour is both terrifying and undeniably evident in societies around the world since 1945 and right into our present day.

The destructive insanity of fascism, specifically in the form of Nazism, is contemplated by one of Dick's characters, Baynes, in light of their ambitions to expand into space:

> The conquering of planets. Something frenzied and demented, as was their conquering of Africa, and before that, Europe and Asia.
> Their view; it is cosmic. Not a man here, a child there, but an abstraction: race, land. *Volk. Land. Blut. Ehre.* Not of honourable men but of *Ehre* itself, honour; the abstract is real, the actual is invisible to them. … They identify with God's power and believe they are godlike. That is their basic madness. They are overcome by some archetype; their egos have expanded psychotically

so that they cannot tell where they begin and the godhead leaves off. It is not hubris, not pride; it is inflation of the ego to its ultimate – confusion between him who worships and that which is worshipped. Man has not eaten God; God has eaten man.[30]

Baynes characterizes the Nazis as agents of entropy, speeding the world prematurely towards its unavoidable ultimate death, advancing God's ultimate design. This is evidence, Howard Canaan points out, not only of Dick's pervasive Gnosticism, but also 'that Nazism is more than a political or historical phenomenon for Dick; it is a psychic or spiritual sickness, a perversion not just of civilization or community, but the true communion'.[31] *The Man in the High Castle* questions our complacency about such constructs as truth and history, and shows that fascism can lead to catastrophes worse than the Holocaust as we know it: the successful and complete eradication of the Jews and Gypsies of Europe and beyond, but also the aforementioned 'huge empty ruin' of Africa, and the potential evisceration of the globe in nuclear war. Thus, *The Man in the High Castle* locates the Holocaust on a scale of comparable atrocity suggesting that it is not temporally inaccessible (it could happen again), nor set apart in its brutality and scale (it could have been / could be worse).

Fatherland (1992), Robert Harris

In a very different way to Philip K. Dick's novel, Robert Harris's *Fatherland* is also a novel about the mutability of history's artifice. It may be the definitive fictional extension of the words Szymon Laks recalls being told by an SS officer while in Auschwitz:

> according to the instructions of the Führer himself, not even one *Häftling* should come out alive from any concentration camp. In other words, there will be no one who can tell the world what has happened here in the last few years. But even if such witnesses should be found – and this is the essence of the brilliant plan of our Führer – NOBODY WILL BELIEVE THEM.[32]

The protagonist of the novel is Xavier March, a homicide investigator in the Berlin Kriminalpolizei (the Kripo), the plain-clothes arm of the city's police force in a 1960s Germany under the rule of a victorious Third Reich. March is investigating the first in what will turn out to be a series of killings or suspicious deaths; when introduced to the reader he is attending a crime scene on the shores of Lake Havel where the first body is found. It is soon revealed that the body belongs to Josef Bühler, a Nazi official who in our history was an assistant to the Governor General of the occupied Polish territories.

Discovering the identity of the body sets March on a course which causes him to clash with his superiors in the Kripo, as well as the even more sinister Gestapo, as he ultimately works his way towards the heart of a conspiracy at the centre of the Reich. In the world of *Fatherland*, Germany successfully conquered Europe and reached an uneasy truce with the United States. The Soviets, though pushed back, are waging a long and bloody guerrilla war, creating a *Nineteen Eighty-Four*-esque eternal struggle in the Urals to the East which is 'dragging on forever'.[33]

> Inside, beyond the SS sentries and the creaky revolving door, a board announced the current state of terrorist alert. There were four codes, in ascending order of seriousness: green, blue, black and red. Today, as always, the alert was red.[34]

Comparisons with George Orwell's classic novel are readily forthcoming, not least the dystopian setting and the didacticism, but also in the limited access which Harris's German citizens have to their own history. March is accompanied for a significant part of the novel by Charlotte 'Charlie' Maguire, an American journalist, a woman who acts as the Julia to March's Winston, a catalyst for his fall from grace.[35] At one point they discuss propaganda:

> The War in the East ... In Berlin we hear only of victories. Yet the Wehrmacht has to ship the coffins home from the Urals front at night, on special trains, so nobody sees how many dead there are.[36]

Charlie informs him that the Pentagon estimates 100,000 Germans killed since 1960. They discuss the relative strengths of the space program in Germany and the USA; in this case it seems the Reich is being truthful when it claims to be ahead of its American rival. March asks if Winston Churchill is alive (he is, living in Canada), then March asks about the Jews. Charlie is reluctant to answer:

> 'Please. The truth.'
> 'The truth? How do I know what the truth is? ... We're brought up to think of Germans as something from outer space. Truth doesn't enter into it.'
> 'Very well then. Give me the propaganda.'
> ... 'They say you scoured Europe for every living Jew – men, women, children, babies. They say you shipped them to ghettos in the East where thousands died of malnutrition and disease. Then you forced the survivors farther East,

and nobody knows what happened after that. A handful escaped over the Urals into Russia. I've seen them on TV. Funny old men, most of them; a bit crazy. They talk about execution pits, medical experiments, camps that people went into but never came out of. They talk about millions dead. But then the German ambassador comes along in his smart suit and tells everyone it's all just communist propaganda. So nobody knows what's true and what isn't. And I'll tell you something else – most people don't care.'[37]

In *Fatherland* the Final Solution for the extermination of the Jews in Europe has been completed and largely covered up thanks to a feat of wilful ignorance on the part of the German population, but as Charlie confirms, also a wilful ignorance, or perhaps innocence, among other peoples too:

The Jews had all been evacuated to the east during the war. Everyone knew that. What had happened to them since was not a question anyone asked in public – or in private either, if they had any sense, not even an SS-Sturmbannführer.[38]

Having served their purpose, Auschwitz and the other extermination camps have been decommissioned and demolished. Under the direction of the head of the SS and de facto ruler of the Reich, Reinhard Heydrich (who survived the Prague assassination in 1942 which killed him in our timeline), the mass extermination of a people is being expunged from history. Ultimately this includes forever silencing those individuals, like Josef Bühler, who attended the infamous Wansee Conference which in 1942 formalized the plans for what would come to be known as the Holocaust.

The word is of course mundane to March, and only occurs once in the novel, in its non-capitalized form, in reference to war crimes committed by Stalin's Russia in the 1930s. Tellingly, this lone usage occurs in the section immediately following Charlie's own description of how events are perceived in Germany:

One by one, as they advanced eastwards, beginning with the bodies of 10,000 Polish officers in the Katyn forest, the Germans had discovered the mass graves of Stalin's victims. Millions had died in the famines, purges, deportations of the 1930s. Nobody knew the exact figure. The execution pits, the torture chambers, the gulags inside the Arctic Circle – all were now preserved by the Germans as memorials to the dead, museums of Bolshevik evil. Children were taken round them; ex-prisoners acted as guides. There was a whole school of historical studies devoted to investigating the crimes of communism. Television showed documentaries on Stalin's holocaust – bleached skulls and walking skeletons, bulldozed corpses and the earth-caked rags of women and children bound with wire and shot in the back of the neck.³⁹

The allusion to the Katyn Forest Massacre is telling; in the absence of a greater atrocity worthy of the capital H, the Katyn Massacre and other war crimes committed by Stalin's regime have become the benchmark for evil. Harris layers the ironies here as the methodological slaughter inflicted at Katyn is considered by some historians to be a direct predecessor to the Holocaust.⁴⁰ Furthermore, the manner in which these atrocities are treated by a post-war Nazi Germany replicate the treatment of the Holocaust in Western consciousness with memorials, museums and schools of historical study.

As an alternate history, *Fatherland* succeeds in challenging our expectations about the truth and the validity of our own historical narrative. By referencing Soviet atrocities as the epitome of (known) evil within the novel, Harris applies a moral relativity to the Holocaust, placing it within a continuity of horrific acts from which it has been frequently excluded by exceptionalist doctrine. In addition, the Nazi vilification of the Soviets to better mask their own crimes mirrors the Soviet eagerness to highlight German crimes both during the war and in its aftermath, including falsely blaming the Nazi government for the Katyn Forest Massacre at the Nuremberg Trials.⁴¹ Similarly, Harris challenges Anglo-American moral superiority vis-à-vis such atrocity both through Charlie's confession that 'most people don't care' and by employing authentic historical artefacts within his fiction.⁴²

In Harris's 1964 a United States led by President Joseph P. Kennedy is making overtures for an alliance with the Reich. In our own timeline, and at least in the West, it is difficult to imagine a world unaware of the Holocaust, or a United States of that period willing to ally itself to Nazi Germany while the rest of Europe is either occupied or being run as a puppet state. Yet, through feasible extrapolation, Harris sketches an alternate route which challenges our concepts of moral superiority and righteousness. Harris weaves genuine historical documents into his counterfactual history, and so, among other relevant material, he quotes real diplomatic memos from our mutual 1938 which record the conversations between the German and American ambassadors to the United Kingdom, the latter of whom was Joseph P. Kennedy. The memo reads:

> The Ambassador then touched upon the Jewish question and stated that it was naturally of great importance to German-American relations. In this connection it was not so much the fact that we wanted to get rid of the Jews that was harmful

to us, but rather the loud clamour with which we accompanied this purpose. ... Kennedy mentioned that very strong anti-Semitic tendencies existed in the United States and that a large portion of the population had an understanding of the German attitude towards the Jews.[43]

The context of this extract within the novel has the added sinister effect of implying that an American suggestion to lower the 'loud clamour' may have contributed to the secretive and conspiratorial nature of what the Holocaust became. As M. Keith Booker remarks, the depiction of the United States in the novel suggests that 'Western democracies are willing to tolerate the brutal oppression of large populations when it is convenient to do so', not only in its tolerance of Nazi Germany, but by foregrounding the real United States' wartime relationship with Russia: 'we ... should not be overly self-satisfied having defeated the real-world dystopia of Nazi Germany, especially as we did so by allying ourselves with the equally horrific dystopia of Stalin's Russia'.[44] Harris's United States may allow German domination over Europe, but in some ways this is only a darker exaggeration of the Allies in our own timeline allowing Stalin's Russia to control the Eastern half. These *realpolitik* attitudes remain relevant given the patchwork and uneven attitude towards dictatorial governments practised by Western nations today.

Harris, a former journalist, adopts the historian's craft by employing accurate historical sources in this manner. Similarly, his author's note takes care to assert that 'biographical details are correct up to 1942', that those 'named as having attended the Wannsee Conference all did so'. He also includes a list of 'authentic' documents used in the novel, including Heydrich's invitation to the conference, the ambassadorial dispatches, railway time tables and more; 'where I have created documents', he continues, 'I have tried to do so on the basis of fact'.[45] Insisting on historical authenticity in a counterfactual or alternate history novel may seem oxymoronic, but it actually reveals a conflation of two sides of Harris's character: that of the careful journalist/historian and that of the novelist.[46] It also asserts the factuality at the core of the novel that is the Holocaust, increasing the extent to which the reader must face up to real-world horrors at the heart of the fiction, while also acting as a response to the lies of Holocaust deniers.[47]

Fatherland further challenges our relationship with history through its characterization of Xavier March himself. March is a veteran of the war, a member of the SS, and yet he is also a sympathetic character who we empathize with throughout the novel. True, he is an SS member by default as all members of the Kripo are inducted into the ranks automatically, he wears the uniform only when he must and is not an actual registered Nazi Party member. Yet he still challenges the cultural homogenous depiction of all members of the SS as being the epitome of evil at the centre of an evil regime. Even within the novel, Charlie admits that she hated him on sight, that the SS uniform 'blots out the man'.[48]

The success of this rehabilitation is questionable, however, as it is unclear how tainted by the Reich March had actually become. Certainly, he is unaware of the Holocaust and is horrified by the revelation, all the more so because of his inadvertent personal connection: a powerful scene in which March learns that the hair from female camp detainees was turned into thread for socks for submarine crewmen such as himself, another genuine historical document among those mentioned above.[49] But perhaps what most undermines his rehabilitation is the fact that he does not appear to be particularly German; indeed Geoffrey Winthrop-Young goes so far as to claim that even his name, Xavier March, 'is almost unpronounceable to Germans; if he really were one, he would more likely be called Xaver März'.[50] Yet regardless of the failures or successes of March as a German SS member, *Fatherland* uses him as an effective protagonist to steer readers through the novel and induce an appropriate level of estrangement to allow us to reflect more meaningfully upon the artificiality of history. Karen Hellekson sums up such relationship-challenging functions of alternate history:

> Alternate histories question the nature of history and of causality ... they make readers rethink their world and how it has become what it is. They are a critique of the metaphors used to discuss history. And they foreground the 'constructedness' of history and the role narrative plays in this construction.[51]

Specifically focusing on *Fatherland*, Gavriel D. Rosenfeld attributes the representation of March to a general process of normalization which is further underlined by the negative depiction of the American government, 'directly challenging traditional notions of Anglo-American moral superiority'.[52] He writes:

> [Harris] used the scenario of the Nazi wartime victory to question the nation's self-congratulatory myths and create a new sense of national identity ... In so doing, [*Fatherland*, and other texts like it] normalize the portrayal of a Nazi victory, depicting the Germans in human rather than demonic terms.[53]

As previously mentioned, by introducing the issue of the Holocaust as the subject of a cover-up, *Fatherland* manages to include substantial elements from the conspiracy thriller mode, and it is worth touching upon them. By making the Holocaust a hidden event, wilfully covered up by the machinations of a government, the novel casts Xavier March in the role of historian, piecing together the evidence for the atrocity while also solving the murder case. Both feed into March's assessment of himself: 'It kept him going, his blessing or his curse, this compulsion to *know*.'[54] March seeks defence in historical knowledge as the novel's principle villain, Odilo 'Globus' Globocnik, interrogates him. March calls out the names he has learnt, the names of the death camps, 'Majdanek! Sobibor! Auschwitz/Birkenau! ... like a shield to ward off the blows'. Globus taunts March, stripping the words of the power they hold in our own vocabulary:

> They're just names, March. There's nothing there any more, not even a brick. Nobody will ever believe it. And shall I tell you something? Part of you can't believe it either.[55]

In a sense, Globus is correct. Through him Harris is evoking the incomprehensibility of atrocity. March is propelled by a desire for an assured and certain truth (as we have seen, itself a nebulous concept at the best of times) but as both a historian and a detective, he is forced to do some of his work backwards. Having already uncovered a narrative, he becomes primarily concerned with uncovering facts. It is this that leads him to his fate at the end of the novel. Documented evidence of the Holocaust having been given to Charlie who is fleeing for the Swiss border, March no longer has any control or influence on the global impact of the revelations he has uncovered. Nonetheless, he is driven by a personal desire to know, to believe, and so he turns to another branch of history, archaeology:

> He bent and picked it up, turned it over in his hand. The brick was pitted with yellow lichen, scorched by explosive, crumbling at the corners. But it was solid enough. It existed. He scraped at the lichen with his thumb and the carmine dust crusted beneath his fingernail like dried blood. As he stooped to replace it, he saw others, half-hidden in the pale grass – ten, twenty, a hundred . . .[56]

The counterbalancing of depression regarding the crime committed and satisfaction at having found hard evidence is an important revelatory moment for both March and the reader as the abstract notion of the Holocaust is given corporeal form in the bricks amid the grass. In ending the novel in this manner,

Harris disproves Globus and the exceptionalists; March believes it now, but he also knows that, as a part of the society which allowed this atrocity, he has blood on his hands.

Conspiracy narratives engage because they appeal to the historian's temptation to disregard the core tenets of their craft and lean more greatly on a pleasing fiction – 'the work of historical self-construction is part of the endless business of beating social determinants to the punch, writing history before it writes you'.[57] In uncovering a conspiracy, as March does, the narratives are also intrinsically anti-authoritarian (a conspiracy is never imposed from below, after all) and so, in the context of Nazi Germany, apt. They are also invariably thrillers and include a romanticized notion of the automatic justification, and indeed morality, of the truth over fiction, playing on the 'paranoid suspicion that any one of us might be hand in glove with the devil, and not know it'.[58] Citing Susan Sontag's take on Oscar Wilde – 'I envy paranoids. They actually feel people are paying attention to them' – David Aaronovitch posits that 'if conspiracism is a projection of paranoia, it may exist in order to reassure us that we are not the totally unconsidered objects of a blind process'.[59] Michael Barkun agrees with this sentiment pointing out that the conspiracy theory is 'frightening because it magnifies the power of evil, leading in some cases to an outright dualism in which light and darkness struggle for cosmic supremacy. At the same time, however, it is reassuring, for it promises a world that is meaningful rather than arbitrary'.[60]

Yet, at the same time, for the historian conspiracies are terrifying because they cede the truth of a narrative to an exterior, normally opposing, force. Conspiracies deliberately undermine the historical record, they are anti-historical, and they imply that certain facts or truths have been concealed from the population by being erased from history. They epitomize a postmodern anxiety of knowledge and history because they centre on an 'unbridgeable gap between historical events and historical narrative'.[61] Fiction both plays upon, and attempts to bridge, that disconnect. In doing so, conspiracy thrillers use their fictionality to call into question the validity of what we call history, and question the artificial and proscribed nature of its construction, yet in a different manner to alternate histories which do not necessarily require the external agency which is a prerequisite of the conspiracy. *Fatherland* inhabits both sub-genres as the conspiracy is orchestrated by an external force, Heydrich, yet the alternative nature of the alternate history is a separate facet, woven into the narrative organically rather than created as part of a plot to steer history in a different direction.

Fatherland's concerns are not solely based on history, however; Harris also uses history, and his alternate history world, to critique current affairs. Harris's Germany is at the centre of a European Community which it dominates. In a lengthy piece of exposition he describes the wider European economic and social position:

> in the West, twelve nations – Portugal, Spain, France, Ireland, Great Britain, Belgium, Holland, Italy, Denmark, Norway, Sweden and Finland – had been corralled by Germany, under the Treaty of Rome, into a European trading bloc. German was the official second language in all schools. People drove German cars, listened to German radios, watched German televisions, worked in German owned factories, moaned about the behaviour of German tourists in German-dominated holiday resorts, while German teams won every international sporting competition except cricket, which only the English played.[62]

The European Parliament is in Berlin, and is dwarfed by the monumental architecture of Albert Speer – 'the flags of the twelve member nations were lit by spots. The swastika which flew above them was twice the size of the other standards'.[63] Europe has a common currency, the Reichsmark, and a flag, twelve gold stars on a field of dark blue.[64] Enough of these details are distortions and exaggerations of our timeline's European Union (EU) to make the comparison explicit, and given that the novel was published in 1992, the year the Treaty of the European Union was signed in Maastricht, it can be seen to reflect British concerns about the future of the continent and particularly Germany's increasing importance in those plans. As Harris wrote in the *New York Times* the same year, Germany's role 'isn't worrying [to the British] in that we fear the jackboot, but … the German mark is what causes us to shiver'.[65]

Nonetheless, in recent years Harris has been more vocally supportive of the European Union, opposing Britain's exit from the group (Brexit), a stance which puts the references in *Fatherland* in a peculiar position. Nothing about them suggests that they are a satire of anti-EU fears; rather they seem a genuine expression of the author's economic and cultural fears, or at least his channelling of the fears he perceived in the British public in 1992. Of course opinions change, and both Britain and the EU certainly changed in the twenty-four years between the book's publication and the Brexit referendum. Nonetheless, *Fatherland*'s negative portrayal of a German-led European community resonates in much of the pro-Brexit discourse, with disgruntled politicians, journalists and others complaining that 'Britain helped liberate half of Europe', that their fathers 'never submitted to bullying by any German', and that if 'our civil service can cope with world war II it can easily cope with this'.⁶⁶ Harris himself attributes much of the Brexit dialogue to 'a divergence between Britain's proud memory of the Second World War and that of other European countries', itself a statement which highlights the presence of parallel and separate histories, particularly as they are understood culturally, and the reality-shaping power of that [mis]understanding.⁶⁷ What is notable in this context is how that divergence of histories has allowed the fuelling of a mythological memory which has served to strengthen the right-wing and the far-right in British politics, at a time of general resurgence. Harris, writing when he was, cannot have foreseen the parallels but the points of comparison with regard to divergent history, national myth and the scapegoating of problems onto other racial or national groups has serious and worrying parallels with Europe and America in 2019 just as it did in the 1930s.

Making History (1996), Stephen Fry

While *The Man in the High Castle* and *Fatherland* use different tactics to alter our relationship with history and reinsert the Holocaust into a relative scale of morality, Stephen Fry's *Making History* uses a time-travel induced alternate history to place Adolf Hitler similarly back onto a moral spectrum, picking at and unravelling the popular conception of him as an epitome of evil.

The novel centres on Michael Young, a final year PhD candidate at Cambridge University writing a history thesis on Adolf Hitler's early life and family. The early chapters of the novel are interspersed with what turn out to be chapters from Michael's thesis, his 'Meisterwerk': 'From Braunau to Vienna: The Roots of Power'.⁶⁸ Michael's academic supervisor Dr Angus Alexander High Fraser-Stuart refers to the thesis as 'effluent. It's not an academic argument, it's a novel and a perfectly disgusting one at that'⁶⁹ because of the presence of these extracts.

The offending sections are indeed novelistic, and by Michael's own account not based on any physical historical record ('I did take a few liberties').⁷⁰ They provide a perspective on Hitler's birth, early years and youth initially from the point of view of his mother and later the future Führer himself. Fraser-Stuart's vitriolic reaction, a nightmare for any PhD student, is that Michael's work is 'garbage. Offal. It's not a thesis, it's faeces! It's pus, -moral slime, ordure'.⁷¹ Such comments represent the threat to the historiographic consensus presented by

Michael's thesis, and thus to Fry's novel (as a representative of alternate history more widely). Yet in his first-person narrator's conversation with the reader Michael seems to think this is exactly what history should be:

> A historian, someone said – Burke, I think, if not Burke then Carlyle – is a prophet looking backwards. I cannot approach my story in that fashion. The puzzle that besets me is best expressed by the following statements.
> - A: None of what follows ever happened.
> - B: All of what follows is entirely true.
>
> Get your head round that one. It means that it is my job to tell you the true story of what never happened. Perhaps that's a definition of fiction.[72]

The quote Michael twice misattributes is actually the famous adage by Schlegel (and a likely inspiration for Benjamin's backward-facing angel of history), another worrying example of his scholarship.[73] That Michael should so readily conflate history with fiction would, and does, make Fraser-Stuart apoplectic; yet a PhD candidate being unable to tell the difference between the two forms also undermines the privilege of 'fact' which we bestow history. Michael's confusion, and his working statements, apply to the story he is telling within the novel: the events never happened because he created and then destroyed an alternate timeline; but they are equally true of any history book.

Michael's statements do not apply to alternate history fiction, and we are not after all expected to believe it as true. This, however, does not preclude many historians from dabbling in counterfactualism, though Fraser-Stuart is unlikely to be one of them. Historians predominantly engage in alternate history under the label of the counterfactual essay, although it is noteworthy that many who do so also distance themselves from their fictional counterparts. Niall Ferguson, for example, writes that 'of course Hollywood and science fiction are not academically respectable'.[74] Andrew Roberts is less dismissive, yet he too refers to 'the difference between a What If and mere science fiction'.[75] Still both historians begin their introductions with descriptions and references to literary and cinematic alternate histories. Richard J. Evans, author of highly acclaimed histories of the Third Reich, is on the one hand consolatory towards fiction, acknowledging that historians' 'counterfactual history essentially belongs in the same world as these other, more obviously fictional works of the imagination, some of which have a much longer track record and came into fashion long before counterfactual histories became commonplace'.⁷⁶ However what Evans gives he also takes away and so he recommends that 'we have to put aside these more baroque products of the imagination and try to pin down more precisely exactly how the counterfactual does relate to the real'.⁷⁷

Michael is, of course, presenting his narrative segments as history (in the most literal sense), not alternate history, but they are simultaneously part of an alternate history novel courtesy Fry's narrative. The alternate enters the novel through the mechanic of a time-travel story. Leo Zuckerman, a physics professor Michael happens to encounter on the same day he has his thesis demolished by Fraser-Stuart, is working on a time machine of sorts. This time machine is one of two crucial plot devices in the novel. The other is a chemical which permanently sterilizes male humans, the product of research by Michael's girlfriend Jane.

Zuckerman and Jane are worthy of attention. Zuckerman is a physicist while Jane is a chemist, but both raise interesting points about morality and truth. Early in the novel Michael visits Jane's lab, and he confesses that '[her] work was a dark mystery to me, which was the way she liked it'.⁷⁸ Yet he also relates to us a typical debate about the ethics of her work with genetics:

> What would you do if you discovered that there really was a gay gene? Or that black people have less verbal intelligence than white? Or that Asians are better at numbers than Caucasians? Or that Jews are congenitally mean? Or that women are dumber than men? Or men dumber than women? Or that religion is a genetic disposition? Or that this very gene determined criminal tendencies and that very gene determined Alzheimer's? You know, the insurance ramifications, the ammo it would hand to the racists. All that?
>
> She would say that she would cross that bridge when she came to it and that, besides, her work was in a different field. Anyway, if you, as a historian, discovered that Churchill was screwing the Queen all through the war, would that be your problem? You report the facts. Shared humanity has the job of interpreting them. Same with science. It wasn't Darwin's problem that God didn't create Adam and Eve, it was the bishops' problem. Don't blame the messenger, she'd say calmly, grow up and look to yourself instead.⁷⁹

Jane places her responsibility on a higher scientific truth that outweighs any moral considerations. This is emphasized to the reader when, breaking into the lab later in the novel, Michael discovers that Cambridge University regularly uses animals in their scientific testing.⁸⁰ In this case a room full of caged dogs:

'the cutest puppies you've ever seen'.[81] Although Michael also offers another suggestion for the absence of her sense of social responsibility, remarking:

> Big business of course, genespotting. You pretend to the world that you are working on a grand scheme called the Human Genome Project, which is worthy and noble – Nobel, in fact – Good Science, Human Achievement, Frontiers of Knowledge, all of that, but really you are trying to find a new gene and copyright the pants out of it before anyone else stumbles across it too. There were dozens of commercial 'biotechnical' companies in Cambridge alone. God knows what kind of bribery and badness they got up to.[82]

Fry's evocation of scientific ethics and responsibilities alludes to the human experimentation conducted by the Nazi regime. Zuckerman's work is similarly tainted; not with capitalist ambitions but with the most indelible taint there is – or at least that is how he himself sees it – the extermination camps. Specifically, of course, Auschwitz.

However, there is a twist in Zuckerman's tale: he is in fact a non-Jew. Through a lie of omission, he allows Michael to believe that he is a survivor, or the child of a victim at least, of Auschwitz, until he finally confesses his true parentage: His real name is Axel Bauer. His father Dietrich Josef Bauer was an SS doctor at Auschwitz. 'His job was to treat the sick amongst the officers and men of the SS and to attend the *Sonderaktionenas* as a medical observer. ... [Also he] continued some medical experiments that had been initiated by [Johann] Kremer. The removal of live organs for study.'[83] Fry, through Leo, expands upon this using the methods of the historian and quotes from Kremer's actual diaries. Bauer Senior's crimes directly relate to the pursuit of science without human empathy or consideration, enabled to an extent by the Nazi doctrine that those he was experimenting on were *untermensch* and thus socially and racially inferior, but they provide an important point of comparison with Jane's attitude towards the unaccountability of scientific progress, presenting the nightmare scenario to which such philosophy can lead.

Through the avatars of Michael and Jane/ Leo, the novel frequently compares history and science, seeking to justify one against the other. Ultimately however it reveals that neither are perfect systems with which to understand the world and, unsurprisingly, a mixed method is probably the best we can aim for.[84] History is called into question by the alternate historical scenario brought into being by Leo and Michael. Leo has built a device which allows him to view an abstract image of the past, a pattern of colours and shapes which represent the atomic structures present at a given moment in time, a Temporal Imaging Machine (TIM).[85] With Michael's help he is able to rig his device in such a way that it can send a small sample of material backwards in time. Using Michael's thesis-level knowledge of Hitler's early life they decide to send a handful of stolen sterilization pills from Jane's lab to the well in Braunau-am-Inn, Upper Austria, from which the Hitler family draw their water, on 1 June 1888, the aim being to sterilize the drunkard father Alois and 'make sure the motherfucker is never born'.[86]

Having succeeded, reality is reset and Michael (presumably because he was the one who physically pressed the button on the machine although it is never really explained) is the only person who remembers the original timeline. There are many differences between the two worlds; first of note for Michael is that he is now American – his parents having emigrated to the United States before he was born – and a student at Princeton University. Technology is also different; information is stored on 'carts', video-like cassettes with an interactive element, rather than on CD-ROMs, and Michael's American friend Steve does not recognize the word keyboard.[87]

This new timeline without Hitler should be a relative utopia, at least that is what Michael expected, once again exposing his historical ignorance or at least his naïvety. He did not account for the circumstances that shaped and enabled Hitler, and thus he did not reckon with Rudolf Gloder. As he comes to realize:

> But in my arrogance I thought I'd generated a better one. I thought if Hitler wasn't born the century would have less to be ashamed of. I suppose I should have known better. The circumstances were still the same in Europe. There was still a vacuum in Germany waiting to be filled. There was still fifty years of anti-Semitism and nationalism ready to be exploited. There was still a Versailles Treaty and a Wall Street Crash and a Great Depression. But one thing at least … this Rudolf Gloder, this Führer. I mean, at least he wasn't as bad as Hitler. From what I could tell of him from that book he was human at least, sane. I mean there weren't any death camps, no Zyklon B, no holocaust, no frothing monomania, no genocide.[88]

Gloder is a creation of Fry's rather than a historical footnote expanded. Our first encounter with him in the capacity of Führer comes as Michael reads an encyclopaedia entry. What follows is a ten-page exposition presenting the potted history of Gloder's life, including his rise to power in the Nazi Party. Unlike Hitler he is described as being 'known for his ready, caustic wit, early rivals dismissed him as a comedian', a leader with 'charm [which] won him the most friends', a man 'naturally endowed with good looks, an athletic bearing and a movie star smile'.[89] Michael's friend Steve, however, takes him to a library where they watch a cart entitled 'The Fall of Europe' which, in another piece of sizable exposition, gives a more detailed history of the 1930s and early 1940s, revealing the devastating implications of the far more cool-headed and calculating Gloder as head of a German Nazi Party.[90]

Gloder's Nazi Party has the same anti-Semitic philosophy, using hatred of Jews among the workers 'as a unifying slogan', yet he is also wary that 'to frighten the Jews away early would be a tactical error' and that such slogans should not be 'at the expense of wasting the vital resources of Jewish science and banking'. 'Swallowing his natural anti-Semitism, Gloder went out of his way to court the physicists of Gottingen University and other centers of scientific excellence, where developments in atomic and quantum physics were reaching far ahead of any comparable institutions outside Germany.' He even goes so far as to hold 'secret meetings with the Jewish community throughout his early years, meetings of which even his most trusted allies were unaware, Gloder was able to convince prominent Jews that his party's anti-Semitism was public posture and that Jews in Germany had less to fear from him than from the Marxists and other rightist factions'.[91]

An unfortunate symptom of this characterization of Gloder is that it portrays the leaders of the Jewish community – scientific, religious and commercial – as hopelessly naïve. It is difficult to credit that, even without the knowledge of potential Holocaust, there were no warning voices such as an Adorno or a Benjamin who could view the long history of anti-Semitism and pogrom in Europe and urge caution or danger as the fascist state of Gloder's Germany assembled itself. Yet because of the incorporation of science and technology, whether Jewish in origin or not (something Hitler was unable to do, to the Allies' benefit given the quantity and quality of European Jewish scientists and engineers who worked on the Manhattan Project among other endeavours), Germany is able to launch a surprise attack on Russia in 1938 (a year after Gloder is awarded the Nobel Peace Prize), detonating atomic bombs which devastate Moscow and Leningrad 'killing Stalin and the entire Politburo'.[92] By the end of the year Eastern and Western Europe, including the United Kingdom, Russia and 'Scandinavia', have capitulated and been folded into the 'First Greater German Reich'.[93]

With Europe under his control and rebellions crushed without mercy, Gloder evicts all of European Jewry to a new 'Jewish Free State' in 1939. The final irony occurs when Michael learns that Gloder discovered the contaminated water supply in Braunau and uses it to sterilize the Jewish population, wiping them out in a single generation. The scientist who isolated the chemical reagent in the well water was Dietrich Bauer, Leo/Axel's father.[94]

Ultimately Gloder is an Über-Hitler: he appeals to all strata of German life, has effortless charisma and is a ruthless rationalist capable of *realpolitik* in a way Hitler never was. His presence is the worst-case scenario for Michael, Germany having even pulled the United States further to the right, with violent homophobia being a norm, enshrined by the criminalization of homosexuality. This becomes a personal issue for Michael as he comes to realize that he and Steve are in a relationship and that in this reality he is himself gay. Europe has been spared the gas chamber but, by the time of the novel's present day, the Jews have been wiped out nonetheless. We do not receive an inside view of this fate.

Making History's contribution to the discussion of the Holocaust, then, comes not from descriptions of terrors, or imaginative spaces opened up by the language of the author, but from the effect of placing Adolf Hitler in a position of relative morality. Removing Hitler from reality, and yet creating a scenario which is even worse, particularly for the long-term survival of the Jewish people, shifts some of the blame from the man to the environment. In this way it undermines the Carlylian 'Great Men' model of history, subscribing instead to a vision of early-twentieth-century Europe more in line with Daniel Jonah Goldhagen's *Hitler's Willing Executioners: Ordinary Germans and the Holocaust* (1996), one of the books which Fry mentions in his acknowledgements, referring to it as 'brilliant'.[95] Goldhagen's book brings with it an element of controversy to *Making History*, and some critics and readers have interpreted it as endorsing the message of *Hitler's Willing Executioners*: that Germans were an exceptional people who were destined to attempt to exterminate the Jews. Rosenfeld, for example, connects Fry's status as the child of a refugee (his mother was an Austrian Jew who fled to England in the 1930s) to his positivity about Goldhagen's book to explain that 'Fry may well have intended this sceptical view of the German people to be the chief message of his novel'.[96]

The implications of Goldhagen's book are disturbing, but for non-Germans they might offer a form of comfort, and thus approach being dangerous. This point can be explained with a quote from Zygmunt Bauman:

> The unspoken terror permeating collective memory of the Holocaust … is the gnawing suspicion that the Holocaust could be more than an aberration,

more than a deviation from an otherwise straight path of progress, more than a cancerous growth on the otherwise healthy body of civilised society; that is, in short, the Holocaust was not an antithesis of modern civilisation and everything (or so we like to think) it stands for.[97]

Bauman identifies a central anxiety surrounding the Holocaust: that we are all culpable for the genocide, not because we failed to stop it (although that's also true), but because it is a progression, evolution and product of the state of modernity that civilization in Europe and America has produced. Goldhagen's work, on the other hand, relocates the blame from a generalized state of modernity to the German state in particular, arguing that Germany had generations of anti-Semitism stretching to Martin Luther, and that this had uniquely embedded itself in politics, culture and German national identity culminating in 'eliminationist antisemitism'.[98] In promoting this controversial thesis, he offers a form of succour to non-Germans, thus exceptionalizing the Holocaust in a different manner – but with similar results – compared to scholars such as Elie Wiesel. Ultimately, by positioning the Holocaust as the moment when Germans 'marked their departure from the community of civilised people', it tells Anglo-American readers it did not happen here and it could not have happened here and suggests that it cannot happen here.[99] Similarly it allows significant moral ambiguity when considering the culpability of those in occupied nations who collaborated in targeting, transporting and exterminating the Jews of their own countries. Nonetheless, as Lilian Friedberg remarks, the success of the book, both in terms of sales and awards, illustrates that 'public flogging of the German people for their willing participation in the melee represents an acceptable and indeed lucrative form of public and academic discourse'.[100]

However, I do not believe that it was Fry's intention to align his novel with a discourse of exceptionalism; that *Making History*, despite clear Goldhagen influences, does not imply a unique complicity for the German people. Rather, the novel combats a different form of evasion – that of placing the Holocaust entirely at Adolf Hitler's feet. As the prime personage at the heart of the Nazi state his own complicity is of course total; however it can be tempting to ease blame from others in order to place it more firmly solely with Hitler, or at least with a core Nazi elite.[101] Hellekson defends historians' counterfactual histories on the grounds that 'they foreground the notion of cause and effect that is so important to historians when they construct a narrative'.[102] Fry's novel poses Hitler not (or not only) as the cause of the Holocaust; rather it presents Hitler and the Holocaust as a product of the social, political and economic climate in Europe at that time.

Making History attracted further criticism for its use of humour and a humorous tone in dealing with its subject matter. Hellekson described *Making History* as 'delightfully funny', and the gently comic tone is consistent not only with Stephen Fry's TV persona but also with the rest of his writings.[103] However *New York Times* reviewer Michiko Kakutani attacked the novel for its 'flippant, tongue-in-cheek tone' and finished her review by stating that Fry 'has tried to make the death of six million people part of his joke, and the joke isn't funny – it's repellent'.[104] Fry himself has remarked on this commentary, suggesting that Kakutani's review was so particularly adversarial because she had not realized he was Jewish; he justifies this opinion by comparing her comments with the 'unbelievably generous and kind' review she wrote for his next book, the first volume of his autobiography *Moab is My Washpot* (1997), in which his Jewish heritage is explicitly discussed.[105] He goes on to relate how he was pressured by his publisher to assert his Jewishness, and how he resisted:

> I know my publishers wanted me to write a foreword to *Making History* saying, 'Look, I am a Jew. I think I have a right to address this.' But once you start having to say, 'Look, this is the number of my family killed in the Holocaust. That gives me the right to discuss it and to think about it,' then it becomes ridiculous. The Holocaust has no meaning if it doesn't affect us all. Anybody has a right to discuss the Holocaust. Because everyone is somehow complicit in it, as much as it was a cultural eruption of the most appalling kind. If we only believe it's something nasty to do with Germans, then essentially, the only answer is to round up all the Germans and put them in ovens. And obviously no one is suggesting that.[106]

Fry's comments raise pertinent points about the ownership of the Holocaust and the perceived 'right' to create fiction about it. He also, here, explicitly universalizes the genocide insisting that it does have meaning for all of us, that 'everyone is complicit in it', and makes explicit the horrifying implications of an extreme form of Goldhagen's thesis.

Conclusion

All three of the novels discussed in this chapter imagine alternate history scenarios in which the Holocaust could have been even worse: in the case of *The Man in the High Castle* and *Fatherland* because Nazi Germany was able to extend its reach and consolidate its military victories into long-term and further reaching domination; in the case of *Making History* by proposing an alternative technique for genocide alongside its alternate history. These alternative genocides imagine a scenario which challenges the Holocaust's status as the incomparable and exceptional ultimate evil by imagining slaughter which outstrips it, implicitly encouraging comparison. By inserting hypothetical genocides beyond the scope of the Holocaust, Dick, Harris and Fry dismiss the unhelpful notion of absolute evil and instead insist upon a type of extreme evil, if we are to use that not unproblematic label at all.

One practical reason for declaring the Holocaust incomparable to other traumatic events is a response to the fact that, as Dominick LaCapra notes, 'certain comparisons may function as mechanisms of denial … they may misleadingly conflate normality with a levelling normalization'.[107] This is a particular concern with regard to what is called the *Historikerstreit*, or Historians' Debate, on which LaCapra is writing in this instance. The debate began in West Germany in the summer of 1986 and centred around attempts by neonationalist historians to diminish the importance of the Holocaust, and thus lessen German guilt, by comparing the genocide to the crimes of the Soviet Union in Eastern Europe and the gulags. As Susan Neiman points out, in this context asserting 'that what happened at Auschwitz was worse than what happened in the gulags was thus to take a stand against rightist attempts to avoid German responsibility for its own crimes by pointing to those of others'.[108]

While Harris as a journalist and historian may have been consciously referencing the *Historikerstreit* in the manner in which his alternate Nazi Germany highlights Soviet crimes in the Katyn Forest (although remembering that Nazi Germany historically did draw attention to the massacre during the war), it is unlikely that Fry is drawing a conscious comparison with the event, and it is obviously impossible for Dick to have been thinking of it. Regardless, by comparing the Holocaust not to the historic crimes of other nations, but rather to hypothetical more severe crimes of the Nazis themselves, all three authors sidestep the neonationalist agenda by refusing to absolve anyone of responsibility. Indeed, as I have shown, if anything rather than diminishing German culpability for the Holocaust, the novels assert a shared responsibility.

The emergence of a shared responsibility does not absolve the Nazis of blame for the Holocaust, but it does prevent us from labelling Germany at that time as evil and thus imagining ourselves sufficiently distinct to the people of that time and place (none of us, after all, consider ourselves to be evil). The novels of this chapter problematize the history of the Second World War and the Holocaust sufficiently to draw attention to this moral othering, forcing us to consider it in light of the historic moral compromises and indeed crimes of our own nations, and against contemporary events. They insist that we face a scenario even worse than our own history in order to understand that evil is not limited to six million dead Jews, nor is it limited to a particular face, or a particular time, and instead it can appear anywhere under circumstances that are worryingly easy to reproduce. We must therefore be ever vigilant, both in our approach to history and truth and in our everyday presents.

3

The Damned and the Saved: *The Boys from Brazil* (1976), *The Portage to San Cristobal of A.H.* (1981), *Hope: A Tragedy* (2012) and *The Yiddish Policeman's Union* (2007)

History is never a closed circuit of distinct inputs and final outcomes, and the Holocaust is no exception to this. While the slaughter ended in 1945 with the liberation of the camps, the survivors were shuffled around Europe in displacement camps, while key perpetrators of the genocide took their own lives or faced tribunal at Nuremberg. Many tried to escape justice; Heinrich Himmler attempted to pass himself off as a Sergeant Heinrich Hitzinger rather than the war criminal and Reichsführer of the SS; when his British captors found out the truth he took his own life with a poison capsule. Other Nazis were luckier in their escapes, exploiting escape routes through sympathetic or allied nations, in particular Franco's fascist Spain, aided by the clergy of the Catholic Church, the International Red Cross, and secret services of other world powers as they navigated 'ratlines' from Germany to South America.[1]

The known identities of infamous Nazi criminals who escaped the Allies provided a fertile imaginative space for writers who hypothesized about the dangers of Nazis, real or fictitious, waiting to strike again from the shadows. The narrative potential of these escapees was only compounded by the absence of Hitler himself from the Nuremberg Trials, the Führer having taken his own life in his bunker as Soviet forces closed in on Berlin, his corpse burnt with gasoline alongside that of Eva Braun. His remains were recovered by Soviet intelligence operatives and removed from Germany, creating ambiguity for some in the West in the initial absence of physical proof of death. This ambiguity was only furthered by Stalin who suggested to President Truman that Hitler was still alive 'in Spain or Argentina', despite knowing this was not the case.[2]

This chapter will address speculative fiction about these escaped Nazis, examining their portrayal as dangerous figures able to exploit the dangers of the new Cold War for their own ends, or strangle the newborn Jewish state in its cradle. I will focus on texts in which attempts are made to bring these escapees to account and show how, just as the texts of the previous chapter problematize history, so too speculative fictions of this time problematize justice and culpability.

The Nazis being hunted in this chapter are the damned; however I also want to examine a second set of texts, ones which do not save Nazis from justice (only to later attempt to capture them), but which save Jews from the Holocaust. A relatively recent trend, these Jews are the saved counterpoints to the damned perpetrators of earlier fictions.[3] Where Ira Levin imagines the malevolent experiments which Auschwitz doctor Josef Mengele might have been conducting while living a new life in South America, Shalom Auslander imagines a scenario for Anne Frank had she secretly escaped to the United States. George Steiner depicts a powerful vision of a mission to bring Hitler to justice, having found him living in secret in the Amazon rainforests, while Michael Chabon imagines a relative safe-haven for Jews which saves millions of lives.

Whether one life or millions, each of the texts in this chapter depicts history which slips beyond what we might recognize as true to pull people beyond the confines of the war years. They distinguish themselves from the texts of the previous chapters by not completely reversing the outcome and allowing the Nazis to win the war, but by suggesting various close-but-not-quite alternatives. In the case of Chabon's *The Yiddish Policeman's Union* (2007) this is still a radically different world, but in Shalom Auslander's *Hope: A Tragedy* (2012) events pass more or less as they do in our history books except for one life, that of Anne Frank, who now lives in secret in the attic of a home in upstate New York. Yet through orchestrating these changes the authors are able to use speculative fiction to tease open enough space to critique the issues of their contemporary worlds while still retaining a frame of reference that has enough similarities to carry the narrative. In doing so each of the writers takes what should be a positive concept (bringing a war criminal to justice, saving someone from the Holocaust), perhaps even utopian (saving millions), and deliberately undermines that positivity.

Understandably, the Holocaust has inspired ample dystopian visions, many of them found in the other chapters of this book. However, this chapter focuses on texts which are interesting because they create a positive event in the midst of the Holocaust and yet are still far from being utopian or, more precisely, uchronian. While it can be said with some certainty that none of these texts were ever intended to be utopian novels, the peculiar juxtaposition of a seemingly utopian concept with dystopian results attracts the eye of the critical reader. Each of these texts, though differing in time of writing, approach, and indeed the extent to which they explicitly concern themselves with the Holocaust, subverts the utopian idea of a diminished Holocaust or of a genocide more neatly and completely brought to justice. In doing so they convey the inextricable nature of the genocide to the Anglo-American culture in which they are writing, demonstrating a level to which we might consider Anglo-Americans scarred, or culturally traumatized, by the Holocaust.

The Boys from Brazil (1976), Ira Levin

The idea of a Fourth Reich being constructed by the remnants of the Third was a very real concern for many: in the final stages of the war, understanding that defeat was no longer an impossibility, many senior Nazis, particularly SS and Gestapo leaders, were issued with false documents by the *Reichssicherheitshauptamt* (RSHA, equivalent to the Interior Ministry of the SS). Simultaneously, wealthy German individuals and industries were funnelling money and materials into neutral or friendly non-belligerent nations. Holocaust survivor and Nazi-hunter Simon Wiesenthal references a US Treasury Report in 1946 which lists some 750 companies set up around the globe by Germans with German money, in Spain, Portugal, Turkey, Argentina, Switzerland and elsewhere. He writes of minor SS officials who were known to have received substantial sums of money as early as 1944 and speculates that, if an SS *Obersturmbannführer* (lieutenant colonel) received an anonymous deposit of 2,600,000 Reichsmark, the sums given to higher-ranking officials must have been vast. To him, he says, 'it proves that before the war ended the Nazis set up large, hidden funds for the building of a Fourth Reich'.[4]

The untraceable nature of the fiscal transactions and the mysterious cloak-and-dagger existence of ODESSA-like groups, who arranged the transport, safety and resettlement of top Nazis, provides ample material for writers of fiction.[5] After all, the basis in fact is proven by numerous Nazis surviving for many years after the war outside of Germany's borders such as the commandant of Sobibor and Treblinka, Franz Stangl, who was arrested in Brazil in 1967; Auschwitz's infamous Angel of Death, Josef Mengele, who lived in South America under his own name from 1950 until his death in Brazil in 1979; and most famously Adolf Eichmann who was captured in 1960 in Argentina. The existence of these historical precedents, and the possibility of others, has provided fuel for speculative fiction plots to which many dramas and conspiracy thrillers have gravitated. Like other thrillers of the Second World War the majority do not explicitly reference the Holocaust nor offer any significant insight into the implications of a Fourth Reich for our relationship with the Holocaust. Instead they follow the pulp-era pattern perfected by *Indiana Jones and the Raiders of the Lost Ark* (1981), focusing on mystical artefacts of power and evoking the now classic atmosphere of Nazi occultism when a member of the US government tells Indiana Jones that for 'the last two years the Nazis have had teams of archaeologists running around the world looking for all kinds of religious artefacts. Hitler's a nut on the subject, he's crazy. He's obsessed with the occult'.[6]

If not occult in nature then the resurgent threat may instead be from outside the known spheres of military power or scientific understanding such as in Stephen Cole and Justin Richards's *Doctor Who* adventure, *The Shadow in the Glass* (2001), which features a child of Hitler being raised alongside a Nazi army in a secret Antarctic base (shaped like a swastika, naturally), or John Wyndham's posthumously published *Plan for Chaos* (2009), as mentioned in Chapter 1. Nonetheless, there are exceptions to this model.

Understandably, the most popular sub-genre of such fiction consists of works that imagine putting Hitler himself on trial. These appeared even before the war had ended with novels such as Max Radin's *The Day of Reckoning* (1943) or Michael Young's *The Trial of Adolf Hitler* (1944) depicting the Nazi leader being brought before a court as a legal benchmark with vast implications, and as a near-divine wish which if fulfilled would redeem mankind, respectively.[7] Jesse Bier's short story 'Father and Son' (1964) explores the possibility of a collective punishment being forced on Germany with over six million Germans being drawn from the general population at random and held in camps. The story takes the form of an exchange of letters between a father in the provisional government and a son working in one of the camps, the latter gradually growing more and more alarmed as he begins to believe he is going to be exterminated like the Jews who had occupied that camp previously. While this turns out to not be the case, this is not revealed until after the son has had a mental breakdown and lost any concept of where or at which point in time he is. Gavriel D. Rosenfeld writes that Bier's story 'offers a pessimistic message about the possibility of atonement after the

Holocaust'.⁸ Rosenfeld cites a personal correspondence with Bier which suggests his writing was motivated by a desire for fantasy rooted in his Jewishness:

> I suppose that as an ethnic Jew, I was at long last – 20 years after WWII – constructing a piece of wish-fulfilment nearest my heart … As I recall, I didn't need the Eichmann trial – but maybe it played its part … the matter of of [*sic*] generic German punishment had always plagued me, simmering, simmering.⁹

Whether consciously influenced by the Eichmann Trial or not, Bier's story forms part of a resurgence of interest in accessing further justice for the Holocaust and the Second World War in ways not accessed at the Nuremberg Trials. His admission that he had been plagued by the 'generic' nature of German punishment suggests a frustration with the repercussion of the Holocaust for Germany, while also implying the exceptional nature of the crime.

Certainly, the length and depth of the Eichmann Trial exposed the shortcomings of previous war-crimes trials, particularly those at Nuremberg, with regard to the Holocaust. As such, it seems only natural that authors should fantasize about such trials being extended to other key figures beyond Eichmann. In non-mimetic fiction the obvious candidate for this is Adolf Hitler himself. Phillipe van Rjndt's legal thriller *The Trial of Adolf Hitler* (1978) has Hitler botch his suicide and escape Berlin and live under a new identity for twenty-five years in a village in Bavaria before revealing himself and being put on trial, attempting to turn the process into a stage from which he can grandstand and sow the seeds of a new Reich. In Joseph Heywood's *The Berkut* (1987) he is captured by Soviet forces and is the subject of vicious torture and abuse, reflecting the experiences of many Soviets captured by the Nazis during the war, but also using the Russians as a screen onto which to project American desires for bloody revenge which circumvents rules of law or moral decency.¹⁰ The Führer of Barry Malzberg's short story 'Hitler at Nuremberg' (1994) changes his mind about suicide (too late for Eva Braun), and is captured and put on trial with the other surviving senior Nazis.¹¹ David Charnay's lengthy *Operation Lucifer: The Chase, Capture, and Trial of Adolf Hitler* (2001) similarly sees Hitler escape and pose as a financier (this time going so far as to have plastic surgery and adopt a Jewish identity), attempting to stir up tension in the Middle East. He is eventually captured and hung.¹²

Perhaps the most famous example of this type of narrative, thanks in no small part to its 1978 cinematic adaptation starring Gregory Peck and Laurence Olivier, is Ira Levin's *The Boys from Brazil* (1976). Rather than supposing that Hitler may have escaped, Levin's novel features Yakov Liebermann, a Vienna-based Holocaust survivor turned Nazi-hunter clearly modelled on Simon Wiesenthal, in pursuit of notorious Auschwitz doctor Josef Mengele. In selecting such a protagonist and such an antagonist, Levin is seemingly reinforcing a dichotomy of heroes and villains between survivor and perpetrator that would therefore seem to be a fairly conventional use of Nazis in a post-war thriller. However, once Mengele's plot is finally revealed so too is Levin's deconstruction of the standard moral dichotomy, particularly the notion of irreducible evil.

Extrapolating from Mengele's well-documented experiments on prisoners in Auschwitz, particularly his known fascination with twins, Levin depicts the doctor as a mad scientist in exile who has not only successfully cloned Hitler, but has also managed to manipulate international adoption systems to place these clones in families all over the world, families which replicate as closely as possible the family in which Hitler himself was born. The adoptive fathers are all older men of some, but not great, authority. What adds drama to the plot is that Mengele is now having these father figures killed to replicate the death of Alois, Hitler's father, when Adolf was fourteen. Liebermann ultimately halts the plot, although not in time to save the eighteenth father; he arrives at the house to warn him only to find Mengele imitating him, 'Mengele! The hated, the so-long hunted; Angel of Death, child-killer!'[13] Liebermann is shot, but Mengele is killed by the father's dogs, sicced on him by the son – the Hitler clone – himself. 'The Fourth Reich is coming – not just a German Reich but a pan-Aryan one,' Mengele boasts before his death, 'I'll live to see it, and to stand beside its leaders. Can you imagine the awe they'll inspire? The mystical authority they'll wield? The trembling of the Russians and the Chinese? Not to mention the Jews.'[14] He tells the boy:

> as you grow and see the world engulfed by Blacks and Semites, Slavs, Orientals, Latins – and your own Aryan folk threatened with extinction – from which *you* shall save them! – you'll come to see that [Hitler] was the best and finest and wisest of all mankind! ... Look in your heart! The strength is there to command armies ... to bend whole nations to your will! To destroy without mercy all who oppose you![15]

Mengele is making explicit the rational fear of a resuscitated Nazi movement, describing the mentality which could produce another Hitler-figure, the original's genetic material or otherwise. *The Boys from Brazil* is thus part of a pattern of texts which suggest an escaped Hitler returning, or his progeny (either biological or ideological) secretly building a powerbase before launching an attack once more. But where Levin's novel differs from its antecedents is its final moral judgement of those successors. Lieberman has a list of all of the adopted clones and their families, spread out around the world, and one of Liebermann's allies, Rabbi Gorin, states that 'there are ninety-four boys ... who have to be killed before they get much older'.[16] He worries that if they do not deal with this potential problem now, that 'when some of them *do* become Hitlers, why, we'll just let our children worry about it. On the way to the gas chambers'.[17] Lieberman, however, cannot bring himself to allow such a thing to happen:

> It could be that none will be Hitler, not ever if there was a thousand of them. They're boys. No matter what their genes are. Children. How can we kill them? This was *Mengele*'s business, killing children. Should it be ours?[18]

Levin, through Lieberman, is taking a stance in the nature/nurture debate around iconic figures of evil such as Hitler. By arguing that the genetics of these boys does not necessarily destine them to be future dictators and instigators of genocide, the novel is therefore arguing that Hitler himself was not destined for that same fate, that were the situation different he might have led an unremarkable life. At the same time by having a Jew, a Rabbi no less, argue for the extermination of nearly a hundred children based on their genetics, raises the prospect of a genocidal act in and of itself, showing the manner in which vengeance can lead to crimes comparable to those that instigate revenge.

Lieberman destroys the list and Gorin confronts him enraged, telling him: 'It wasn't your list ... It was ... everybody's! The Jewish People's! ... It's Jews like you ... that let it happen last time.' Lieberman retorts that 'Jews didn't "let" it happen ... Nazis *made* it happen. People who would even kill children to get what they wanted'.[19] Lieberman equates Gorin's actions with the Nazis, making their morality comparable. Lieberman's response also addresses the intellectual problem of victim passivity, a problem from which springs the question asked of survivors across the range, from war-crimes trials to classrooms: 'why didn't you fight back?'[20] Primo Levi identifies the sentiment as part of a 'family of questions' that 'as the years go by ... [are] formulated with ever increasing persistence, and with an ever less hidden accent of accusation'.[21] The response deflects from a victim-blaming culture which makes the victims of the Holocaust complicit in its execution, while at the same time highlighting the small increments of moral compromise which could lead to a genocide occurring. After all, while Gorin's intentions to prevent another Holocaust are noble his methods are not.

Nonetheless, Levin steps back slightly from Lieberman's argument in the final scene of the novel, a short two-page chapter, in which the previously encountered clone – the only one to have had his genetic identity revealed to him by Mengele – has taken up painting (Hitler was of course an artist), a Strauss waltz playing in the background, and is at that moment engaged in painting a fantasy of a stadium full of people, a man on a platform holding their attention. 'Not just a singer or comedian; someone fantastic, a *really good person* that they loved and respected ... He could hear the people cheering, roaring; a beautiful growing love-thunder that built and built, and then pounded, pounded, pounded, pounded. Sort of like in those old Hitler movies.'[22] The final line evocation of Hitler, the sense of aspiration in the boy, ends the novel on an ominous tone: a pessimism which compounds the cool manner in which the boy commands the dogs to kill Mengele, and his unshaken manner in dealing with the corpse of both the Nazi doctor and the father Mengele killed when he arrived. However, this does not undo Lieberman's moral stance. Rather, Levin is complying with the genre conventions of the thriller format which he is writing within. This final scene is the literary equivalent of the final scene of a horror movie where the defeated monster's hand twitches as the heroes ride off into the distance. Furthermore, it offers no definitive evidence that Lieberman was wrong, only leaving open the possibility of it.

Michael Butter argues that the novel occupies 'a middle position between the postmodernist texts of the early 1970s and the realist ones written only a few years later. [It] negotiates conflicting conceptions of Hitler in American culture and explores their potential for self-critique and affirmations'.[23] Expanding upon this, Butter writes that *The Boys from Brazil* suggests: 'Genes might not be the decisive factor in the creation of a new Hitler ... but American culture's obsession with images of and narratives about the Nazi past, which distract from rather than draw attention to racism within the United States.'[24] The novel utilizes the speculative fiction trope of cloning Hitler, alongside a Josef Mengele occupying the stereotype of an evil scientist, in order not to express real fears that this is a realist scenario that might have been happening in South America in the 1970s, but to examine and undermine our self-perceived moral authority, and our notions of exceptionality: both that the lead Nazis were evil monsters different from the rest of humanity, and that the Holocaust was above and beyond the most evil act committed by one set of mankind upon another.

The Portage to San Cristobal of A.H. (1981), George Steiner

Gavriel D. Rosenfeld cites *The Boys from Brazil* (albeit, the 1978 cinematic adaptation) as a 'modified form' of the Hitler survival premise, texts which 'posited Hitler's survival in order to indulge in the fantasy of killing him, thereby holding him accountable for his misdeeds'.[25] The most powerful example of the Nazi survivor/ Hitler on trial texts, however, is *The Portage to San Cristobal of A.H.* (1981) by linguist and literary critic George Steiner, which seems to undermine the entire sub-genre. It begins portentously:

> — You. Is it really? *Shema*. In God's Name. Look at you. Look at you now. You. The one out of hell. … It is you. Isn't it. We have you. We have you. Simeon is sending the signal. Everyone will know. The whole world. But not yet. We have to get you out of here. Ours. You are ours. You know that don't you. The living God. Into our hands. He delivered you into our hands. And it came to pass. You. … Silent now? Whose voice. They say your voice could.
> The boy had never heard it.
> — Burn cities.[26]

The very old man is of course Adolf Hitler, but he is named sparingly within the novel. Even the title of the book only grants him initials. To deliberately avoid the name further invokes a mythic malevolence akin to a being of Lovecraftian ritual or, to read anachronistically, J. K. Rowling's Lord Voldemort.[27] While we are familiar with the proverb that warns 'speak of the Devil and he shall appear', given the readily blasphemous content of the novel it also equates Hitler with the unspeakable name of God. Furthermore, just as this opening exchange between the anger of youth and silence of history labels him the 'living God', so Hitler is presented as performing a sinister twisted messianic role to the Jews.

The team sent to bring Hitler out of the jungle are younger, modern Jews, born out of a post-Holocaust age, but they are dispatched and commanded by Emmanuel Lieber who is not. Lieber is based in Israel and communications with the jungle team are fragmented as the conditions corrode the search party's radio equipment. As such it is often unclear which communications are being received and which we are able to read but are being uttered into a void. One such communication from Lieber takes the form of a whole chapter of the book and it reinforces the mythic elements of Hitler's character. Though

I quote it here at considerable length, the following is merely a short portion of the tirade:

> Listen to me. You must not let him speak, or only few words. To say his needs, to say that which will keep him alive. But no more. Gag him if necessary, or stop your ears as did the sailor. If he is allowed speech he will trick you and escape. Or find easy death. His tongue is like no other. It is the tongue of the basilisk, a-hundred-forked and quick as flame. As it is written in the learned Nathanial of Mainz: there shall come upon the earth in the time of night a man surpassing eloquent. All that is God's, hallowed be His name, must have its counterpart, its backside of evil and negation. So it is with the Word, with the gift of speech that is the glory of man and distinguishes him everlasting from the silence or animal noises of creation. When He made the Word, God made possible also its contrary. Silence is not the contrary of the Word but its guardian. No, He created on the night side of language a speech for hell. Whose words mean hatred and vomit of life. Few men can learn that speech or speak it for long. It burns their mouths. It draws them into death. But there shall come a man whose mouth shall be as a furnace and whose tongue as a sword laying waste. He will know the grammar of hell and teach it to others. He will know the sounds of madness and loathing and make them seem music. ... Do not let him speak freely. You will hear the crack of age in his voice. He is old. Old as the loathing which dogs us since Abraham. Let him speak to you and you will think of him as a man. With sores on his skin and need in his bowels, sweating and hungering like yourselves, short of sleep. ... You will think him a man and no longer believe what he did. That he almost drove us from the face of the earth. That his words tore up our lives by the root.[28]

Lieber associates Hitler with the sirens whose songs drag sailors onto the rocks, and with the basilisk – the king of serpents – thus tapping Greek myth that predates even Abrahamic. He associates Hitler with God as a being capable of speaking hell's language, the antithesis to the Word of creation. As a serpentine infernal being who makes speech like music but who actually brings death, destruction, madness and suffering, Hitler is associated with the snake in the Garden of Eden. He is the subject of divine prophecy, the Antichrist of the Jews who has somehow come before their Messiah. He is as old 'as the loathing which dogs us since Abraham', giving him an eternal quality and a retrospective hand in the anti-Semitism that preceded him as well as that which continues on. He is 'so obscene as to be sacrosanct'.[29]

The obsession-driven trek through stinking swamps and humid jungles to find a single man evoke Joseph Conrad's *Heart of Darkness* (1902), and despite deifying Hitler and imbuing him with a singular mythic power unprecedented in human history, Steiner thus invites comparisons between the Holocaust and other genocidal atrocities. As Hitler himself says, when finally roused to speak at the novel's conclusion:

> I was not the worst. Far from it. How many wretched little men of the forests did your Belgian friends murder outright or leave to starvation and syphilis when they raped the Congo? ... Some *twenty* million. That picnic was underway when I was newborn. What was Rotterdam or Coventry compared with Dresden and Hiroshima? I do not come out worst in the black game of numbers. Did I invent the camps? Ask of the Boers.[30]

Here, Hitler himself relativizes his war crimes by comparing them to the actions of others, specifically the nations of the Allies, some of which preceded him such as the British concentration camps in the Boer War or the Belgian exploitation of the Congo, the latter of which again invites comparisons between this novel and Conrad. In the same speech Hitler invites comparisons between himself and Stalin, citing an 'unimpeachable witness', 'the holy writer, the great bearded one who came out of Russia and preached to the world. ... The man of the Archipelago ... the sage of the Gulag', who though Hitler does not name him we must imagine to be Aleksandr Solzhenitsyn, of whom Steiner is a great admirer.[31] Paraphrasing his witness, and it is worth noting that Steiner cannot bring himself to put Solzhenitsyn's exact words, or even his name, into Hitler's mouth, the former Führer remarks: 'Stalin had slaughtered *thirty* million. That he had perfected genocide when [Hitler] was still a nameless scribbler in Munich.'[32] He continues:

> How many Jews did Stalin kill – your savior, your ally Stalin? Answer me that. Had he not died when he did, there would not have been one of you left alive between Berlin and Vladistok. Yet Stalin died in bed, and the world stood hushed before the tiger's rest. Whereas you hunt me down like a rabid dog, put me on trial (by what right, by what mandate?), drag me through the swamps, tie me up at night. Who am a very old man and uncertain of recollection. Small game, gentlemen, hardly worthy of your skills. In a world that has tortured political prisoners and poured napalm on naked villagers[33]

Hitler here invites comparisons with not just the Soviet Union and Stalin but with the United States and its actions in Vietnam. Most cutting and most controversial of the points Steiner's Hitler speaks in his defence, however, is his final one which Norman Finkelstein refers to as an 'apocalyptic speech' in which 'we face a terrible reversal of transcendental justice and the most excruciating of human failures'.³⁴ Again, it is worth quoting at some length:

> Would Palestine have become Israel, would the Jews have come to that barren patch of the Levant, would the United States *and* the Soviet Union, *Stalin's* Soviet Union, have given you recognition and guaranteed your survival, had it not been for the Holocaust? It was the Holocaust that gave you the courage of injustice, that made you drive the Arab out of his home, out of his field, because he was lice-eaten and without resource, because he was in your divinely ordered way. … Perhaps I *am* the Messiah, the true Messiah, the new Sabbatai whose infamous deeds were allowed by God in order to bring His people home. 'The Holocaust was the necessary mystery before Israel could come into its strength.' It is not I who have said it: but your own visionaries, your unravelers of God's meaning when it is Friday night in Jerusalem. … The *Reich* begat Israel.³⁵

Steiner assigns Hitler a near omniscience in his speech; he has stayed unnaturally well-informed on the world outside the jungle, despite the evidence in the book that the jungle itself is a barrier to all forms of communication and a significant hindrance to travel. Gavriel Rosenfeld remarks that Hitler's impassioned defence of his actions, and of his person, 'proves himself once again to be the dangerous demagogue he always was'.³⁶ Rosenfeld is critical of using fiction to elevate Hitler, even a fictional Hitler, to a messianic status. Finkelstein however defends the use of the Hitler character as an expression of Steiner's own doubts about the Jewish faith, suggesting the ethical and ideological risks Steiner's Hitler presents are worth taking for the intellectual value of, 'in midrashic fashion', casting the problem back to the reader.³⁷ Efraim Sicher writes that 'Steiner's representation of Hitler … points to the danger anti-Semitism poses to civilization, but it also risks validating its arguments'.³⁸ This is a sentiment expressed by numerous commentators and places *The Portage to San Cristobel of A.H.* in an unusual situation, as perhaps the only novel I discuss in this book to have been considered potentially dangerous, as a result of a perfect storm of author credibility and the text's critical and commercial exposure.³⁹

Hitler's lengthy speech is the last dialogue of the novel, or almost: Teku, a Brazilian native who, despite not understanding any of the words, feels the 'brazen pulse [which] carried all before it', and jumps to his feet to exclaim 'Proved'.⁴⁰ At this point the helicopters arrive to take them away and the novel ends; the extraction team are allowed no rebuttal and we gain no insights into how they are affected by Hitler's speech. 'So rhetorically powerful is his self-defense', writes

Rosenfeld, 'that it rings true at a pre-linguistic, emotional, level. ... By declaring Hitler the de facto victor, Steiner suggested that humanity's attempt to bring Hitler to justice is destined to fail.'[41] This has the additional effect of 'sound[ing] a cautionary note about the perils of memory'.[42] As an artefact of history, made into fact within the novel's fiction, Hitler's character encapsulates the problems of memory versus history. Lieber too is a symbol of this conflict, solely driven by his desire to possess Hitler. As one member of the extraction team, Gideon, remarks: 'He's the one that needs Hitler most. Lieber. They need each other like the breath of life. ... A man strangling his own shadow. Because without Lieber there would be no Hitler. Not any more.'[43] In many ways this comment anticipates Hitler's closing remarks, just as the deification of the opening exchange and Lieber's mythologizing of the Führer find their echo in Hitler's claims to the status of messiah. In pairing Lieber and Gideon in this way he is making a more specific case for another point he makes when he says: 'I know when Hitler will die. ... When the last Jew is dead. ... To be a Jew is to keep Hitler alive.'[44] In both of these instances Gideon is remarking on a symbiotic relationship between Hitler and the Jews, or Hitler and Lieber. If Lieber is a stand-in for a Jew of a particular mindset, not only a survivor but someone who looks backwards to memory rather than history, and Hitler is synecdoche for the Holocaust, then Gideon is also making important claims about the intertwined nature of Holocaust memory and Jewish identity.

Hitler's monologue is part of a mock trial conducted by the extraction team; while there is presumably an official Eichmann-style event in his future, Steiner withholds it from us. The amateur event is the only one to which we bear witness. However, as S. Lillian Kremer notes, 'although the only overt trial in *Portage* is Hitler's, the international community is also on trial and judged corrupt through authorial selection'.[45] Steiner uses scenes set outside the jungle, asides to the main action, to display the conflicted interests of the international community, and through their responses to the news of Hitler being found alive is able to critique the post-war relationships of those nations (the UK, US, France, West Germany, the Soviet Union) to the history of the Second World War and specifically the Holocaust.

Richard J. Evans in his survey of counterfactual and alternate histories comments on the fictions, particularly from the United States, which 'have focused on making up for the frustration felt by many that Hitler had not been personally brought to account for his crimes'. He goes on to identify such narratives as having been 'inserted into a political critique of the relative failure of governments across the world to bring old Nazis to justice'.⁴⁶ Steiner and others use the techniques of speculative fiction to examine notions of culpability and justice, targeting Germany but particularly Hitler. However, the texts also offer a more nuanced position which examines the relative moralities of the Western position, both during and after the war. In this instance speculative fiction insists upon a catalogue of atrocity which may or may not include the actions of the United States or United Kingdom, but which certainly suggests an alternative to the idea that the Holocaust is incomparable with any other event. They may not offer any insights into the specifics of the Holocaust itself, thus contributing to our understanding of the event, but they do undermine the notion of evil as a metaphysical characteristic of the perpetrators, showing them to be human, frail and – to reference Hannah Arendt – 'banal'. That said, by using speculative fiction to attempt to enter the mental space of a Nazi, or even a Hitler, as in Steiner's *Portage*, we can perhaps approach a realization of the levels of mental gymnastics required to relocate our cognition from our safe moral space into theirs. The truly disturbing element of many speculative fictions of the Holocaust is the realization of how easy this can sometimes be.

Hope: A Tragedy (2012), Shalom Auslander

Perhaps as an inevitable side effect of time's passing and the retreat of the Second World War and the Holocaust from living memory, narratives of Nazis hiding and plotting their return to power are now something of a rarity. It's not that Nazis are not still being hunted and brought to trial, because they certainly are, although before too long that too will necessarily end. Rather the incongruity between the nonagenarians standing trial and narratives of powerful war criminals hiding to unleash fresh evil upon the world seems to date such fictions, and so most writers have located their narratives in entirely fictional alternate timelines.⁴⁷ Shalom Auslander's *Hope: A Tragedy*, however, is an interesting example of a twenty-first-century text which takes the format of the hidden Nazi novels and inverts it, presenting instead a hidden survivor story. Specifically, a hidden Anne Frank story.

Anne Frank may be the single person most synonymous with the Holocaust in Western (and possibly global) imagination. She is certainly the most synonymous Jewish victim. From a single diary, published by her father after she and her sister died in Bergen-Belsen, she has become a figure of popular consciousness that has been represented in every medium of art from theatre and film to graphic novels and manga. In June 1989, to coincide with what would have been her sixtieth birthday, the then mayor of New York Edward 'Ed' Koch officially declared the week beginning 12 June as Anne Frank Week.[48] Naomi Alderman compares her to Richieu, Art Spiegelman's older brother who died during the Holocaust before Art was born, his absence in the present-day sections of *Maus* a haunting (and on some level taunting) presence, a spectre of childhood potential that Art has always felt himself measured against and necessarily fallen short of. So too, Alderman writes of Anne Frank:

> She, with the translucent ghosts of her unwritten books on the shelf, will always be a better writer than us, with our tawdry, mundane, completed works, each one a small failure. She, with all the suffering, will always deserve success six million times more than us – we have survivor guilt for managing to do what she could not. She, with her purity, her innocence, will always be there to say, in the back of our minds: 'how can you write that? I would have written it different, better. My books should take the place of yours.' Yes, if we're going to be Jewish writers, we're going to have to talk about Anne Frank.[49]

A single figure who looms so large over contemporary Jewish writing, and who is like Richieu a blank-slate of sorts. Yet Frank is also a paradoxical figure, writing about the Holocaust without writing about it. Hidden with her family, Frank has moments where she imagines a future for herself. The Anne Frank of the diaries had not yet experienced the worst that the Holocaust could provide. As Lawrence Langer writes:

> She is in no way to blame for not knowing about what she could not have known about. But readers are much to blame for accepting and promoting the idea that her *Diary* is a major Holocaust text and has anything of great consequence to tell us about the atrocities that culminated in the murder of European Jewry.[50]

Perhaps the absence of the Holocaust's most extreme realities, and yet the knowledge that they exist beyond the pages, in Frank's future, explain the enduring popularity of the *Diary*. Regardless, Anne Frank is now well and truly a figure of collective cultural memory and imagination. With so much unrealized potential it is hardly surprising that speculative fiction has also been produced to imagine a potential future for the young girl.

Prior to Auslander's novel, perhaps the most famous example would be the fantasies within the otherwise realist *Ghost Writer* (1979) by Philip Roth in which the protagonist Nathan Zuckerman becomes obsessed with a fantasy that the young woman he's met, Amy Bellette, is in fact a mature Anne Frank. Zuckerman imagines marrying Anne and thus putting his Jewishness beyond doubt, it having been called into question by the publication of a story which seemed to confirm certain racial stereotypes and, despite its success, had drawn the ire of his family and the influential community rabbi. Frank is thus presented as a redeeming force and a paragon of Jewishness, as Zuckerman imagines:

> Oh, marry me, Anne Frank, exonerate me before my outraged elders of this idiotic indictment! Heedless of Jewish feeling? Indifferent to Jewish survival? Brutish about their well-being? Who dares to accuse of such unthinking crimes the husband of Anne Frank![51]

Elsewhere, Zuckerman supposes that Anne Frank might be 'some impassioned little sister of Kafka's, his lost little daughter'; in saying so he is blurring the lines between literary criticism and fantasy, imagining a scenario whereby this might be true. Invoking Kafka is not only the invocation of another titan of twentieth-century Jewish literature (the novel also features appearances from fictitious authors who Zuckerman regards with almost equal awe), but also a titan of the non-mimetic form.[52] In *Ghost Writer* Roth is clearly toying with speculative fiction while not completely committing to the mode. Yet, his deliberate gestures in that direction are visible in Amy/Anne's first appearance in the text: immediately after the resident author, Lonoff, insists 'I've been writing fantasy for thirteen years'.[53]

Shalom Auslander's *Hope: A Tragedy* (2012) is more overtly fantastical in its narrative which imagines the protagonist, Solomon Kugel, relocating his young family out of New York to the rural location of Stockton. The Holocaust is a constant presence in the novel, and Kugel's mother is a caricature of the second-generation American Jewish relationship with the Holocaust: she respects it, is in awe of it, and on one level feels robbed of the formative experience of being a part of it. In one of the more dramatic instances of this, George Steiner described himself as 'maimed for not having been at the roll call'.[54] Kugel himself is a mess of indecision, paranoia, morbidity, and the perfect embodiment of someone surrounded by the 'cloud of neurosis' which Henri Raczymow called the post-Holocaust Jews' 'only legacy'.[55] The true shock of the novel, however, and its break from realism, comes when the family find Anne Frank still alive in their new farmhouse attic. But gone is Anne Frank the hopeful youth snuffed out at the very moment of her blossoming; sixty years have passed and this Anne Frank is a foul-mouthed geriatric who eats dead birds and the neighbour's cat to survive, ceaselessly typing.

The novel is woven with controversial approaches to the Holocaust which vary between thoughtful and humorous, all of which have a normalizing effect on the genocide. For example, when Kugel is discussing hope with his psychiatrist, Professor Jove, who considers Hitler the last century's greatest optimist:

> Hitler was the most unabashed doe-eyed optimist of the last hundred years. That's *why* he was the biggest monster. Have you ever heard of anything as outrageously hopeful as the Final Solution? ... The only thing more naively hopeful than the Final Solution is the ludicrous dictum to which it gave birth: Never Again. How many times since Never Again has it happened again? Three? Four? That we know of, mind you. Mao? Optimist. Stalin? Optimist. Pol Pot? Optimist.[56]

Such moments, including almost every interaction with Kugel's mother, relativize the Holocaust. In the above example it is through re-inserting it into a chronology of genocide that suggests it was not the first and shows it was not the last atrocity, highlighting the ineffectiveness of an empty gesture of 'Never Again'. The re-contextualization of the Holocaust attempts to reverse the exceptionalism that declares the Holocaust unique and inexplicable, or at least to question the process which led to that point, through the treatment of Hitler and the notion of the Final Solution not as an infernal evil unparalleled in human history but as some manner of twisted joke. When Kugel as a child is taken to visit Sachsenhausen concentration camp by his mother he automatically smiles for the camera when she takes a photo of him next to the ovens. She storms off telling him: 'I hope you're happy ... You ruined the whole concentration camp for me, you know that? You ruined the whole damn camp.' This is one of many funny scenes in the novel, and yet it is set in and around a concentration camp (a real one, popular with tourists for its easy access, being just north of Berlin), and chooses as its target the controversial phenomenon of Holocaust tourism. Kugel's mother's enthusiastic passion for all things Holocaust goes beyond fanaticism and slips into mania. She is a caricature of the overzealous post-war American Jew of the kind described by Ruth Wisse as '[having] lately appropriated the Holocaust to their own needs of self-identification, and begun to wrap themselves in its historical mantle'. Wisse goes on to warn that 'commemorating the Holocaust does not require its placement at the center of

Jewish experience. A community otherwise so ignorant of its sources that it becomes preoccupied with death and destruction is in danger of substituting a cult of martyrdom for the Torah's insistence on life.'[57]

The totalizing symbol of this normalizing critique however is the treatment of Anne Frank. Even Kugel's mother, previously her most devout attendee, calls her a 'lying old whore', a 'bitch', after reading her most recent manuscript and finding it ill-fitting of the idealized Frank: 'Anne Frank would never write those things,' she insists. 'Anne Frank would never *think* those things.'[58] Through Anne Frank as a character, speculative fiction is able to tell stories which are not set in or around a concentration camp but are still very much about the Holocaust as an event. Emily Miller Budick writes that novels such as *The Ghost Writer* and *Hope: A Tragedy* expose 'not only the manipulative, fantasizing, exploitative dimension of the public's imagination of Anne and the Holocaust but also a parallel obsession with Anne and the Holocaust on the parts of even those writers who are critical of the public fascination with Anne'.[59] Though I reject the implication that to fantasize is necessarily synonymous with exploitation or manipulation in the negative sense, Budick's point does convey the self-entangling nature of writing about the Holocaust creatively, and of critiquing contemporary relationships to it. Such stories are the speculative fiction equivalent of a story such as Nathan Englander's 'What We Talk About When We Talk About Anne Frank' (2012). The characters in Englander's story talk about Anne Frank and discuss who might hide them if they needed to try to survive a Holocaust event, and if one of them were gentile would they hide the others, but they are really talking about contemporary American and Israeli politics, about Jewishness and Jewish identity, about the stereotypes that Jewish humour is based on, and about the difference between generations.[60] Yet even Englander's characters still employ a 'what if?' hypothetical question, the cornerstone of speculative fiction.

The Yiddish Policeman's Union (2007), Michael Chabon

For some writers of speculative fiction altering the fates of emblematic individuals allows them to comment on the Holocaust and its cultural position. Putting Hitler on trial or putting words in his mouth in order to examine not his own guilt (unquestionable as it is) but the guilt of Britain and America for failing to prevent the genocide, or of post-war generations who allowed subsequent atrocities to occur and were perhaps even complicit in them either directly or through the mechanisms of Western democracy. Or reviving Anne Frank not to examine her as a person or historical figure but to examine our relationship with her as a symbol, a fetishized avatar of suffering through whose innocence we can feel like we can safely get close enough to validate our own consciences and tell ourselves that we have become informed and are better people for it.

Michael Chabon takes a very different approach in his novel *The Yiddish Policeman's Union* (2007), an alternate history novel which analyses the Holocaust through the lens of a diminished catastrophe. Rather than taking one specific and named figure from the history of the Holocaust and placing them in a different time and place, he takes some of the nameless millions and saves them. This is achieved through Chabon's twist of a historical footnote into an epoch-altering event: the Alaskan Settlement Act. Despite isolationist and anti-Jewish sentiments in America at the time (those same sentiments capitalized on by other writers of alternate history – for example see Philip Roth's *The Plot Against America*, discussed in Chapter 4), there were members of the Roosevelt administration, including Interior Secretary Harold Ickes, who favoured creating 'a haven for Jewish refugees from Germany and other areas in Europe where the Jews are subjected to oppressive restrictions' to which end Interior Undersecretary Harold Slattery composed a report called 'The Problem of Alaskan Development', now better known as the Slattery Report.[61] Ultimately, the bill died in the committee hearing phase, partly because of xenophobic or anti-immigration rhetoric such as that printed in the editorial to an Alaskan which was anxious that the new arrivals would be 'an outcrop of bunds and other foreign groups that would exalt the alien idea instead of the American'.[62] The most vocal, and influential, opponent of the bill was Anthony J. Dimond, who argued that with the restrictions on movement the bill would impose upon refugees (partly to ease concerns about Alaska becoming a gateway for immigrants to access the mainland United States), it 'would set the territory off from the rest of America, making it one of the world's largest and most expensive penal colonies'.[63] Chabon's solution is to remove Dimond through 'the fatal intervention on a Washington, DC, street corner of a drunken, taxi driving schlemiel named Denny Lanning – eternal hero of the Sitka Jews'.[64] With Dimond absent the 'Alaskan Settlement Act of 1940' is passed and immigrants carry 'an "Ickes passport", a special emergency visa printed on special flimsy paper with special smeary ink'.[65] Life in Alaska is of course harsh, and even without Dimond the Jewish immigrants are placed under restrictions which mean they cannot leave the territory, and Chabon conspires to further skew history:

> Their mother was taught the rudiments of agriculture, the use of plow, fertilizer, and irrigation hose. Brochures and posters held up the short Alaskan growing season as an allegory of the brief duration of her stay. Mrs. Shemets ought to think of the Sitka Settlement as a cellar or potting shed in which, like flower bulbs, she and her children could be put up for the winter, until their home soil thawed enough to allow them to be replanted there. No one imagined that the soil of Europe would be sowed so deeply with salt and ash.[66]

The ashes are the ruins of an even more prolonged conflict in Europe, culminating in the nuclear bombing of Berlin. They are also the ashes of the Holocaust, known to the Jews in this novel as 'the Destruction', a more faithful translation of the Yiddish *churbn*, reflecting the status of Yiddish as the first language of Sitka and their residents.[67] This, however, neither eliminates nor diminishes the image of the Holocaust/Destruction survivor, as represented by Isidor Landsman, the father of the novel's protagonist Mendel:

> One warm September afternoon ... Landsman's father had just arrived in Sitka, alone, aboard the *Williwaw*, fresh from a tour of the death and DP camps of Europe. He was twenty-five, bald, and missing most of his teeth. He was six feet tall and weighed 125 pounds. He smelled funny, talked crazy, and had outlived his entire family. He was oblivious to the raucous frontier energy of downtown Sitka ... He walked with his head down, a hunch in his shoulders, as if only burrowing through this world on his inexplicable way from one strange dimension to the next. Nothing penetrated or illuminated the dark tunnel of his passage.[68]

The presentation of Isidor as a strange transient figure, no longer truly belonging to our world, highlights the historical wrongness of the existence of Yiddish Sitka, a 'strange' city which for the reader does not exist and has no real parallel. It also emphasizes the status of the extermination camps as Other, as a site of erasure, evoking 'Planet Auschwitz' and '*L'Univers Concentrationnaire*'. Excavated from his psychological tunnel by his friend Hertz Shemets, Isidor remains a damaged figure who finds solace only in the game of chess and even that proves insufficient, a painful experience which he plays 'like a man with a toothache, a haemorrhoid, and gas'.[69] Isidor marries Hertz's sister, Freydl, and fathers two children, but he ultimately commits suicide by overdosing on the barbiturate

Nembutal. He leaves a suicide note: 'Six lines of Yiddish verse addressed to an unnamed female ... an expression of regret for his inadequacy. Chagrin at his failure. An avowal of devotion and respect. A touching statement of gratitude for the comfort she had given him, and above all, for the measure of forgetfulness that her company had brought to him over the long, bitter course of the years.'[70] The natural assumption is that this is a suicide note to Freydl, an apology for failing to live up to her attempts to lift 'the choking, low-hanging black pall of the Destruction'.[71] However, Landsman later notices that 'if you put together the first letters of each of the six lines of the poem, they spelled out a name. Caissa'. The goddess of chess players.[72] By making his final devotion through an acrostic to a pagan goddess of a rational and intellectual pursuit, Isidor performs the roles of both the secular survivor and the pagan, disavowing traditional Jewish faith. Not only does this set up Landsman himself as the secular detective amid the novel's central plot, which revolves around Zionist Jewish fundamentalism, it also reflects the post-Holocaust crisis of faith represented in texts such as Elie Wiesel's *Night* (1958): 'Never shall I forget those moments that murdered my God and my soul and turned my dreams to ashes.'[73]

The theological crisis continues in later religious and philosophical thought by writers such as Richard Rubenstein.[74] It represents not only the physical trauma of starvation and beatings, nor only the psychological trauma of confinement, torture and the death of ones loved ones, but is in fact also a spiritual trauma; the search for God and either failing to find him, or finding him inadequate. This inadequacy or irrelevancy finds expression in numerous works of Holocaust literature, for example in Thane Rosenbaum's *The Golems of Gotham* (2002) when two Holocaust survivors commit suicide in New York, years after the genocide:

> God would have no say in this matter. He had become irrelevant, a lame-duck divinity, a sham for a savior, a mere caricature of a god who cared. That's the price you pay for arriving late at Auschwitz, or in his case, not at all; you forfeit all future rights to an opinion. Yes, it's true: The taking of human life is a sin in the eyes of God. But this was a God who had already blinded himself. It mattered little to the Levins whether he approved of what they had done under his watch and that's why they showed no fear in taking the liberty of poking God's eyes out one last time.[75]

The inadequacy of God is also represented in *The Yiddish Policeman's Union* through the human failings of the potential messiah, the *Tzadik ha-Dor* Mendel

Shpilman, being unable to save himself, let alone the Jewish people. Mendel's fate is a mirror for the Yiddish society as a whole, corrupted and despondent. The most powerful and sacred family in the community, the Verbovers, are both pious Jews and gangsters, metonymically known as the 'black hats', yet they too are products of the Holocaust:

> They started out, back in the Ukraine, black hats like all the other black hats, scorning and keeping their distance from the trash and hoo-hah of the secular world, inside their imaginary ghetto wall of ritual and faith. Then the entire sect was burned in the fires of the Destruction, down to a hard, dense core of something blacker than any hat. What was left of the ninth Verbover rebbe emerged from those fires with eleven disciples and, among his family, only the sixth of his eight daughters. He rose into the air like a charred scrap of paper and blew to this narrow strip between the Baranof Mountains and the end of the world. And here he found a way to remake the old-style black-hat detachment. He carried its logic to its logical end, the way evil geniuses do in cheap novels. He built a criminal empire that profited on the meaningless tohubohu beyond the theoretical walls, on beings so flawed, corrupted, and hopeless of redemption that only cosmic courtesy led the Verbovers even to consider them human at all.[76]

The non-human Othering, with which Chabon suggests the Verbovers think, is just one example Chabon posits of the Jews not learning from the Holocaust and instead absorbing the mentality of their persecutors in order to inflict it upon others. For example, their relationship with the Native Americans, the Tlingit people, is demonstrated by the discrimination felt by the half-Tlingit, half-Jewish detective Shemets, and exemplified by the Synagogue riots:

> Jews want liveable space. In the seventies some of them, mostly members of small Orthodox sects, began to take it.
> The construction of the prayer house at St. Cyril ... was the final outrage for many Natives. It was met with demonstrations, rallies, lawyers, and dark rumblings from Congress over yet another affront to peace and parity by the overweening Jews of the north. Two days before its consecration, somebody – no one ever came forward or was charged – threw a double Molotov through a window, burning the prayer house to its concrete pad. The congregants and their supporters swarmed into the town of St. Cyril, smashing crab traps, breaking the windows of the Alaska Native Brotherhood hall, and setting spectacular fire to a shedful of Roman candles and cherry bombs. ... The Synagogue Riots remain the lowest moment in the bitter and inglorious history of Tlingit-Jewish relations.[77]

The Jewish search for liveable space here has echoes of *Lebensraum* but also, especially given the reference to the seventies, of the Israeli settlers of occupied Palestinian territories, although Chabon himself denies such comparisons.[78] Chabon's use of the Tlingit also taps into wider literary traditions: Rachel Rubinstein shows in her study of the Native American in Jewish literature that the symbolism of the Native Americans as peoples displaced from their rightful land has been used repeatedly as a symbol by both Zionist and Palestinian writers.[79] Thus *The Yiddish Policeman's Union* invites us to connect three traumas of displacement: the Jews, the Palestinians and the Native Americans; and uses the Holocaust as the means of bringing these three groups into focus with one another.

As it turns out the 'somebody' who threw the Molotov was a Jew, working in secret. Hertz Shemets, the shadowy figure working for the FBI, commissioned an expert to bomb the prayer house to absolve the Jews; he explains:

> Those Jews, those fanatics, the people moving into the disputed areas. They were endangering the status of the entire District. Confirming the Americans' worst fears about what we would do if they gave us Permanent Status.[80]

The same bomb expert is employed at the novel's end to bomb the Dome of the Rock, framing alternate Arab/Muslim groups in the process in order to sow disharmony in Jerusalem and prepare the way for the return of the Jews to the lands of Israel and the coming of the Messiah. The novel revolves around these two burning temples, one in the past, the other in the future for most of the book, echoing the destruction of the two temples in Jerusalem which are central to Jewish history. The destructions in the novel are both false flag operations, designed to assign blame to another group of people in order to benefit the Jews in the long term. In doing so they not only confirm the image of the secretive machinating Jew, such as the subjects of the *Protocols of the Elders of Zion*, but also they do it by utilizing the same false flag tactic employed by the Nazis themselves.[81]

To return briefly to Mendel Shpilman's downfall, he spirals into a cycle of drug abuse, but the trigger for this decline stems not from the pressure to take on the role of the messiah, but more because, as Helene Meyers states, 'he cannot imagine a way to negotiate his complex spiritual and erotic desires' while also adhering to the necessary ultra-orthodox regimen of the Verbover community.[82] In portraying Mendel in this manner, highlighting that even someone as remarkable as he could not hope to remain within the community while remaining true to his sexuality, and given the context of the novel, we are reminded that homosexuals were also victims of the Nazis – the pink triangle identifying someone in a camp as much as a yellow star.

Chabon's novel is a warning about tolerance. Permeating the book is the Yiddish experience, that of the displaced population and the persecution of the Jews over their long history but particularly in Europe in the recent century. The threat of returning to that world, of a whole nation about to be ejected from their homes with no place left to go, looms over the narrative. A threat illustrated with dark humour by Landsman (whose name is of course also of ironic significance), when urged to cut down on drinking by an Indian doctor from the Asian subcontinent:

> Doctor ... I respect your keenness, but tell me, please, if the country of India were being cancelled, and in two months, along with everyone you loved, you were going to be tossed into the jaws of the wolf with nowhere to go and no one to give a fuck, and half the world had just spent the past thousand years trying to kill Hindus, don't you think you might take up drinking?[83]

The intolerance faced by the Yiddish-speaking people of Eastern Europe is undeniable, yet Chabon colours this with the mutual intolerance of the Yiddish residents of Sitka and their Tlingit neighbours, as well as Mendel's seemingly intolerable sexuality. In doing so *The Yiddish Policeman's Union* is a reminder that tolerance works in both directions, as does intolerance. Through the figure of the Verbover rabbi, and the natural moral murkiness of the hard-boiled detective genre, Chabon raises questions of morality and its lack of relativity. The experience of persecution, and ultimately of genocide, does not imbue an individual, or a group, with an intrinsically superior morality or moral cause. Chabon clouds any attempt at deriving a moral message from the novel by wrapping these questions up around a persistent chess metaphor later revealed to be that of 'Zugzwang' or 'no good moves' – the Yiddish people of Sitka have no good options left to them. Yet we, like Landsman, are left unconvinced that the course chosen, to destroy the Dome of the Rock and incite war so that the Jews can force their way back into the lands of Israel, is really the best bad choice.[84]

Chabon may only partially undo the Holocaust but he completely undoes the state of Israel, underlining the inextricable link between the genocide and the foundation of the nation. In particular Chabon draws attention to the extent to which the United States is enmeshed with Israel, not only through the machinations of a character such as Hertz Shemets, but also through the world-building of the alternate history:

> Israel collapses partly because the United States, having done this grand gesture, doesn't feel the same sense of guilt and the same pressure to do something to help the Zionists in Israel.[85]

There is a narrative expediency in removing Israel as it means the Sitka Jews, if denied American citizenship, really do have nowhere else to go. Sitka is a limbo between two states (figuratively and literally), not a permanent solution. The heightened tension for the Jews which results from the absence of Israel reflects Chabon's feelings about the role Israel plays in the Jewish psyche among non-Israeli Jews. As a child Chabon considered Israel to be a fallout shelter, an option of last resort for the Jews of the world. As he grew older, he became increasingly disillusioned with Israel; part of the reason for writing *The Yiddish Policeman's Union* was to 'build [himself] a home in [his] imagination'.[86] That this home is fleeting and temporary perhaps reflects the insecurity and doubt centuries of anti-Semitism, channelled through the Holocaust, has instilled in the Jewish popular consciousness.

Chabon first struck on the idea of an alternate history of Alaskan Yiddish Jews when he encountered a Yiddish phrasebook in a bookshop, 'like a book in a story by Borges, unique, inexplicable, possibly a hoax'.[87] The book listed an original publication date of 1958, 'a full ten years after the founding of the country that turned its back once and for all on the Yiddish language, condemning it to watch the last of its native speakers die one by one in a headlong race for extinction with the twentieth century itself ... it seemed an entirely futile effort on the part of its authors, a gesture of embittered hope, of valedictory daydreaming, of a utopian impulse turned cruel and ironic'.[88] A phrasebook for a land which never existed, Chabon was particularly entranced by 'Can I go by boat/ferry to _____'; the blank space is a void which his imagination demanded he fill, the antithesis of the empty spaces of the Holocaust. The extinction of Yiddish was not trauma, at least not for Chabon or the Anglo-American popular consciousness, but rather a poignant imaginative opportunity. Nonetheless, the two are inextricably linked.

The Yiddish Policeman's Union fuses alternate history with the stylized genre of the hard-boiled detective mystery in order to craft a narrative which draws numerous historical reference points into relative positions. The detective novel is a particularly adept partner for alternate history as it presents the reader with a double mystery: the crime, and the mechanisms of the alternate world.[89]

By inviting us to consider the real-world displacements of Native Americans and Palestinians alongside the Jewish diaspora and the Holocaust, Chabon places the act of genocide against the Jewish people alongside other atrocities. Through its use of a speculative fiction setting, *The Yiddish Policeman's Union* is able to employ the Holocaust as a lens through which to examine historic relationships between the United States and those three groups, but also through which to consider contemporary politics and social relations. In this way, Chabon's novel is more subversive than previous novels which seek to undo the Holocaust completely. By merely diminishing the genocide, Chabon places the Holocaust among the realms of other atrocities, and so highlights the extent to which the promotion of the Holocaust's exceptionalism influences the world.

The most recent novel to attempt a level of subversion and displacement akin to Chabon's alternate history is Lavie Tidhar's *Unholy Land* (2018). It takes as its inspiration the proposed 'Uganda Scheme' to resettle Europe's Jewish population in a nation of their own, not in Palestine but carved out of British East Africa. The proposal, already the subject of a novelette by Tidhar in 'Uganda' (2007), was an early-twentieth-century idea which drew the support of prominent Zionist Theodor Herzl and British Colonial Secretary Joseph Chamberlain, among others.[90] The scheme got so far as to commission a survey of the proposed land, conducted in 1904, which reported negatively on the prospects for the territory, recommending that no Jewish settlement be established. In the introduction to *Unholy Land*, Tidhar reports of 'a perhaps apocryphal story' that one of the members of the expedition, Nahum Wilbusch, by now an old man was 'flying over the territory many years later, ruefully reflecting that the Holocaust might never have happened had the plan gone ahead'.[91] Like Chabon's novel, Tidhar takes the creation of this might-have-been alternate Jewish nation as his starting point. Unlike Chabon, however, Tidhar does not fully commit the narrative to the alternate reality. Instead Tidhar layers alternate realities over each other, allowing characters to move between universes from one that looks very like ours to another in which the Uganda Scheme has birthed a Jewish nation in Africa called Palestina, with brief forays into others besides. Some characters wilfully move between these worlds and defend them against others who might seek to cross over, adding a spy-thriller element to the novel; others seem to cross more accidentally: the writer Tirosh who finds himself thrust into the middle of the action and at times unable to identify which reality is his native one having memories of an identity belonging to each.[92] Another character recounts stumbling upon some Nazis in the Palestina forests, 'but there were no Nazis', he opines as he tries to work it out, 'there have been no Nazis since the Hitler assassination, and that was in '48 ... What are Nazis anyway? ... We were not involved with the war in Europe. The Nazis never did a thing to us'. Special Agent Bloom, who is aware of the layering of reality and its permeable boundaries, tells the man that 'they were Nazis ... it was just that they were not from around here'.[93]

As the Jews of Palestina displace native Ugandans and Kenyans, and build a wall around their young nation and its most disputed land to protect settlers and enforce their territorial rights, when a terrorist attack occurs and 'innocent labourers and naturalised tribespeople would be locking their doors and praying to see the morning undamaged' fearing retaliatory attacks and reprisals, Tidhar's parallels to contemporary Israel are clear to the point of being blunt.[94] However, in writing the novel Tidhar infuses it with his typical brand of narrative trickery; the layering of realities diminishes the authority of all of the universes, undermining the supposition that a world in which the Holocaust was avoided would lead to a better long-term solution for the Jewish people than our world, or indeed that it would lead to a worse one.

Like Chabon, the role of the detective is compared to that of a historian, as both 'must go around asking questions, banging on doors, interrogating unwilling witnesses. They must piece together a story from conflicting tales, from clues ... to give meaning to a series of what were, essentially, just meaningless events'.[95] However, 'the problem was that everyone had a different story. The same place could have multiple names: Jerusalem, Ursalim, Yerushalaim. Each name came with a different and competing history'.[96] History, Tidhar suggests, is not as neat as the plot of a detective fiction, not a closed circuit, just as reality is not as neat as history can suggest. Narratives are formed by privileging certain types of information over others, sifting to create a story with some manner of cohesion. This process is fundamental to fiction and the translation of imagination to text, but while equally necessary in historicism it is not unproblematic.

Tidhar's novel has more to say about Israeli politics than it does about the Holocaust, being more explicitly and unabashedly concerned with the contemporary world and the political than *The Yiddish Policeman's Union*, but it continues a trend seen in Chabon's novel of connecting the Holocaust to recent history, recognizing it as both a beginning and an end, as an event inextricably woven into our contemporary world.

Conclusion

The texts I have selected to discuss here are not the only works of fiction to try to create a positive scenario out of the Holocaust: the closure of putting Hitler on trial, the saving of Anne Frank, the saving of millions of lives. The Second World War as a whole event, including the Holocaust, doesn't occur in a considerable number of alternate history novels.

For example, Norman Spinrad's provocative *The Iron Dream* (1972) features a world where Adolf Hitler fails in politics and becomes a writer of pulp science fiction. It presents a novel within a novel which illustrates Hitler's psychosexual violence of Nazism while satirizing science fiction and fantasy fandoms' attraction to militaristic and hyper-masculine role models which are themselves fascistic in nature. The book is layered with paratextual information, the most dominant of which is the afterword which 'to make damn sure that even the historically naive and entirely unselfaware reader got the point, [Spinrad] appended a phony critical analysis of *Lord of the Swastika*, in which the psychopathology of Hitler's saga was spelled out by a tendentious pedant in words of one syllable'.[97] Through this analysis we learn of the world in which the novel was written, one in which Communists seized power in Germany instead of fascists. We read about the 'rabid heights' of anti-Semitism in the Greater Soviet Union, and the deaths of 'five million Jews' in recent decades, suggesting an inevitable doom for the Jewish population of Europe, Nazi or otherwise.[98]

In his novella 'The Three Armageddons of Enniscorthy Sweeny' (1977), R. A. Lafferty uses speculative fiction to remove not only the Holocaust but all of the major traumas of the twentieth century including both world wars and the Great Depression. However, in typically elusive fashion, Lafferty finds a way to avoid these traumas yet still experience them. In his narrative, the titular Enniscorthy Sweeny, is some manner of magus with nebulous reality-bending powers. Sweeny demonstrates his capacity to change the world through the composition of three operas: the titular Armageddons. Each of the Armageddons coincides with a World War in our own timeline: Armageddon I is first performed in Vienna in 1916, Armageddon II opens 'simultaneously in twelve capitals of the world' in 1939, while Armageddon III – representing a third and final conflict – is produced in Palestine in 1984.[99] Yet some people who go to see these operas come out of them as traumatized as if they had lived through the event itself, convinced they've lost limbs or loved ones. Lafferty's complex and twisting novella seems to suggest the inescapability of the terrible destruction contained in the last century, like a freight train which has been gathering speed for some time.

The inevitability of war is demonstrated through the inevitably warlike character of Germany in another novel, Jerry Yulsman's *Elleander Morning* (1984). In this novel, the titular character uses force of will to transport her consciousness back in time, occupy her own body at the beginning of the century, and travel to Austria to kill Hitler. Removing Hitler prevents the war, however the assassin's daughter comes into possession of a two-volume illustrated history of the Second World War from our timeline and its revelations, revealed decades later, are exploited by a German elite as evidence of an international Jewish-led conspiracy against them. A leader rises to power who favours 'special Teutonic attribute[s]' and has a predilection to extermination based on racial criteria. Despite some seventy years between the assassination of Hitler and the events of the novel, the spirit of fascism, hunger for conquest and drive to genocide still inhabits the hearts of the German people.[100]

These three novels contain events which should be positive: they avoid the Second World War and the Holocaust. Yet like those texts that make up the preceding pages of this chapter, they are unable to create positive worlds out of their speculations. For all of these fictions it seems any attempt to defuse the Holocaust, or to diminish it, is doomed to create not a potential utopia but a different dystopia. 'What can be more disturbing than considering whether the holocaust may not have happened or may have happened on a smaller scale?' asks Elana Gomel, 'Are we not skirting perilously close to Holocaust denial in such exercises?'[101] But these texts make no attempt to confuse real and fictional histories, and feature very clearly alternate worlds. What's more they do not even seem able to create anything good out of the Holocaust, even in a diminished or altered state.

In rewriting the narrative of history and the Holocaust these texts presented not utopian (or, uchronian) global societies, but texts which offer a bleak commentary on the human condition, on the destructive drives of particularly European society, and in some cases on the nature of Jews and Germans themselves. While the notion of the German people as being inclined to barbarism and genocide may have fallen away in recent decades (but still present in Yulsman's *Elleander Morning* in 1984), the notion that the Holocaust or some similar catastrophe was unavoidable persists. Even should it be delayed by preventing the Nazi rise to power, these narratives suggest that the toxic combination of nationalism, racism (specifically anti-Semitism), and imperial ambitions or posturings were building pressure which had to explode into genocide at some point.

The texts of this chapter suggest the impossibility of positivity, the denial of the happy ending. Or, at the very least, the denial of the clean ending. They demonstrate that history cannot be contained in neat packages, that the process of historiography is a packaging of events which is necessary for its easy consumption, but that is too often presented as definitive and neat. Speculative fiction is limited only by the imagination, yet by refusing to find a route to utopia through the twentieth century, the writers of these texts are either proposing that our imaginations are not up to the feat, or perhaps equally, that we are not deserving of such an ending.

In an inversion of the unimaginability of Auschwitz, in these texts the Holocaust cannot be un-imagined, it remains an indelible stain on the imagination which imposes itself on the seeds of positivity we might expect in finding justice, saving lives or avoiding conflict. In this sense the Anglo-American mindset has so internalized the trauma of the Holocaust that the culture itself has undergone a form of trauma whereby even writers completely detached from the event itself can no longer escape from its gravity.

4

Reimagining Horror: *The Plot Against America* (2004), *Farthing* (2006), *A Man Lies Dreaming* (2014) and *J* (2014)

A significant challenge for Holocaust studies in the twenty-first century has been how the field will develop in a post-survivor era. As we have already seen, one of the significant strengths of speculative fiction's approach to the Holocaust is its capacity to reimagine and reframe the atrocity for us to reconsider it in alternative contexts. The texts of this chapter embrace the dystopian power of the Holocaust, utilizing it to craft speculative fictions which implicitly (and sometimes explicitly) draw the Holocaust into comparison with our relationships to other traumas and catastrophes. Philip Roth's *The Plot Against America* (2004), for example, creates a fictionalized biography of the author's own childhood growing up not in a United States under the presidency of Franklin D. Roosevelt and sympathetic to the plight of Britain and France, but rather under the presidency of Charles Lindbergh and friendly with Nazi Germany. In creating this alternate history Roth finds an outlet for the fears of the time, the 1930s, about the rise of fascism and the naked violence of anti-Semitism, and the dangers that posed to American democracy as well as world peace. But Roth's novel also speaks to the dangers of right-wing politics in the American system more generally, with numerous commentators drawing comparisons to the post-9/11 America of George W. Bush when the book was first published, and to Donald Trump more recently.

Similarly, Jo Walton's 'Small Change' trilogy, and particularly the first novel in that series, *Farthing* (2006), creates an alternate history where an establishment elite assume power in the United Kingdom after Dunkirk and force an armistice with Germany. In this new peace British society is dragged to the right, and Walton uses the conventions of the stately home detective novel to both expose the unsettling ease with which such a scenario might have come about and also to comment on xenophobia, anti-Semitism and scapegoating. In turn, she explicitly acknowledges that the books were a reaction to the shift to the right in

British politics and a comment on how far we were willing to sacrifice liberty for often illusionary security.

More recently, two novels first published in 2014 gave very different speculative fiction approaches to the Holocaust yet both authors presented texts which spoke to concerns about contemporary society as much as to the Holocaust itself, although both also point to worrying markers of a common history of political shifts, anti-Semitism and distrust of institutions which are found both in the early years of twentieth-century fascism and in our own time. Howard Jacobson's *J* does this through an inventive dystopian novel set in a vaguely near-future, possibly alternate historical, England. While Lavie Tidhar's *A Man Lies Dreaming* centres his alternate history novel on figures from the Nazi Party, specifically Hitler himself, now living in exile in the United Kingdom following communism's rise to power in Germany.

These texts take the Holocaust and imagine a potentially worse version of it, an act which as we've already seen in Chapter 2 forces us to confront the genocide on a spectrum of relative morality; but unlike the 'Hitler Wins' scenarios already examined, they do so not by depicting Nazi Germany winning the war or attaining global domination, but by demonstrating the insidious creep of right-wing politics, the manner in which fascism can present itself as attractive to certain populations at certain times, and the realities of anti-Semitism and xenophobia. In doing so they are very demonstrably important texts both of the Holocaust then, and of our time now.

The Plot Against America (2004), Philip Roth

Opening in an alternate 1940, Philip Roth's *The Plot Against America* tells the story of 'America's international aviation hero' Charles Lindbergh, speaking out against American intervention in the Second World War and gaining the Republican nomination for the presidency.[1] Ultimately he wins by landslide on an anti-war platform and immediately signs a treaty of non-interference with Hitler's Nazi Germany (the Iceland Understanding) and Imperial Japan (the Hawaii Understanding). Following the Iceland Understanding, Lindbergh makes a short speech expressing American isolationism:

> It is now guaranteed that this great country will take no part in the war in Europe.
> … We will join no warring party anywhere on this globe. At the same time we

will continue to arm America and to train our young men in the armed forces in the use of the most advanced military technology. The key to our invulnerability is the development of American aviation, including rocket technology. This will make our continental borders unassailable to attack from without while maintaining our strict neutrality.[2]

Roth's novel does not depict an expansion of fascism, anti-Semitism and Nazism to the United States through conquest but through established historical advocates assuming positions of power. He showcases home-grown fascism, rather than the philosophy of a hostile invading enemy, and the capacity for the United States to succumb to the same fate as Germany, Italy, Hungary, Spain and other nations.

Roth's novel was not the first to take this approach. Jack London's *Iron Heel* (1908) is remarkable for predating the rise of fascism, even anticipating a moment of global crisis and a war which would precipitate divergent political systems of socialism and what he terms oligarchy. London dates this crisis as 1913, he was off by a year. More directly tuned to the specific politics of Nazism and twentieth-century fascism was Sinclair Lewis's *It Can't Happen Here* (1935), a bestseller at the time which was also adapted for the stage, with eighteen American cities staging adaptations in 1937, including a Yiddish production in New York and a Spanish-language version in Tampa, Florida.[3] The novel has experienced a resurgence in popularity recently. Its depiction of a swaggering populist winning through to the presidency and introducing a fascist dictatorship, despite warnings in a liberal press, found resonance with readers and reviewers in 2016.[4] Roth makes explicit reference to Lewis's novel in an earlier work, *American Pastoral* (1997), one of the characters referring to it as 'a wonderful book'.[5] Less acclaimed but still of note, Dennis Easterman, a nom-de-plume for the Irish academic and writer Denis MacEoin, published *K* (more commonly referred to as *K is for Killing*) in 1998. *K* anticipates Roth's novel by also putting Lindbergh in the White House in Roosevelt's place, but his influence is quickly subsumed beneath the Ku Klux Klan who quickly rise to prominence. In structure and tone, however, the novel hews closer to the conventions of the standard thriller than the literary memoir.

The Plot Against America is narrated by a young Philip Roth – an alternate version of the author, inhabiting the alternate history, with a very similar background to the real Philip Roth in our own timeline. Both boys were/are seven years old as the novel opens in June of 1940; they are living in the Weequahic neighbourhood on the edge of Newark, New Jersey. As a member of a Jewish family he is immediately placed into the position of extreme uncertainty and thus imbues the rise of Lindbergh's government with a new urgency both in terms of the characters' reactions and because of the foreknowledge readers have about the potential fate of our young Jewish narrator. Indeed, Stefanie Boese connects *The Plot Against America* to *The Diary of Anne Frank*, remarking that the novel 'reads like an American rewriting of the famous Holocaust narrative'.[6] Similarly, by being a first-person narrative, Roth's novel more effectively conveys the trauma experienced by young Philip. Indeed, the novel opens with a recognition of the effects of trauma in shaping the narrative:

> Fear presides over these memories, a perpetual fear. Of course no childhood is without its terrors, yet I wonder if I would have been a less frightened boy if Lindbergh hadn't been president or if I hadn't been the offspring of Jews.[7]

This opening paragraph also draws attention to the novel's alternate history by inviting further speculation on alternate realities. One, where Lindbergh was not president, potentially leads back to our world, while the other invites us to imagine a non-Jewish Philip Roth, experiencing the events of the novel in a less personal and more detached manner, a reminder for non-Jewish readers of the privilege of their status.

In an interesting irony, the anti-war America First Group, of which Lindbergh was a prominent figure and which propels him to the Republican candidacy in *The Plot Against America*, referenced a form of counterfactual thought themselves in their official announcement of the dissolution of the movement following Pearl Harbour in 1940. The statement asserts the following:

> Our principles were right. Had they been followed, war could have been avoided. *No good purpose can now be served by considering what might have been, had our objectives been attained.* We are at war. Today, though there may be many important subsidiary considerations, the primary objective is not difficult to state. It can be completely defined in one word: Victory.[8]

While asserting that their position could have avoided the conflict, and then shutting down debate on the subject by denying the use of counterfactual thinking, the America First Group were seeking to reclaim some vestige of the moral high ground they had claimed was their position in advocating for American neutrality. That Roth's novel exists, and indeed that all the other alternate history texts in this thesis exist, is a rebuttal of the claims made in this statement and serves as a reminder that in fact speculative and counterfactual considerations of history are invaluable tools for not only re-evaluating that history on its own standing, but for learning new lessons from it that we can take into our own understanding of the present and our vision for the future.

The Plot Against America is not Roth's only foray into Holocaust speculative fiction.[9] By blending his own biography with that of alternate Philip, Roth collides the more traditional alternate history (which takes its cues from historical fiction) with memoir, verging on a new genre: that of alternate memoir. Comparisons can be made with a text such as Jo Kubert's graphic novel *Yossel, April 19, 1943* (2003), in which Kubert imagines what his life would have been like had his parents not emigrated from a shtetl in Poland to New York in 1926, when Kubert was still just two months old.[10] Kubert's *Yossel* however, like Roth's prior forays into the genre, is an alternate history on a micro, one-person, scale. The larger course of history is unaltered by the changes in the biographies of these single historical figures. Non-mimetic narratives in mimetic worlds. *The Plot Against America*, in contrast, takes memoir-esque explorations of self and places them in a completely speculative fictive world.

Ultimately, Roth doesn't go so far as to fully actualize an alternate Holocaust in the United States, though he lays sufficient groundwork to leave beyond doubt the possibility that the persecution and despotism on display could be extended to genocide should the circumstances develop sufficiently. As it is, *The Plot Against America* restores historical continuity in its ending, although it comes closer to the brink of apocalypse in doing so. Lindbergh is elected on a platform of non-intervention, tinged with the rhetoric of his historically accurate Des Moines speech (which Roth includes in full in the novel's extensive postscript material).[11] Among the initiatives which President Lindbergh enacts is his 'Homestead '42' program. Under the auspices of the new Office for American Absorption, and chaired by Quisling-esque Rabbi Lionel Bengelsdorf, Jewish families are relocated from their urban communities and dispersed in more rural locations, 'steeped in our country's oldest traditions where parents and children can enrich their Americanness over the generations'.[12] The Roth family learn they are to be relocated to Danville, Kentucky.

The episode throws into stark contrast a moment from earlier in the novel when Philip's father turns down a promotion, and a chance to earn enough money to buy their own home, when the family takes a drive through the suburban borough of New York that they would live in, a mere six miles West of their current home, and realize that theirs would be 'the house where the Jews live'.[13] By contrast, if they moved to Kentucky the Roths would be not only the only Jews in their immediate area but among very few in the whole town, or even the state. 'There are very few', Philip's father tells his mother, 'All I can tell you is that it could be worse. It could be Montana, where the Gellers are going. It could be Kansas, where the Schwartzes are going. It could be Oklahoma, where the Brodys are going. Seven men are leaving from our office, and I am the luckiest, believe me.'[14] Homestead '42 is presented by the government as 'a program designed to broaden and enrich the involvement of America's proud Jewish citizens in the national life' ('proud' of course can be both an insult and a compliment); in fact it is 'a fascistic strategy to isolate Jews and exclude them from the national life', to break up communities and thus the powers of representation both culturally and politically that such communities have in a borough, city, state, or indeed, nation.[15]

However, it is only after the president goes missing while flying his own plane from Louisville, Kentucky, to Washington D.C. that things become darkest and most terrifying for the Roth family and their Jewish friends. In Lindbergh's absence his vice president Burton K. Wheeler becomes acting president and imposes martial law throughout the United States before announcing to Congress that the FBI have uncovered evidence that Lindbergh has been kidnapped. The Nazi German state radio declare they have evidence that the kidnapping is the result of a conspiracy:

> masterminded by the warmonger Roosevelt – in collusion with his Jewish Treasury secretary, Morgenthau, his Jewish Supreme Court justice, Frankfurter, and the Jewish investment banker Baruch – and that it is being financed by the international Jewish usurers Warburg and Rothschild and carried out under the command of Roosevelt's mongrel henchman, the half-Jew gangster La Guardia, mayor of Jewish New York City, along with the powerful Jewish governor of New York State, the financier Lehman, in order to return Roosevelt to the White House and launch an all-out Jewish war against the non-Jewish world.[16]

The acting president is called upon jointly by the Grand Wizard of the Ku Klux Klan and the leader of the American Nazi Party 'to implement extreme measures to protect America from a Jewish coup d'etat'.[17] Despite the curfew and presence of National Guard, anti-Semitic riots erupt in eleven states in the South and Mid-West, setting fires and resulting in the deaths of 122 American citizens. Conspiracy theories and counter-theories circulate; some claim Britain is aiding the Jewish coup, others that Germany has staged the entire affair; all are fanned by the press, leading to prominent Jewish figures in the establishment being arrested and the First Lady Mrs Lindbergh, thus far a voice of reason and calm, being institutionalized in an army hospital for 'extreme nervous exhaustion' while Mayor La Guardia and Roosevelt himself are also taken into custody.[18] America prepares to declare war on Canada, to wrest it from British control while Churchill warns of German plans to invade Mexico to secure their southern border. Tanks roll into New York and troops occupy all news rooms and radio stations in the city.

While these historical alterations have globe-altering implications, the anticipation and fear is contained to a personal sphere, that of young Philip Roth and his family. It is also, understandably, felt primarily by the Jewish population of Roth's Newark and there is less evidence of foreboding among the limited quantity of non-Jewish characters encountered:

> 'Look', I said, 'I don't want to do this. Not now. There's a lot going on outside that's not so great, you know.'
> But he was oblivious of what was not so great, either because he was Catholic and had nothing to worry about or simply because he was irrepressible Joey.[19]

Yet the novel's world is pulled back from the brink of disaster by the escape of the First Lady and her impassioned speech, broadcast across the nation every half hour, urging the armed forces to stand down, the FBI to release its prisoners and the police to vacate illegally-occupied media outlets. She denounces the acting president and calls on Congress to call a special election. Roosevelt is duly swept into office and undoes all of the damage caused. Within a month, the Japanese launch a surprise attack on Pearl Harbour and the United States declares war on Germany and Japan, a year later than in our own timeline but seemingly setting history back on track nonetheless.

The Plot Against America emphasizes the feelings of existential dread that authoritarianism provokes, particularly in minority groups, but its ending is not entirely satisfying. David Brauner notes that First Lady Lindbergh 'functions as an unlikely *deus ex machina*', describing the alacrity with which young Philip's narration is suddenly interrupted by extracts 'Drawn from the Archives of Newark's Newsreel Theatre' which infodump the which detail Wheeler's brief incumbency as acting president and the quick dismantling of his police state.[20] The 'happy ending' comes so suddenly that it jars considerably with the preceding narrative which so effectively and resonantly evokes a climate of foreboding. Gavriel D. Rosenfeld notes that despite the 'upbeat conclusion' to the novel, it 'hardly diminishes the horror of the Third Reich and makes no attempt to normalize its legacy'.[21] He further notes that the happy ending makes *The Plot Against America* somewhat of a return to future histories of the 1940s such as Fred Allhoff's *Lightening in the Night* (1940), 'which also tempered their cautionary lessons about the Nazi menace with happy endings so as not to demoralize the public'.[22] Yet, the novel backtracks towards this somewhat and it is notable that despite the chronological ending being a happy one with the resumption of normal history, the novel rewinds itself and gives a personal perspective from young Philip Roth of the darkest hours as news of America's planned invasion of Canada is announced. This final chapter, entitled 'Perpetual Fear', reflects the manner in which this alternate Roth will return to these days throughout his life. By giving the title the same name as the subject of the opening line ('Fear presides over these memories, a perpetual fear'), Roth creates a narrative loop, suggesting his alter ego will forever be living these days. History may have been restored to something like its normal self but the alternate Roth, and others affected by it, are indelibly traumatized.

After the Second World War alternate history narratives in which the United Kingdom or the United States allied itself with Nazi Germany because of the rise of their own brands of fascism were rare, with most authors preferring to set their narratives in occupied nations (including an occupied UK or US), or in Germany itself. More recently, however, we have seen a resurgence of this type of narrative (see the below discussion of Jo Walton's *Farthing* for further examples). Roth himself denied any reason for this rooted in contemporary allegorical meaning, yet the notion that the erosion of liberties in Western democracies has hallmarks and precedents that should be feared and recognized seems too prominent to ignore. One of the most powerful things about alternate histories of the Second World War is that they can emphasize the terrible dangers that fascism poses; and they remind us how close our way of life came to destruction, and they keep those memories alive by reinventing them in a manner which discourages complacency. Native fascism narratives do all of this particularly well, as they also remind us that the dangers do not necessarily lie on distant shores but that 'for want of a nail' it could have happened here, and it still could.

Such alternate histories have further implications on the moral superiority of post-war readers because they address a long-established moral taint in both nations which until recently popular images of history preferred to cast as an outdated footnote which never amounted, and never could have amounted to anything in the United Kingdom or United States: anti-Semitism. *The Plot Against America* shows that in the correct circumstances, in this instance the bringing to power of a government willing to endorse and even participate in Nazi-like behaviour, anti-Semitism can be stirred and become a force to actively threaten Jews on a national level, just as in mainland Europe. Roth's novel is particularly potent in this regard, detailing the days and weeks in which a young Jewish boy gained a sense of identity not through learning, cultural blossoming or exploration of self, but through being identified as different from any other 'American child of American parents in an American school in an American city in an America at peace with the world', rupturing 'that huge endowment of personal security that [he] had taken for granted'.[23] Indeed, *The Plot Against America* highlights that this anti-Semitic strain has always been there, it was not imported by an invading Nazi Party. Even before Lindbergh's presidency, this is the America of the Ku Klux Klan, 'those days of unadvertised quotas to keep Jewish admissions to a minimum in colleges and professional schools and of unchallenged discrimination that denied Jews significant promotions in the big corporations and of rigid restrictions against Jewish membership in thousands of social organizations and communal institutions'.[24]

Nonetheless, Roth explicitly denied any attempts to link his novel to the post-9/11 sociopolitical climate in the United States. Gabriel Brownstein writes that 'the references to George W. Bush's America are impossible to miss', highlighting numerous supporting quotes not least the fact that 'when the boyish, pious president wants to rally, he dresses up in a flight suit and hops in a plane', a reference to President Bush's infamous 'Mission Accomplished' speech delivered from the flight deck of the USS Abraham Lincoln on 1 May 2003 for which the president arrived (as a passenger) in a S-3B Viking jet.[25] While Michael Schaub suggests:

> [It is, perhaps,] not a coincidence that *The Plot Against America* is being published just weeks before the 2004 American presidential election. ... Roth has stated clearly his disdain for the current president, and it's easy to read echos of George W. Bush in Charles Lindbergh. Even the name of Lindbergh's final solution ('Just Folks') hearkens to Bush's false good-ol'-boy style.[26]

The representation – or perception – of the book as topical was a significant factor in its success, according to Michael Wood, with readers interpreting even the title as a topical allusion, playing simultaneously upon 'the global plot of al-Qaida against the evils of capitalism, substantively and symbolically centred in the US' alongside 'the plot of the Bush administration to abolish the civil liberties and concentrate autocratic powers in the hands of the president'. Instead Wood asserts that Lindbergh's plot is not a true representation of either of these: 'The plot in the novel is not against America as an imperial nation or America as the land of liberty, but against America as an increasingly battered utopia of tolerance, an always threatened and never fully accomplished vision of shelter and respect for all.'[27] Dan Shiffman points out that comparisons with the Bush-era are imperfect, 'While it does not make sense to read *The Plot Against America* as a protest of the war in Iraq – President Bush's foreign policy was the opposite of Lindbergh's [isolationism]', although he goes on to note that the novel is very much a post-9/11 text with its dramatization of 'isolationism and of living in an invulnerable America'.[28] Meanwhile Brett Ashley Kaplan notes that the Office for American Absorption echoes the Department of Homeland Security, created in response to 9/11.[29]

Yet despite the reality that, as Catherine Gallagher has noted, 'alternate-history fictions always reflect and often satirize their conditions of production',[30] Roth himself attempts to close down use of the novel as allegory or warning:

> I can only repeat that in the 30's there were many of the seeds for its happening here, but it didn't. And the Jews here became what they became because it didn't. All the things that tormented them in Europe never approached European proportions here. Nor is my point that this can happen and will happen; rather, it's that at the moment when it should have happened, it did not happen.[31]

There is an unusual note of appreciation of good fortune here. Roth not only believes that a Holocaust situation could have happened in the America of the 1930s/1940s, but that it should have happened and yet somehow did not. While he may dispute its allegorical status, it is hard to believe that Roth was not inspired by the events of 9/11 and the changes that day had on American people's perception of the world; it seems too perfect a coincidence that he chose to write this book at this time, and chose this alternate president (who in reality never even stood as a candidate for the Republican nomination, let alone the presidency); after all the infamous Des Moines radio speech 'Who Are the War Agitators?' was delivered, Roth helpfully points out in his extensive appendices, on 11 September 1941.[32]

Regardless of Roth's motivations and conscious decisions regarding allegory, *The Plot Against America* undermines complacency about democracy in the

United States and demonstrates that the American population could be just as susceptible to populist fascism as various nations of Europe were in the 1930s.

Farthing (2006), Jo Walton

Second World War alternate history fictions set in the United Kingdom are even more likely to be narratives set during or after an invasion by Nazi Germany than their American counterparts, simply because an invasion force crossing the English Channel to mainland Britain feels far more feasible than such a force successfully crossing the Atlantic. However, like Roth's *The Plot Against America*, it is only more recently that writers have focused on the possibility that a fascist government take power in the United Kingdom not as a result of invasion but because of its own domestic politics.

Ian R. MacLeod's novella 'Summer Isles' (1998) is set in an alternate 1940s in which the United Kingdom lost the First World War and thus takes the place of Weimar Germany in history, a fascist leadership taking advantage of resulting crises and resentment of outsiders to take control and turn the nation into a fascist state by the 1930s. The novella highlights its artificial historicity through its protagonist: an Oxford University history tutor and closeted homosexual.[33] MacLeod's contribution is particularly interesting because it is a rare example of the fortunes of Britain and Germany being reversed in such a way that fascism develops in the United Kingdom instead of Germany, rather than in parallel.

Another example of self-installed fascism in the United Kingdom can be found in *Superman: War of the Worlds* (1999), a comic in which H.G. Wells's Martians fight 1930s Superman, leading to massive destruction on a global scale after which 'with its royal line extinguished, the masses of Great Britain [turn] to the native-born fascist Sir Oswald Mosley for leadership'.[34] Mosely is a common feature in alternate history, often the preferred figure to be installed as the head of a German-led puppet state as in Harry Turtledove's *In the Presence of Mine Enemies* (2003).

Mosley is also the titular villain in journalist and historian Guy Walters' *The Leader* (2003). In that novel Mosley rises to power contemporaneously with Hitler. The scenario is enabled by the actions of King Edward VIII, a familiar plot point in alternate histories both because of his decision to abdicate and the environment in which he did so, something heightened by the former king's purported sympathies for fascist causes and personal admiration for prominent

Nazi figures.³⁵ This admiration seemingly ran both ways: Albert Speer quotes Hitler as having remarked that he was 'certain through him [Edward] permanent friendly relations could have been achieved. If he had stayed, everything would have been different. His abdication was a severe loss for us'.³⁶ In *The Leader* Edward refuses to abdicate in favour of his brother, and goes ahead with his plans to marry Wallis Simpson. The prime minister, Stanley Baldwin, resigns his government and forms a pact with the Labour and Liberal Parties that none of them will go into government until the king does the right thing. The stalemate leaves the British government in limbo, causing economic instability in the United Kingdom, in the midst of the Great Depression. Groups on both the extreme right and the extreme left capitalize on the chaos this causes, drawing members into the British Communist Party, and into Mosley's British Union of Fascists. An attempt to form a 'King's Party' of those who still support the monarch fail when Winston Churchill, leader of this group, cannot win a majority of seats in the House of Commons. In the resulting hung parliament, Mosley's Fascists make up a significant bloc and are the most vocal in their advocacy of the king's position. King Edward, true to his characterized pro-Nazi leanings, asks Mosley to try and form a government; Mosley does so and even wins emergency powers from the House of Commons allowing him to bypass the House and reshape the country into a defacto fascist state.

The protagonist of *The Leader* is Captain James Armstrong, a hero of the First World War, chief whip of the now ineffective Conservative Party. The combination of these two facets of his character mark him out to be a true hero of the traditional conservative establishment and even his name evokes the feeling in a thriller that this is someone we can trust to get the job done. Armstrong comes to lead a rebellion formed primarily from union agitators and other left-wing agitators (who gain a grudging respect from the Conservative Armstrong); with support from friends and supporters in the military they plan a coup, to be crowned by the killing of Oswald Mosley. After a last-minute change in seating arrangements means that the planned bomb would kill President Roosevelt rather than Mosley, Armstrong is forced to pursue the Leader in person; 'they all knew that killing the American president would have an even worse outcome than leaving the Blackshirts in place'.³⁷ Armstrong tries to reach Mosley during the procession to Edward's coronation, resulting in a chase scene through London (on horseback) and a sword fight in which the protagonist finally bests the titular dictator, despite Mosley's referenced historical prowess as a fencer. While forcing the surrender of his foe, Armstrong extolls his superior morality, remarking to Mosley that 'unlike you, I don't believe in summary executions', despite his previous willingness to blow him up Westminster Abbey and resolve to 'kill him before he gets to the Abbey' when that ceases to be a viable option.[38]

Mosley is arrested and put on trial, and found guilty of 'countless' crimes; he is spared execution by hanging in order to avoid making a martyr of him and so is instead sentenced to life imprisonment, as is his wife Lady Diana and his four most senior surviving accomplices. The king, despite protests from his wife, and encouraged by a delegation of politicians freshly released from prison, including Winston Churchill and Stanley Baldwin, finally abdicates in favour of his brother the Duke of Windsor, and goes into exile. The novel draws to a close, in the spring of 1938, with history placed more or less back on the rails of our own timeline:

> [Armstrong] said that he had had enough of politics and that there were plenty of capable men in Parliament who could run the country and see to it that Germany did not dominate the continent; men like Neville Chamberlain, for example.[39]

The knowing-wink irony of these lines is completely in line with the tone of the novel which, adhering to the conventions of the thriller genre, and like Roth in *The Plot Against America*, reassures us that everything will be resolved in a familiar fashion.

One of the most effective demonstrations of the potential for native fascism in the United Kingdom comes from Jo Walton's novel *Farthing* (2006), the first in her 'Small Change Trilogy' of alternate histories, a book inspired by her growing awareness of the unexplained historical incongruities in Josephine Tey's otherwise mimetic mystery novel *Brat Farrar* (1949).[40] The trilogy's title is a play on the titles of the composite novels: *Farthing* (2006), *Ha'Penny* (2007) and *Half a Crown* (2008). It is also a reference to the alternate history generally: the change in this case is Rudolph Hess's mysterious flight to the United Kingdom being accepted by the British establishment and a member of the aristocracy, Sir James Thirkie, returning with him to Berlin in 1941 and negotiating with Hitler a 'Peace with Honour'.[41] The novel opens in 1949 at Farthing, a stately home in the English countryside which gives its name to the Farthing Set of upper-class socialites and politicians (analogous to the Cliveden Set in our own timeline, also named after a house and also referring to aristocratic proponents of appeasing Hitler).

Narration of *Farthing* is split equally, in alternate chapters, between two characters. The first is Lucy, the young eight-month-wed daughter of the Eversleys, owners of Farthing. Her marriage has resulted in her being effectively disowned by her parents because her choice of husband is a Jew, David Khan. Her father acknowledges that 'he was born in England, he's a war hero, his family are very wealthy' but counters 'with the fact that he was educated on the Continent, he's a Jew, and not one of us'.[42] Despite this, Lord Eversley is one of the more moderate members of the set with regard to his anti-Semitism and he approves of the marriage so long as Lucy is sure it is what she wants and is happy. An analeptic discussion between him and Lucy shows him throwing multiple problems and scenarios at his daughter, but more to check she has considered the implications of the society they live in rather than to properly discourage her:

> '... We share a name that we didn't do anything to earn but which we inherited from our Eversley ancestors, who did. It is a name that opens doors for us. You're talking about giving that up to become Mrs. Kahn-'
>
> 'Kahn means that David's ancestors were priests in Israel when ours were paining themselves blue with woad,' I said, quoting – probably misquoting – Disraeli.
>
> Daddy smile. 'All the same, what it means to people now and in England will close a lot of doors in your face.'
>
> 'Not doors I want to go through,' I said.
>
> Daddy raised an eyebrow at that.[43]

Yet they have been invited back to Farthing for the weekend to participate in what Lucy refers to as 'one of Mummy's ghastly political squeezes'.[44] The purpose of their invitation quickly becomes clear in its sinister intention, however, when Sir James Thirkie is found dead, a dagger through his chest pinning to him 'a square of navy blue cloth on which was embroidered a six-pointed yellow star'.[45] Suspicion instantly falls on David for being Jewish despite there being no evidence or motive, beyond Thirkie's role in appeasing Hitler.

The second narrator of the novel is Inspector Peter Anthony Carmichael. His sections are narrated in the third person, in contrast to the first-person perspective of Lucy. He is the police detective sent to Farthing to head the murder investigation. Like David, and (by marriage) Lucy, he is an outsider in Farthing; not merely because he has never been there before but because he is a working-class Northerner from the Lancashire of 'bleak northern uplands of moorland and fell'.[46] He is also, as is eventually revealed and becomes increasingly significant in the later novels of the series, a secret homosexual in a society almost as homophobic as it is anti-Semitic. *Farthing* borrows from the Golden Age detective novel trope of a murder at the big house to create an atmosphere familiar to readers of Agatha Christie or Dorothy Sayers.[47] Walton says of writing the trilogy:

> I had read a lot of cosy mysteries, Tey, Sayers, Christie, Heyer, and considered the interesting fact that they were about sudden violent death and yet they were written in a way that made them safe, indeed cosy. I thought I could use this to write about fascism, and not in a closed known historical context where we're safe and sure of the ending either.[48]

In an article published in 2005, Walton remarks that the label 'cosy catastrophe' is perfect for Wyndham's novels, suggesting that 'the difference between a cosy catastrophe and a horror or disaster novel is just like the difference between Miss Marple and Hannibal Lecter'.[49] In *Farthing*, Walton is very specifically channelling Marple but retains an awareness of a masked evil, albeit the evil being fascism and anti-Semitism rather than cannibalism.

The solution of the whodunnit rapidly becomes secondary (we can be fairly sure it was one or all of the Farthing Set, it almost does not matter specifically who) to the implications of the murder.[50] The novel therefore gains a second impetus; Carmichael must now race to not only uncover the murderer, but to also somehow nullify the national political ramifications of the murder. But, in the end, he can do neither. Riding national sympathy and political outrage, Mark Normanby, the foreign secretary and key Farthing Set member, becomes leader of the Conservative Party and by default the prime minister. The rest of the set fill out other key government posts: the Home Office, the Foreign Office, the War Office; Lucy's father becomes chancellor despite convention dictating the position should not go to a peer while other figures, now shuffled to the fringe of the party, are given or offered more minor positions. The newly-deposed Anthony Eden is given Thirkie's old post of minister of education and Churchill is offered, but turns down, commerce, and 'so on all down the line, the plum for the Farthing people and the others either in the wilderness or given the unimportant hard work'.[51] Even while Carmichael is still conducting his investigation, Normanby makes a radio broadcast condemning the 'cowardly Jew' who killed Thirkie, and other 'cowardly terrorists' like the Bolsheviks, announcing that 'extreme measures' will be taken against them:[52]

> What 'drastic measures' [sic] meant, according to *The Times* the next morning, was that they were taking on powers the next thing to dictatorial, in the name of

protecting themselves and the country from the Jewish Bolshevik Menace. *The Times* rather approved of it, from the tone of their editorial.[53]

These measures include the deportation of foreign nationals who cannot find three British sponsors, the banning of the Communist Party and its newspapers, and the vetting by MI5 of the Labour Party for Communist sleeper agents. Fixed-term Parliaments are introduced with four-year terms, and identity cards are introduced:

> The identity cards we had all carried ever since the war were to be tightened up, to prevent forgery, and they would carry photographs, which would help the police, and more information, such as religion. Apparently a young Labour hothead called Michael Foot had leapt up at this and said it amounted to persecution of Jews and Catholics, which Mark had answered by sneering that nobody was talking about making anyone wear yellow stars, it was equitable, we would all have our religion marked on our cards. *The Times* seemed very concerned about what atheists would put, though I didn't see why 'atheist' couldn't just go on the card. I immediately thought that it's what I'd suggest David say he was – after all, he was racially Jewish, but hardly religious.[54]

Lucy and her old governess Abby both refer to the situation as a 'Reichstag fire', underlining (a little too severely for some reviewers), the parallels between the new government and Hitler's rise to power, thus equating the fascistic elements of Britain's parliament with those in Germany in 1933.[55]

More than one reviewer has compared *Farthing* to Kazuo Ishiguro's *The Remains of the Day* (1989) because of the way they both cast light onto the 'pro-fascist feeling that infected significant sections of the British establishment in the 1930s'.[56] So too when Lucy and David talk to Mrs Smollett (the Polish-Jewish cook whose real name is Szmolokiewitsz), Walton is using her story about being a Jew in Warsaw in the 1930s to convey something of the refugee experience in Europe in our own timeline as surely as W. H. Auden's 'Refugee Blues' (1939). As Mrs Smollett talks about her restaurant, David, in his capacity as a money lender, offers to lend her the money to set up a new restaurant in Britain. He hopes that besides creating a profitable business, fulfilling Mrs Smollett's dream, maybe Londoners, 'instead of saying from ignorance that the Jews are greedy and cowardly, push to the front of queues, take seats on buses, will say on reflection that they are not so bad; Mrs. Smollett cooks pancakes to make the heart glad and David Kahn lends money to poor people to start businesses, and he fought all through the Battle of Britain'.[57] Mrs Smollett pierces this rose-hued dream (particularly idealistically naïve given that David is in the midst of being framed for murder and an anti-Semitic far-right politician has just become prime minister) telling him that his vision will never come to pass: when the Germans invaded Poland the citizens of Warsaw did not stand up for the Szmolokiewitsz family because her pancakes were good, or because her son was a doctor, or her husband a loyal patriot in the army: 'When they smashed the window of my restaurant, it was not the Germans who did it, it was the Poles. And one of them who was in the front with stones in his hand was a customer, who I had served my special dumpling soup only the week before, and given his little son a candle on his crème brulée because it was his birthday. But now his face was screwed up with hate and he would have smashed me as well as the window if I had not run.'[58] Her husband was killed in action as a Polish soldier fighting the German army, her daughter was shot while they were fleeing across France, and her son Yusef died 'in 1946 in a camp called Treblinka'.[59] The name Treblinka does not have particular resonance to Lucy or David, perhaps not even for Mrs Smollett herself, besides being a German concentration camp. They cannot imagine its true horrors. For the reader however, this is a name we know, the second deadliest extermination camp for Jews after Auschwitz itself. Her son died there in 1946, a year after the war ended in our timeline (and two years after the camp was liberated in 1944 by Soviet forces, although the Germans destroyed much of the camp on their retreat). Thus, despite a speech which some critics considered to be as 'cloying and unsubtle' as it is horrific, Mrs Smollett is both representative of all refugees from the Nazis and an emblem of the human cost of the 'peace with honour'.[60]

The Small Change Trilogy is sometimes referred to by its alternate name, proposed by Walton, 'Still Life With Fascists'.[61] Like Small Change this alternate title has multiple meanings; it is both a reference to the gentle, cosy pace of the three books as well as a signal that life continues under fascism (for most, at least). While the subsequent novels display the calcification of the fascist state in Britain, and despite *Ha-penny* moving the action from a purer detective format at a (more or less) single location to something closer to spy fiction set in London, *Farthing* best displays the anti-Semitism of the country: 'polite, poisonous anti-Semitism; which anybody who reads 1920's mysteries falls across all the time. ... You don't have to be smashing windows to ruin people's lives'.[62] All three novels are written in different genres; Walton refers to *Ha'Penny* as a thriller and *Half a Crown* as dystopia, yet all three share a cosy tone and a naïve female first-person narrator who shares the narrative with Carmichael's third-person sections.

Ha'Penny's narrator is Viola Larkin, one of a set of contrasting sisters analogous to the Mitford sisters in our own timeline, while *Half a Crown* jumps forward to 1960 and is narrated from the point of view of Carmichael's teenage ward, Elvira, who feels able to exclaim: 'We're all fascists now, surely? ... And anyway, what's wrong with fascism? It's fun!'[63] Among many faults he finds with the series, John Clute describes these 'airhead' narrators, alternating chapters with Carmichael's detective plots, as creating the effect of 'matter and natter'.[64] Yet other reviewers consider the female characters integral: J. G. Stinson describes *Farthing*'s Lucy as 'the perfect narrator for this', owing to the contribution their naivety and sheltered privilege (a unifying factor of the three) has to creating the cosy feeling of the novels.[65]

Clute also identifies another meaning in 'Still Life With Fascists' when applied to the trilogy as a whole:

> this triumph [of fascism] has been so *fixative* that Walton's new dystopian Britain hardens instantly without demur into pharaonic rigor mortis: between 1941 and 1949 – bar a gradual worsening of conditions for scapegoats – *nothing changes*, the engines of transformation that had wracked and given hope to the real Britain between (say) 1930 and 1950 are frozen shut, without a word.[66]

Chief among the targets for Clute's ire in this regard is the complete absence of any form of visible resistance, or indeed disgruntlement, from the 'vast middle of the nation' to their democracy being hijacked in the manner the novels describe, especially once we leave the insulated and isolated climes of Farthing house. Clute suggests, though instantly withdraws on finding a lack of evidence in the text, that Walton may have been proposing an effect similar to Burdekin's *Swastika Night*: 'that a Nazi dystopia is not only evil but Ground Zero, that is, in fact, a Still Life'.[67] In fact, it seems Joan Gordon has the measure of Walton's intent more accurately when she writes that 'Walton's novels do something very few novels about the Holocaust do – they remind us how cozy it feels to be the ones who belong, how easy it is to close ranks'.[68] Walton, then, is plotting a course more along the lines of Martin Niemöller's 'First They Came for the Jews' than Burdekin's novel.[69]

Clute's final criticism of the trilogy is the manner in which it ends. Like *The Plot Against America* it does so with a *deus ex machina* appeal to the people of the nation who, seemingly as one, see the evils of the government for what they are, and throw off their proverbial shackles. Carmichael and his ward, Elvira, make earnest appeals to Queen Elizabeth II to examine the workings of the government who rule in her name, and warn her of a planned coup to place her uncle the Duke of Windsor (that is, the abdicated pro-fascist King Edward VIII as features in *The Leader*) on the throne in her place. Elizabeth makes a televised address to the nation announcing the attempted coups, as well as the arrest of the Duke and of Prime Minister Mark Normanby whom she reveals to be the murderer of James Thirkie, calling for an emergency general election and the release of all political prisoners and 'Jews and others presently detained under the Defence of the Realm Act'.[70] Writes Clute: 'Meanwhile the middle classes of Britain – completely silent since 1941 – begin to riot in the streets. They listen reverently to the Queen when she speaks to them all by radio. And it's yah-boo for Nazi Britain. The cards tumble down. The novel ends. There were a few minutes of elatedness ... but a souffle elatedness: because the truth of the matter is that the ending of *Half a Crown* must be an insult to any reader who thought Small Change was going to have something adult to submit about the matters it purports to address.'[71] Aside from being unsatisfying in terms of the overall narrative, Clute points out that an easy ending to such a series has more dangerous implications:

> What seems to be said here is not only that Small Change is a game ... but that anti-Semitism and tyranny are similarly a house of cards: that they represent nothing inherent in human nature or the retentivenesses of tyranny that a good plot-twist can't cure. ... She cannot allow the cost of dystopia into a tale in which dystopia dissolves, like the Wicked Witch of the West, as soon as Queen Elizabeth II opens her mouth.[72]

Clute, either deliberately or otherwise, here evokes the spirit of historian E. H. Carr's dismissal of counterfactual histories as a 'parlour game' and have 'nothing to do with determinism ... Nor have they anything to do with history'.[73] Yet where Carr sees the mode as harmless (if a waste of time), Clute instead accuses Walton of gamifying her narrative and thus making light of anti-Semitism and tyranny; essentially, he is echoing accusations levelled at Stephen Fry of not treating the material with sufficient seriousness. Aside from the problems presented by the best hope for our democracy being the unelected head of state, there is indeed a fairy-tale childishness in the day being saved by an innocent girl asking the queen for help, almost reminiscent of the same action being taken by Sophie and the titular giant in Roald Dahl's *The BFG* (1982).

There is some defence against Clute in pointing out that the novel ends before it can show us any form of 'retentiveness'. In *The Plot Against America* the pieces of the game are tidied away by the end of the novel and the implication is that history is back on its intended course. However, in Walton's trilogy world history has been irreparably altered. Even if Britain returns to a democratic state more similar to ours, that state and the role it has played in global affairs, has been missing for almost twenty years. Hitler is still in power in Europe, and the implications of that for the people of countries under his control, especially for Jews, Romani and others, are profound and morbidly permanent. Despite the upbeat ending to the trilogy, which, to return to Clute, 'almost explicitly echo the last phrases of at least two Dickens novels', there is no sign that the global situation has any possibility of reverting to normality.[74]

Underlining the bleak situation of the world in *Farthing*, and perhaps in a nod to *The Plot Against America*, Walton twice refers to President Lindbergh of the United States, as well as the fact that 'they don't allow Jewish people into America, not any'.[75] There is no corresponding gesture towards the subject material of Guy Walters' *The Leader*; indeed as Jack Deighton has pointed out, Mosley and the Union of Fascists (Blackshirts) are conspicuous by their absence, 'though Walton's conspirators echo them clearly enough'.[76] Nonetheless, the close proximity of the three novels, on the rare topic of Anglo-American natively fascistic alternate history, in successive years from 2003 to 2005 (to 2007 if we include Walton's trilogy as a whole), suggests a response, conscious or otherwise, to an external stimulus. Unlike Roth who denies such attempts to suggest contemporary allegory, Walton herself is not coy about this connection to her present:

> it was 2003, I was politically, kind of ... really pissed off, because a government that I had voted for was waging an unjust war in my name, and I could do nothing about it ... The Small Change books were really about that.[77]

> Nothing is written in a vacuum. I wrote these books during a dark time politically, when the US and the UK were invading Iraq without a Security Council resolution on a trumped up casus belli. I was brought up by my grandparents, and the defining event of their lives was WWII, it cut across them like a knife. To find a government I had voted for waging a war of aggression really rocked my expectations. If I'd been in Britain I'd have marched and protested, but I was in Canada, which kept out of that unjust war. My husband is Irish, and Ireland wasn't doing it either. I think it was my isolation on this that went into writing these books.[78]

And, indeed the dedication to *Farthing*:

> This novel is for everyone who has ever studied any monstrosity of history, with the serene satisfaction of being horrified while knowing exactly what was going to happen, rather like studying a dragon anatomized upon a table, and then turning around to find the dragon's present-day relations standing close by, alive and ready to bite.[79]

This foregrounding of contemporary concerns within *Farthing*, and the Small Change Trilogy as a whole, earns praise from some reviewers such as J. G. Stinson who notes that: 'Much talk has been made of how a democracy could never slide into fascism or tolerate it in a neighbouring country. Walton gives a very good example of how this could, indeed, happen all too easily, and along the way reminds us that there is a very high cost for selling out the soul of a nation – and the souls of its people. These days, regardless of one's politics, that's a worthwhile reminder.'[80] Kincaid notes that the novel 'is not an overt satire, but parallels do seem uncomfortably close … this is an alternate history of genuine and chilling power.'[81] Cory Doctorow is adamant that '*Farthing* is clearly a parable about Britain and America in the wake of the 9/11 and 7/7 attacks, when commonsense, humanism, and a commitment to liberty and justice has been easily set aside in a fury of bloodlust and a dismal, shrugging apathy'.[82] But the author's lack of subtlety in this regard has also drawn criticism: 'Walton is clearly also aiming at present-day targets, and it thus suits her to write polemic rather than poetry' writes Dan Hartland, continuing, '*Farthing* is a clever murder mystery but a rather simplistic political statement. "This is exactly how Nazi Germany started!" is not precisely a nuanced contribution to the current debate … It's a shame that Walton couldn't resist the pull of the direct parallel … Walton can write, and write well, but in seeking to teach us a rather blunt lesson, she comes close to breaking her novel's promise.'[83]

The Plot Against America, Walton's trilogy, and indeed *The Leader* draw on the imagery and threat of a fascist police state, anti-Semitism and the Holocaustic potential of such an environment. In doing so, relatively early on in the post-9/11 environment, they draw comparisons with the tightening of security measures, the limiting of personal liberties (the trade-off between liberty and security), increased Islamophobia and the increase in refugees from the Middle East. In so doing, all three texts implicitly relativize the Holocaust by encouraging comparisons with other atrocities and the historical treatment of refugees. They also invite comparisons between the practices and trends of governments, encouraging a view of totalitarianism and fascism that is a sliding scale rather than a binary switch; the same can be said of the comparisons they invite with regard to discriminatory practices by the media and the public more generally, primarily anti-Semitism, although the contextual post-9/11 analogies encourage comparisons between anti-Semitic and anti-Muslim, or Islamophobic, attitudes.

By presenting the largely legal takeover of fascistic regimes in the United Kingdom and United States in a broadly realistic manner, all of the texts undermine the 'it can't happen here' complacency and moral superiority of Anglo-Americans. Gavriel D. Rosenfeld notes that other recent, specifically British, alternate histories challenge post-war foundational myths, specifically 'that the fight against Nazism represented the British people's "finest hour"'.[84] They challenge the assumption that just because our democracy didn't veer strongly towards fascism in the 1930s (or indeed towards communism), that it is inherently stable and never could.

However, the reliance on happy endings, particularly of the *deus ex machina* variety, has worrying implications with regard to these analogies as it creates an imperfect system of thought whereby we are encouraged to believe there is a simple or single solution which can (perhaps even will) pull us back from the brink before the worst can happen. In doing so they somewhat, but not completely, counter the major message of the texts, reinforcing a naïve and complacent view of democracy, specifically Anglo-American democracy. *The Plot Against America*, with its false ending, circling back to darker moments in Philip's experience of the events of the novel, does the least damage in this regard. Both the opening and ending of the novel reinforce a certain permanency of effect for Philip, a trauma, even if overall there seems to be no change to the results of history.

Yet, texts like *The Plot Against America* and Walton's trilogy demonstrate that the Holocaust was far more than the gas chambers and extermination camps. Specifically, following on from Daniel Goldhagen (as discussed with regard to Stephen Fry's *Making History* in Chapter 2), they examine the crippling possibility of such genocides happening anywhere, not just in Germany (or German-occupied territory), and the roots of the Holocaust in casually accepted xenophobia, inaction and complacency. In doing so, and by demonstrating the democratic potential and weakness to fascism, they extend a complicity in the Holocaust beyond the SS, or the army, to all citizens who harboured anti-Semitic feelings, or favoured the Nazi Party. While it seems harsh to expect pre-war Anglo-Americans to have been able to envision the Holocaust when even those caught up in the genocide thought it an incomprehensible impossibility, these texts remind us that their attitudes cost lives and that their presence, and indeed increasing prevalence, in modern society are still being paid for in human lives.

A Man Lies Dreaming (2014), Lavie Tidhar

A more recent novel, Lavie Tidhar's *A Man Lies Dreaming*, is also an alternate history that has more to say about fascism and right-wing politics in the United Kingdom than it does about a Nazi occupation. This is because like *The Plot Against America* and *Farthing*, there is no invasion, at least not in the conventional sense. In Tidhar's novel, Hitler and his fellow Nazis, having failed to achieve their aims in Germany and being defeated in the 1936 elections by the communists, have gone into exile in the United Kingdom. Hitler himself has become a Raymond Chandler-esque private eye in London. There are cosmetic similarities with Norman Spinrad's *Iron Dream*: a Hitler with a new non-political and seemingly non-threatening new role among the Anglo-American peoples who in our own timeline are his antagonists. Yet the similarities are indeed only cosmetic, *A Man Lies Dreaming* is a far more nuanced work than its predecessor.

The bulk of the novel concerns Hitler, now working under the *nom de guerre* 'Wolf', a down and out private eye who in classic hard-boiled fashion is approached by a young woman with 'long black hair and long pale legs' who hires him to find her missing sister who was last heard of trying to escape Communist Germany.[85] The twist, one of many, is that this femme fatale is Jewish, Isabella Rubinstein, daughter of a rich Jewish Banker, Julius Rubinstein:

> One of the Jewish gangsters who grew rich and fat on the blood of the working man in Germany, before the Fall. His like always survived, like rats abandoning a sinking ship they fled Germany and re-established themselves elsewhere, in clumps of diseased colonies.[86]

This short quote is a sample of the writing style adopted through much of the novel, giving direct voice to Wolf's thoughts via a diary. It makes for uncomfortable reading, as the narrative is shorn of the fantastic imagery which accompanies Hitler's open seething racism in *The Iron Dream*, for example. It typifies the language we might expect from a Hitler whose world view has been compounded and hardened by defeat, decline and a fast slide into obscurity: the paranoid conspiracy theories about Jewish power, the simultaneous casting of them as rats and a disease. However, there is also the hint of Tidhar's irony through the reference to them surviving, evoking the survivor of a Holocaust Wolf cannot know. The novel weaves between two narrative styles and three points of view: there are first-person sections, Wolf's diary entries and third-person narrated sections; some sections following Wolf, some following a mysterious killer who is obsessed with Wolf and is killing prostitutes while trying to reawaken Wolf's 'greatness' and, crucially, there is the narrative of a man named Shomer. The Shomer narrative is ostensibly the framing narrative for the alternate history portions of the novel, although the term is a gross simplification of the complexity of the text which Tidhar has created.

Shomer shares his name with a real *shund* writer.[87] The historical Shomer, Nokhem-Meyer Shaykevitch, died in New York City in 1905.[88] Although Tidhar acknowledges the real Shomer in his afterword as way of an introduction to the concept of shund itself, separately he admits 'it was the meaning of the name I was interested in, not the historical author'.[89] Shomer means guardian or watchman. Tidhar's Shomer is interred in Auschwitz 'in another time and place', but is also a 'purveyor of Yiddish *shund*, that is of cheap literature or, not to put too fine a point on it, of trash'.[90] Dislocated in time and space from his historical namesake, Tidhar's Shomer is the titular man dreaming the Wolf narrative. As Shomer's sections progress, it becomes apparent that on a conscious or subconscious level, he is using the shund world he has created as an escape from the brutal realities of camp life. Nor is this the only escape-through-fantasy available to him: he is accompanied through the day-to-day routine of the camp by the imaginary presence of Yenkl, his former bunkmate, who has died, 'his inert form outside … in the snow, where he lies as fat and peaceful as a snowman, with his eyes closed and his hands like twigs … At last the ordeal is over and the boys of the Sonderkommando take Yenkl away'.[91] As such the lines between fiction and reality are constantly blurred, between the obviously fictional world of Wolf and the terrifyingly real Auschwitz coloured by Shomer's hallucinations and imaginations.

In addition to the presence of Yenkl, there are other characters Shomer encounters in Auschwitz who add to the surreal experience of the camp. For example, through this blurring of historical realism and delirious fantasy, Tidhar is able to contrive a meeting of two contrasting voices of Holocaust literature. Shomer is a witness to a debate between two prisoners: 174517 and 135633, Primo Levi and Ka-Tzetnik:

'And how can we write this rent in the world,' [Levi] says … 'Only by science, by using a language as accurate and dispassionate as possible can we describe the atrocities, for it is a scientific genocide we are subject to, with gas they are killing us, with charts and lists they record us, and in Mengele's lab they dissect us like animals. And this must be recorded, for future generations, to never forget, and for that the novelist must employ a language as clear and precise as possible, a language without ornament.'[92]

The language here harmonizes with the style of writing in Levi's own works. It also emphasizes his vocation as a chemist, with its focus on science, recording, precision. Ka-Tzetnik replies in a torrent of vivid imagery and metaphysical language which resembles his testimony, as Yehiel Dinur, at the Eichmann Trial. He says:

But there you are wrong, for this is no longer the world you knew, the world any of us knew. That world is dead, everything is divided, Before-Auschwitz and the Now, for there is only now, even to think of a life beyond is to indulge in fantasy. But to answer your question, to write of this Holocaust is to shout and scream, to tear and spit, let words fall like bloodied rain on the page; not with cold detachment but with fire and pain, in the language of *shund*, the language of shit and piss and puke, of pulp, a language of torrid covers and lurid emotions, of fantasy: this is an alien planet, Levi. This is Planet Auschwitz. ... We have no names. We have no parents and we have no children. We do not dress the way they dress on Earth. We were not born here and we do not give birth. We breathe by different rules of nature. We do not live by the laws of Earth and neither do we die by them. Our name is a number.[93]

Ka-Tzetnik is clearly the greater influence on *A Man Lies Dreaming*, as demonstrated through his ready adaptation of the *shund* imagery to describe Auschwitz. Now little known, much of his work out of print in English, and his status in schools and educational programmes neglected in favour of writers such as Levi himself, Wiesel and Borowski. Tidhar has Ka-Tzetnik reproduce some of the key phrases from his testimony at the Eichmann Trial, in particular the crucial phrase 'Planet Auschwitz'.[94] They do speak a different language on Planet Auschwitz and the experiences related from there are imperfectly translated. However, the phrase also evokes a different set of ideals to the contemporary reader, which Tidhar is very conscious of.

The concept of Planet Auschwitz exerts an influence upon historians. In the introduction to her book *The Holocaust: The Destruction of European Jewry, 1933–1945* (1968) Nora Levin, founder of the Holocaust Oral History Archive at Gratz College, writes that the Holocaust is incomprehensible because 'ordinary human beings simply cannot rethink themselves into such a world and ordinary ways to achieve empathy fail. ... The world of Auschwitz was, in truth, another planet'.[95] The image of Planet Auschwitz is one meant to convey the truly incomprehensible nature of the Holocaust (for which Auschwitz has become a metonym). If the 'foreign country' of the past is difficult to understand then the alien world of the Holocaust is impossible.[96] Arthur A. Cohen writes:

> The death camps are a reality which, by their very nature, obliterate thought and the human program of thinking. We are dealing, at the very outset, therefore, with something unmanageable and obdurate – a reality which exists, which is historically documented, which has specific beginnings and ends, located in time, the juncture of confluent influences which run from the beginnings of historical memory to a moment of consummating orgy, never to be forgotten, but difficult to remember, a continuous scourge to memory and the future of memory and yet something which, whenever addressed, collapses into tears, passion, rage.[97]

The entreaty to remember in the face of the 'continuous scourge to memory', an event which 'obliterate[s] thought' recalls Orwell's conception of history in the hands of Big Brother as 'a palimpsest, scraped clean and re-inscribed exactly as often as was necessary'.[98] Yet rather than being at the mercy of an insidious regime – ironically – the Holocaust requires continuous attention because of the manner in which it induces a sense of obtuseness, a deficit of understanding, in those who approach it. It is a constantly shifting cipher, revealing something awful about humanity's capacity for cruelty, one that Wiesel denies us the possibility of being able to crack: 'We speak in code, we survivors, and this code cannot be broken, cannot be deciphered, not by you no matter how much you try'.[99] Elsewhere he writes that the Holocaust is 'beyond our vocabulary'.[100] To some extent language is always an insufficient tool to capture the reality of an experience, which is why non-mimetic impulses need to be harnessed to some degree alongside their mimetic counterparts to achieve any semblance of communication. Ultimately, we cannot argue when Hayden White reminds us that 'real events do not offer themselves in the form of stories'.[101] However, similarly to Wiesel, Primo Levi writes of the specific inadequacy of words such as 'hunger', 'tiredness' and 'pain': 'They are free words, created and used by free men who live in comfort and suffering in their homes. If the Lagers had lasted longer a new, harsh language would have been born; and only this language could express what it means to toil the whole day in the wind, with the temperature below freezing, wearing only a shirt, underpants, cloth jacket and trousers, and in one's body nothing but weakness, hunger and knowledge of the end drawing nearer.'[102]

The moniker Planet Auschwitz also evokes something of B-Movie and exploitation-cinema sensibilities. This is in keeping with the pulp sensibilities of Tidhar's novel, themselves lifted from crime noir and *shund*. The contrast of high and low culture, Holocaust literature and pulp, is central to the debate between Levi and Ka-Tzetnik and at the core of Tidhar's philosophy when writing the novel:

> That is, the conflict between 'popular' or populist genre fiction and the 'high' art of literary fiction. The book tries to interrogate those two modes, while making fun of them, though its sympathies are quite likely with 'low' art[103]

Tidhar's intentions here speak to the heart of this book's assertion that the Holocaust is not solely the domain of 'the "high" art of literary fiction', nor should it be. Only by engaging art across the spectrum of human capacity can we come to capture something of human experience; this applies to any topic but takes on a new urgency when discussing an issue such as the Holocaust where the need to understand is tangible, driven by a fear of repetition. For Tidhar, 'genre tools allow us to look at reality in a different way, to defamiliarise it'.[104] This becomes a powerful prospect in the face of Holocaust normalization:

> What makes me angry ... is that we may use the Holocaust to absolve *ourselves* of responsibility. Ethnic cleansing, mass murder, the industrialisation of death, these are all ongoing things. We must never forget the Holocaust! – one may cry – and in the same breath curse at the damned immigrants coming over here. Or invade a country for a made up reason ... Or build a huge separation fence to keep another nation in a ghetto and then bomb it.
>
> Do we normalise the Holocaust? We *have* normalised it. We're saturated by images of death and cruelty.[105]

Tidhar is thus consciously relativizing the Holocaust, using it to teach and learn moral lessons applicable to our everyday politics, ethics and ideology. Yet he simultaneously rails against normalization, the numbing of its impact, and sees in non-mimetic fiction an impulse of literature which can help to turn the tide, to give the genocide back its horror, power and Otherness.

The seriousness of this point is made apparent in the grim fantasies to which Shomer retreats: the world of Wolf is not a utopia where the Nazis never came to power and the Holocaust never happened. Instead, it is a world of uncertainty, the threat of communism looming over Europe and shifting the acceptable mainstream dialogue of Western democracy further to the right. As such, through Wolf's sections, we enter a world of people smuggling, xenophobia, police brutality, anti-Semitism, conspiracy, and, at the end, potentially, genocide.

Wolf suffers, as hard-boiled private detectives are prone to do, but Tidhar reserves an extra level of punishment for his detective. In one scene, for example, Wolf stumbles into a Nazi-themed brothel and is placed in restraints and a ball-gag before being whipped by a dominatrix.[106] Such an image could be gratuitous, and perhaps is, but it also serves another purpose. Rather than simply delighting in torturing Hitler for the sake of vengeance-by-narrative, Tidhar is drawing attention to the proliferation of Nazi imagery in 'low' culture. For example, the brothel scene speaks to the fetishization of right-wing language, uniform and other paraphernalia. The fact that the dominatrix is the alternate history's Ilse Koch is also significant as Koch, 'The Witch of Buchenwald', is the inspiration for numerous Nazisploitation fantasies, most infamously *Ilsa, She Wolf of the SS* (1974).[107]

Similarly, the Jewish Gangster Julius Rubinstein has some thugs beat Wolf up for his continued association with Rubinstein's daughter, culminating in his forced circumcision:

> They had me the way they wanted me. I was too weak to struggle, and the men were too strong. My legs were spread wide, my private parts exposed to Rubinstein's scrutiny. ... Rubinstein grabbed Wolf's penis in his hand. ... Rubinstein, almost gently, pulled on Wolf's cock, drawing forth Wolf's foreskin until it protruded, pulling it still, with Wolf shaking and shaking above him and the two men holding him down.
>
> 'Filthy thing,' Rubinstein said, dispassionately. He pulled, sharply, then with almost the same smooth easy movement, almost as though he had had plenty of practice he brought the knife up to the penis and sliced neatly through the foreskin.[108]

There is of course the black comic irony of forcing history's most famous anti-Semite to undergo a mutilation which is among the most predominant stereotypical markers of Jewishness, but once again Tidhar includes this scene not merely for laughs or revenge. While Wolf is a repulsive human being, with a toxic ideology, in the alternate history of the novel he never had a chance to implement his ideas or become a real danger to anyone; as such the vindictive violence wrought against him is particularly cruel. Counterfactual statements within the counterfactual world bring us closer to his true potential – 'Imagine only if he had succeeded; if Germany was his, its military and its citizens, to wield as he saw fit: what would have happened to the Jewish people then?' – but these are shadows which the other characters in Wolf's world cannot see.[109] The flattening out of morality in a world without a Hitler to occupy its lowest point is emphasized by Rubinstein's reference to Nazis as 'cock-sucking opportunists ... rats growing fat having jumped a drowning ship', repeating the same imagery as the Nazis themselves, including in Wolf's own description of Julius Rubinstein earlier in the novel. Such language, and the violent act of circumcision, mark an inversion of alternate-Hitler into the role of non-alternate-Jew, except that where for many Jewish victims of Hitler their life would end in a train journey and gas, he was forged in it. In a moment of flashback he remembers his experience of the First World War (the only World War):

> Six hundred miles by train from the front to the small hospital near the Polish border. Blind – he had been blinded! ... Wolf was on a train, in absolute dark, and he was terrified. Remembering the attack, the whistle of mortar, the gas – the gas![110]

It is not quite the reverse timeline of Martin Amis's *Time's Arrow*, but the point that Hitler was gassed during the war is an overlooked biographic note which takes on a sinister irony when compared to Auschwitz. There is a different sort of irony in *A Man Lies Dreaming*, given that Hitler is still gassed in the alternate history but the Jews escape it. When Wolf converses with a woman on the bus who is railing against an unidentified group, his interest is peaked when she says they should 'gas the whole lot of them. Put them in camps and gas them'.[111] Interest soon turns to revulsion when he realizes her sentiments are aimed towards Germans rather than Jews. When, at the novel's conclusion, Oswald Mosley is elected prime minister by riding a wave of xenophobia and fear, it is perhaps an irony too far for Tidhar to have a far-right government begin to profile and ultimately exterminate Germans in the United Kingdom. Instead, in his inauguration speech at Trafalgar Square he publicly allies himself with a German chancellor-in-exile:

> 'Germany is not our enemy. Communism is. That, and the bankers behind it all. I think you know their real names.'
> 'Jews!' – 'The elders of Zion!' – 'Shylocks!' – 'Yids!'
> 'We must help Germany in its time of need! ... I have news, news we could not share before with you. At nineteen hundred hours today, Germany, with

Russian help, has invaded Poland. ... Our bilateral agreement with Poland dictates a response ... It is my duty to you as your prime minister, to let you know that we are at war'[112]

Tidhar is signalling to the endemic anti-Semitism that was present in Britain before the Holocaust, undermining any sense of moral superiority that this could not have happened here. In doing so *A Man Lies Dreaming* conforms to the self-critical form of alternate history which Gavriel Rosenfeld identifies as one of the significant trends in British depictions of Nazi victory.[113] The twist being that here there is no Nazi victory. Mosley introduces the German chancellor-in-exile to the crowd and Wolf, among them, wonders which of a cast of Nazis it could be; it cannot be Hess (who by this point is dead), but could it be Goebbels, or Himmler, or Bormann, or Heydrich? No, it is Adolf Eichmann:

> 'Who?' someone beside me said, bewildered.
> 'Who?' I screamed. A tallish thin man with a vulture's face and thinning hair came onto the stage and solemnly shook Prime Minister Mosley's hand.
> 'Who the fuck is Adolf Eichmann!' I said.[114]

Eichmann, for Wolf, is an unknown – a bureaucrat who never had the chance to rise to a role of any importance in the alternate history. Yet for us he is unfalteringly connected with Arendt's phrase, the banality of evil. In addressing the crowd, Eichmann announces that he has a solution to the Jewish problem, a 'final solution to the Jewish question', one which Mosley hails as being 'innovative' and 'creative'.[115] The dark turn towards the possibility of a Holocaust happening in this alternate world further undermines British exceptionalism, although that the Germans, and particularly Eichmann, are still involved does offer some small moral escape hatch. Regardless, the absence of Hitler from the proceedings normalizes his evil somewhat and presents a more complex set of structural causes behind the Holocaust than merely one man's whim. This sets the novel in opposition to those who share the sentiments of Milton Himmelfarb who expressed his position succinctly in the title to his 1984 essay 'No Hitler, No Holocaust'.[116]

That such an apocalyptic scenario should come so close to the climax of the novel is particularly strange if we consider the narrative's framing device. The Wolf plot of *A Man Lies Dreaming* is a metatext, or so we have been led to believe, framed by Shomer's experience in Auschwitz. Yet if fantasy is escapist, this world is not one that he would seem to be better off escaping too. Wolf, however, does escape: his circumcision proves to be his painful rebirth as a Jew.

Over the course of his investigation he creates a fake identity as a Jew, Moshe Wolfson, complete with passport – 'My face stared back at me, severe and mute, from the photograph. It was the face of a Jew.'[117] As the novel approaches its endgame, Wolf finds himself more and more inseparable from the Wolfson identity, to the extent that as everything else is stripped away from him, 'He was no one. He was nothing', he assumes it completely:

'I'm a Jew,' he said, and laughed; but like Wolf himself, the sound meant nothing.[118]

Moshe Wolfson boards a ship, *The Exodus*, which sails from London as part of a small flotilla, to Jaffa and Palestine. Perhaps through this conversion and escape, Shomer too can escape the horrors of Auschwitz, except that Tidhar has one more twist. Shomer, like most concentration camp prisoners, has been used as slave labour by the Nazis:

Shomer builds doors; endless doors come down the production line: small doors, big doors, house doors, prison doors, dollhouse doors and cage doors, and oddly shaped doors that fit no blueprint Shomer can imagine.[119]

As his conversations with Yenkl show, Shomer's reality is already weak. Perhaps in Auschwitz, that other planet, other universe, the laws of reality work differently to our contemporary situation. In any case, 'Shomer builds doors, until his entire world is contracted into one rectangular shape, always hovering before his eyes, calling out, an impossible promise, until he reaches out to the handle just attached, and pulls'.[120] Shomer steps through the door and into a world of corridors and doorways; he too has escaped and is now fleeing. The doors lead him into his past where he sits for a last meal with his family, they lead him to Wolf's London, and finally to a beach:

Opening and closing doors Shomer tumbles through half-worlds and fraction-worlds, 'No, this isn't it,' falling down trapdoors and out through endless corridors, 'No, this isn't it, either,' for how long he cannot tell, for there is no time here, where there is not space, until:

He opens the door and steps out onto a beach. The sand is yellow, coarse. Dust fills the sky. The air is humid, warm, scented with citrus trees and late blooming jasmine.[121]

In the morning the guards come for Shomer, 'but Shomer wasn't there'.[122] The possibility remains that he has had a mental break, dissolved into his fantasy under the pressures and tortures of Auschwitz; still possible again is that he has died and that these doorway scenes are some sort of traversal through to an afterlife. However, given the thinness of reality with which Tidhar imbues even the Shomer sections of the novel, it is more likely that Shomer has actually entered his fantasy fully, like Alice entering Wonderland, whom the scene of tumbling timeless doors resembles.

Tidhar says that the novel is 'about escape and, ultimately, about the impossibility, the futility of escape'.[123] Yet, Shomer seems to manage to escape; Wolf is the perennial escapee, escaping Berlin and now London. The escape that seems to be futile is from the Holocaust itself. Individuals may manage to survive but the world cannot be spared, not even a fantasy world where Hitler could not rise to power. James Young writes: 'It is almost as if violent events – perceived as aberrations or ruptures in the cultural continuum – demand their retelling, their narration, back into traditions and structures they would otherwise defy.'[124] In this case, and indeed for all of the novels in this chapter, the structure that should defy something as monstrous as genocide is utopia, yet the utopian ideal of undoing the Holocaust cannot withstand the 'aberrations or ruptures' of the violence itself, and thus the Holocaust is written back into these failed idealisms.

I do not suggest that any of these authors would have been surprised to find the Holocaust working its way back into the novel in which they had initially undone it. Such was, of course, their authorial intention as a deliberate plot point of each narrative. But so many novels points to a trend, indicative of a wider issue. Each of these novels, in undoing the Holocaust, has sought to call into doubt a moralistic view of history, adding complexity to simplistic or idealistic views of perpetrators, survivors and bystanders. They have also relativized the Holocaust by placing it back within a historical timeline from which exceptionalism strives to see it removed. They position it alongside other historical or personal traumas, not as a method of ranking or comparing severity (as Norman Finkelstein writes, 'to make our *moral* distinctions between "our" suffering and "theirs" is itself a moral travesty'.[125]) but as a means of drawing attention to the hypocrisy of a society that would condemn one genocide while turning a blind eye towards another or, worse, committing one itself.

J (2014), Howard Jacobson

Maximillian Edwards writes with regard to Tidhar's *A Man Lies Dreaming* that 'the Holocaust is beyond understanding, and yet we must try to understand it as best we can. It forces alternate worlds as a coping mechanism, and yet all roads lead back to Shomer, to Auschwitz, to the pain and horror that the fantasy is escaping and diverting [sic] upon the figure of Hitler'.[126] The final text I'll examine here, *J* by Howard Jacobson, deliberately expunges the biographies of the Holocaust: the Shomers and the Hitlers, as well as the familiar names and identities which alternate history uses for its handholds, the Lindberghs and Mosleys, for example. Instead, Jacobson creates a dystopia which attempts to access something of the wider nightmare of genocide, to reclaim the Holocaust and bring focus back from the plight of general refugees and persecuted persons to the specific plight of the Jewish people. Set on the British Isles (although no longer a United Kingdom), the novel argues not only – as the previous texts insist – that the Holocaust could have happened here, but that it still could. By focusing the novel specifically on anti-Semitism, Jacobson is seeking to highlight not only the continuous presence of this old and dangerous xenophobia, but also its potential for a violent resurfacing.

The plot of *J* primarily focuses on Kevern Cohen and Ailinn Solomons who are brought together under suspicious circumstances but fall in love. The novel portrays their relationship and slowly unveils how and why they have been encouraged to meet. The majority of *J* takes place in 'Port Reuben', somewhere in the far South-West of the British Isles. The seaside setting, and the importance of the sea as a site of forgetting and the erosion of both land and memory (Kevern's mother destroys her own mother's writings by throwing them into the sea, among other references), combined with the debauched amoral character of many of the port's inhabitants, and the novel's black comedy, evokes a sense of macabre-twee akin to a Jewish cousin of Dylan Thomas's *Under Milk Wood* (1954).

J is set in a country slowly consuming itself with violence and dissatisfaction. Throughout the book there are references to a terrible event in the past, roughly three generations ago (significantly, as far removed from the novel as we are from the Holocaust), referred to as 'WHAT HAPPENED, IF IT HAPPENED'. The vagueness of this nomenclature reflects the disdain for history that the society of the novel has: each household is only allowed a single item over a hundred years old; the only literature anyone reads are rags-to-riches memoirs, cookbooks and romances; the only artworks anyone produces are painted landscapes; the only recorded music anyone listens to are modern ballads. This is not a legal requirement, though at various points in the novel characters are aware they could potentially get into trouble for harbouring multiple older items, or reading unconventional material. For example, Kevern hoards his father's collection of jazz and swing albums; these things are 'not banned – nothing was banned exactly – simply not played. Encouraged to fall into desuetude, like the word desuetude. Popular taste did what edict and proscription could never have done'.[127]

WHAT HAPPENED, IF IT HAPPENED is referred to by Kevern's late father as 'THE GREAT PISSASTER or THE PISSFORTUNE TO END ALL PISSFORTUNES or simply THE PISSASTROPE'.[128] Professor Edward Everett Phineas Zermansky refers to it, within the privacy of his diary, as 'Twitternacht', firmly placing the event in our contemporary sphere while simultaneously evoking *Kristallnacht*, the so-called Night of Broken Glass, the pogrom in November 1939 that is such a significant moniker in the early history of the Holocaust:

> Art wasn't the cause or centre of the great desensitisation, for which, of course, all artists apologise, but WHAT HAPPENED, IF IT HAPPENED – or TWITTERNACHT, as I like to call it when I am feeling skittish, by way of reference to ... well to many things, one of them being the then prevailing mode of social interaction that facilitated, though can by no means be said to have provoked it – WHAT HAPPENED, IF IT HAPPENED, I say, happened, if it did, because as a people we'd anaesthetised the feeling parts of ourselves, first through the ugly liberties with form taken by modernism and second through the liberties taken with emotion by that same modernism in its 'post' form. I say 'we' because there is nothing to be achieved by saying 'they', indeed there is much to be lost, given that 'they' is a policed pronoun today, but when I am certain no one is looking (I mean this figuratively) I poke a finger at the alien intellectualism that brought such destruction first on itself and then, as an inevitable consequence, on all of us. Thus, again, the felicity of my TWITTERNACHT *jeu d'esprit*, twitter like much else in the same vein that was then the rage, having proceeded from the alien intelligences of the very people who were to lose most by it. Call that irony, a concept of which they, in particular, were overfond, which is an irony in itself.[129]

Euphemism and metaphor are omnipresent in discussions and descriptions of the Holocaust and Nazi Germany. At the risk of further clouding the issue by deploying a metaphor to described metaphors: they are a double-edged sword. Nazi rhetoric is loaded with linguistic elements which aid in the dehumanization of its victims; thus Jews are referred to as rats, vermin, bacterium, a rot or a plague, placing them within a conceptual framework which makes them less-than-human and thus easier to exterminate. In this way euphemism and metaphor form a lexicon of death which helps to obscure the implications of actions for the perpetrators and bystanders, but which also compounds difficulties of comprehension in modern readers. Thus Primo Levi relates an episode from a work site during his experience of Auschwitz, during which a young and inexperienced *Kapo* announced his squad to an SS supervisor as '83rd Kommando, forty-two men'.[130] 'Flustered as he was, he had actually said "*zwei-und-vierzig Männer*", "men". The SS corrected him in a reproachful, paternal tone: that's not what you say, you say "*zwei-und-vierzig Häftlinge*", forty-two prisoners. He was a young *Kapo* and therefore forgivable, but he must learn the trade, the social conventions and hierarchical distances.'[131] Jane Yolen makes use of this lexicon of distances in her novel *The Devil's Arithmetic* for example:

> But do not let them hear you use the word *death*. Do not let them hear you use the word *corpse*. Not even if one lies at your feet ... A person is not killed here, but *chosen*. They are not cremated in the ovens, they are *processed*. There are no corpses, only pieces of *drek*, only *shmattes*, rags.[132]

The other side to this is the creation and use of euphemism and metaphor by victims and survivors themselves, either in the midst of the Holocaust or when writing about it later. In this way, metaphor and euphemism are the earliest attempts to grapple with the issue of the Holocaust's incomprehensibility. 'The highest priority for concentration camp prisoners was to lessen the alien character of their experience,' writes Andrea Reiter. 'The metaphors used in the camp reports may be roughly grouped into two functions: either they serve to describe impressions, or they incorporate experience into a horizon of meaning.'[133]

The metaphor of the double-edged sword breaks down, as so many metaphors do when we apply them to the Holocaust, when we realize that there are not two distinct edges – Nazi euphemism vs. Survivor metaphor – but rather that the two states bleed into one another, producing a language of the concentration camp that incorporates both the dehumanized language of the Nazis, and the attempts at comprehension of the survivors, as well as the natural polyglot of so many individuals being quickly and forcibly thrown together from disparate language groups across Europe. This new language likely achieved different things for different users; for the SS working in the camps it eased their conscience on some level by removing the camp internees from the general population on a linguistic level, yet for the detainees themselves this same language may have distracted from the sense of inevitable doom, allowing a precious few to go on living daily and eventually transmute into survivors.

Primo Levi, again, reports of 'the "Lager jargon", sub-divided into a specific sub-jargons peculiar to each Lager [camp] and closely related to the old German of Prussian barracks and the new German of the SS ... Lager jargon [in Auschwitz], as is only natural was strongly influenced by other language spoken in the Lager and its surroundings: by Polish, Yiddish, Salesian dialect, later on by Hungarian'.[134] This polyglot blend is mirrored in the language of Jacobson's *J*. All of the characters have Jewish surnames, as do all the place names, for example Port Reuben and the nearby Bethesda. These are not the original names of these locations, and the family names are not the historic names of the different characters, though the reason behind this remains obscured for much of the first half of the novel. Names are multiplicitous in *J*; Port Reuben has its hidden original name while Densdell Kroplik, the town's self-styled sage and drunk, relates it to Wagnerian saga and says it was 'in its glory days called Ludgvennok', immortalized in Wagner's opera *Der Strandryuber von Ludgvennok*.[135] The peculiar situation of intermittent states of being: a historic English, the Jewish, some German (particularly Wagnerian, although German phrases appear throughout the novel), and part-Celtic (Port Reuben is in Cornwall, while Kevern carves lovespoons – a Welsh tradition – and insults are slung in Irish) add to the confusing situation about what exactly has forged this situation, a confusion and uncertainty reflected by the characters themselves.[136]

The novel is also heavily couched in stories. It opens with a fable, 'The Wolf and the Tarantula', which Aesop-like depicts a bet between the titular animals about whose predatory method is better: the tarantula's habit to sit back and allow its prey to fall into its trap, or the wolf's hunting in a pack with his family. The wolf later returns and claims he has won the bet, the tarantula goes to view the evidence and finds 'that of all the wolf's natural prey not a single creature remained'. The tarantula is impressed but wonders what the wolf will now eat; the wolf bursts into tears and confesses he has had to eat his wife and soon will have to eat his children before eventually he will have no option but to eat himself. The moral, the fable closes by telling us, is 'always leave a little on your plate.'[137]

Such metatextual references – *Moby Dick* is another oft-quoted text in the novel – not only perform the standard functions of metatext, 'self-consciously and systematically draw[ing] attention to its status as an artefact in order to pose questions about the relationship between fiction and reality',[138] but also in the context of the novel draw attention to the tradition of the Hasidic tale, a reminder of the storytelling traditions of the Jewish people and a reference to the original 'People of the Book'.

Another important story within the novel is 'The Allegory of the Frog'. Unlike 'The Wolf and the Tarantula', this allegory is familiar to readers as well as being known to characters in the novel; it is explicitly referenced in letters between Ailinn's mother, Rebecca, and grandfather:

> 'What do you take me for?' the frog said, jumping smartly out. 'Some kind of a schlemiel?'
>
> The following day the frog was lowered gently, even lovingly, into a pan of lukewarm water. As the temperature was increased, a degree at a time, the frog luxuriated, floating lethargically on his back with his eyes closed, imagining himself at an exclusive spa.
>
> 'This is the life,' the frog said.
>
> Relaxed in every joint, blissfully unaware, the frog allowed himself to be boiled to death.[139]

The insertion of the Yiddish 'schlemiel' into the familiar story leaves no doubt about who the frog is in this story. As Rebecca tells her father in one of the letters, 'if I remembered the Allegory of the Frog I would never stay anywhere for five minutes at a time. If I remembered the Allegory of the Frog I would never know a moment's peace.'[140] The exchange of letters conveys the dilemma of Jewish existence throughout recent history, but especially in the post-Holocaust contemporary world. Rebecca is uniquely positioned within a generation who came after the Holocaust, while also pre-dating the new catastrophe that we as readers, and Ailinn who reads along with us, know is coming. Thus her father is able to refer back to the Holocaust itself in order to presage the forthcoming catastrophe:

> 'Here? Don't make us laugh. Anywhere but here.' Until the eleventh hour, until eleven seconds before the eleventh minute before the clocks stopped for us, as you've told me a thousand times, they ignored the warning signs, laughed at those who told them it was now or never, refused what stared them in the face. Here? Not here! … Yes, Daddy, I know their fate, and I owe it to the memory of all those who suffered that fate – whom you speak of as though they were family though none of our family perished, I remind you – never to forget it. But that was then and now is now. And that was there and here is here. You used to laugh at me when I came home from university – 'Here she is, our daughter, life president of the It Couldn't Happen Here Society.' And I called you, Daddy,

'honorary chair of the Never Again League'. Well, I don't disrespect you for believing what you believe. It is right to worry. But you cannot compare like with unlike.[141]

The letters are one of several insights into the time of WHAT HAPPENED. At another point in the novel Kevern learns that ice-cream vans were repurposed to carry signs around the country with slogans such as 'Leave Now or Face Arrest', a notion perhaps inspired by the 'go home' vans briefly employed by the UK government in 2013 to encourage illegal immigrants to leave the country. Jacobson's use of ice-cream vans in particular adds to the sense of macabre-twee that permeates the novel, while the juxtaposition of the chimes the vans played while displaying these signs (from Beethoven's *Symphony No. 5* and *Für Elise* to *Greensleeves* and *You Are My Sunshine*) is another reminder of the exchange and interplay between Anglo-German cultures.[142] Elsewhere this revelation is referred back to and compared to the music of the orchestra at Auschwitz, asking of both, 'what was the logic? To pacify or to jeer? Or both? ... The vans, for now, are better than the trains, some say. Shame there isn't actually any ice cream for the children, but be grateful and sing along. Others believe the vans are just the start of it. We have heard the chimes at midnight, they believe'.[143]

The image of the vans as a precursor to the trains, itself an echo of the 'gas vans' as precursors to the gas chambers, is a reminder of the movement towards genocide by increments. No society simply wakes up one day and decides upon extermination, it is a gradual process taking years, if not generations, of incremental steps. Thus, Jacobson is highlighting the potential danger of the 'new anti-Semitism' which he perceives as becoming increasingly prevalent in British society, and indeed globally.

In his essay 'When Will Jews be Forgiven the Holocaust', based on a speech given at the B'Naith B'rith World Centre in Jerusalem in 2013, Jacobson expands upon points put forward in various articles and commentaries. He proposes that a new anti-Semitism is revealed in contemporary attitudes to the Holocaust and the State of Israel. In particular, he highlights the use of one to attack the other as the clearest indication of this phenomenon. This accusation of anti-Semitism is not limited to the right-wing or fringe, but in fact can be found in equal measure on the left of the political spectrum:

> The latest strategy – dear to the hearts of liberal intellectuals and to my mind the most heinous – accepts the enormity of the Holocaust without demur, but accuses Jews of not emerging from it as better people: the proof of that failure

being the occupation, Gaza, the settlements, etc. ... the Holocaust becomes a sort of university, an educational experience – a great learning opportunity, you might say – from which Jews were ethically obliged to have graduated with First Class honours.[144]

In an article from 2009, Jacobson points to Caryl Churchill's short play *Seven Jewish Children* (2009) as a typical instance of this attitude being placed on display without apparent concern for its implications, the latest example of 'the hatred of Israel expressed in our streets, on our campuses, in our newspapers, on our radios and televisions, and now in our theatres'.[145] Jacobson makes a reading based on his understanding of new anti-Semitism: that rather than legitimate criticism of Israel (Churchill's play was written in response to the 2008–2009 Israel military action in Gaza), Churchill's play demonizes Israeli actions and characters while ignoring, or worse condoning, the actions of Palestinian militant groups such as Hamas, and is thus an example of anti-Semitism. In Jacobson's article he repeats variations on the rhetorical question 'Anti-Semitism? No, no Just criticism of Israel' as well as the phrase with which he closes the piece, 'Not here, though. Not in cosy old lazy old come-easy easy-come England'.[146]

It could well be that Jacobson was already planning his dystopian future, but either way his ironic invocation of the 'not here' echoes the 'it can't happen here' of the previous section of this book, with the added urgency of a speculative scenario set not in an alternate past, referencing our history, but in our future, referencing our present.

Thus, while references to contemporary society abound in *J*, the references to Israel are particularly significant, tying the novel to a nation where the new anti-Semitism has become the accepted norm. The victims of WHAT HAPPENED are referred to as 'foreigners themselves and had what they called a country only by taking someone else's';[147] a country, 'which they call their ancestral home (but which few of them except the most desperate appear to be in any hurry to repair to)'; and pre-WHAT HAPPENED references to 'a recent exchange of prisoners with one of their many enemies in which, for the sake of a single one of their own – just *one* – they willingly handed over in excess of seven hundred! The mathematics make a telling point'.[148] Just as the Jews are the unmistakable victims of the persecution at the heart of the novel, so too is Israel clearly the target of these references and others like them.

At the time of the novel it is clear that nothing like Israel still exists, so too Jewishness itself in *J* is an absent presence, like the struck through letter J which is the novel's eponymous symbol.¹⁴⁹ It is 'a redacted form of Jewishness ... a struck through and stricken form'.¹⁵⁰ This deletion without total erasure (when information is redacted we still see the gaps in a text where words once were) provides space not only for survivors, but for an acknowledgement of the role hatred has played, and continues to play, in constructing our society.

Again in *When Will Jews Be Forgiven the Holocaust?*, Jacobson contemplates the role which anti-Semitism has had in the formation of Christian identity in formerly pagan communities, and the implications of this role still being felt in modern Europe and beyond. Jacobson cites Freud's theory, provided in *Moses and Monotheism* (1939), that anti-Semitism persists most strongly in those Northern and Eastern regions of Europe which were converted relatively late, and while Jacobson makes only a passing reference Freud's point is worth quoting here in full:

> It might be said they are all 'mis-baptised'. They have been left, under a thin veneer of Christianity, what their ancestors were, who worshipped a barbarous polytheism. They have not got over a grudge against the new religion which was imposed on them; but they have displaced the grudge on to the source from which Christianity reached them. The fact that the Gospels tell a story which is set among Jews, and in fact deals only with Jews, has made this displacement easy for them. Their hatred of Jews is at bottom a hatred of Christians.¹⁵¹

'The consequence of this for Jews', writes Jacobson, 'is that we end up being the meat in the sandwich, responsible for the paganism *and* responsible for the Christianity, depending which way the wind is blowing. Forcing us to ask: are not some instances of Christian anti-Semitism simply expressions of Christian dissatisfaction with Christianity itself?'¹⁵² Jacobson also references the French Catholic philosopher Jacques Maritain's description of the 'monstrosity' of Christian anti-Semitism; in *The Range of Reason* (1952) Maritain writes that 'Christians who are anti-Semites ... are seeking an alibi for their innermost sense of guilt, for the death of Christ of which they want to clear themselves: but if Christ did not die for their sins, then they flee from the mercy of Christ! In reality they want not to be redeemed. Here is the most secret and vicious root by virtue of which anti-Semitism dechristianizes Christians, and leads them to paganism'.¹⁵³ Jacobson finds this idea 'enticing' when applied to Nazi Germany:

> In the way of the Third Reich's fantasy of a pagan reawakening lay Judaism *and* Christianity, but it could hardly be seen to jettison Christianity. By attacking the Jews in the language long favoured by the Church, however, it

was able to appear to honour Christianity, while at the same time freeing itself to stage its heathenish parades. For the Nazis, you could say, Jews were proxy Christians on whom they offloaded all they hated about monotheistic religion, so alleviating what remained of their guilt about it.

It is a profoundly important thought, anyway, it seems to me, that the Jew serves as an *alibi* for Christian guilt. For acting against the Jew then becomes something like a sacred obligation – a debt you must pay to the Christ to whom you do not want otherwise to be beholden.[154]

With its blending of Wagnerian and Celtic paganism, this acknowledgement is also seen in *J*. However, in a twist typical of the perverse, almost child-like, nature of many of the novel's characters, the wrong lesson is taken from it. Esme Nusbaum has tracked Kevern and Ailinn, manipulates their circumstances to encourage them to meet and fall in love, and wants to save them and their child, 'like Noah'.[155] However she does not want to save Jews to make amends for the crimes of her forefathers; to attempt to make a gesture towards undoing a genocide, she wants to save the Jews to give society someone to hate:

> WHAT HAPPENED, IF IT HAPPENED was only, after all, a partial solution. They don't expect a uniformity of response. ... a few well-judged publicity photographs, the odd teaser interview, not giving too much away, in celebrity and gossip magazines – should begin to restore the necessary balance of societal antagonism. 'Just give us some titbits we can definitively leak,' they tell her, meaning that the wedding, the conception, and the birth can wait. The child of course is crucial – *For unto us a child is given* – but even the promise of it should suffice for the moment.[156]

A 'partial solution' of course invokes the Final Solution, while the references to celebrity gossip magazines suggest the 'necessary balance of societal antagonism' is something very much more contemporary to our society. At the same time, the reference to Isaiah 9:6 'For unto us a child is born, unto us a son is given', recalls that this is a Christian society and that the child of Kevern and Ailinn, while not Jesus Christ the son of God (himself the child of Jews), is still regarded as a saviour by the administration, who need someone to loathe and fear in equal measure, at least as characterized by Esme.

This understanding of anti-Semitism lies behind depictions of the church within *J*, an institution which has not fared much better than the Jews themselves, as shown by the small cathedral city of Ashbrittle, 'at one time home to more ecclesiastical dignitaries than any other town in the country' but now 'you can smell the disuse'.[157] The gargoyles on the cathedral's edifice are telling markers of the society's relationship both to the church as an institution and to its history as a Christian nation and more generally:

> 'The gargoyles have been defaced,' Kevern noted, looking up. 'They have no features. No bent noses, no bulging eyes, no pendulous lips.'
> 'Years of bad weather,' Ailinn guessed.
> 'Well that's a kind interpretation. But I bet this is deliberate. They've been smoothed over – made to look like nothing and nobody.'
> 'Botoxed, you reckon?'
> He laughed. 'Morally Botoxed. Rendered inoffensive.'[158]

The image of a moral botoxing, of removing anything that might be deemed offensive, is itself a thinly-veiled critique of political correctness. However, more pressing here is the defacing of the cathedral as an erasure of history. In the society of *J* remembering the past is only a superficial gesture: remembering WHAT HAPPENED, IF IT HAPPENED but without remembering necessarily what that event is, or as the modifier indicates, whether it occurred at all. Thus, references are made to our own society as: 'the bad old days', when '"never forget" was a guiding maxim – you couldn't move, I've heard tell, for obelisks and mausoleums and other inordinately ugly monuments exhorting memory – but this led first to wholesale neuroticism and impotence and then, as was surely inevitable, to the great falling-out, if there was one'.[159]

At a time when the manner and method of memorialization for the atrocities of the past century are a topic of debate, controversy and revision, the characterization of our society in this manner is both timely and powerful. 'Never Forget' is one of the few maxims which might be more ubiquitous in popular discussions of memory and history than a variation on Santayana's warning about repeating history. Jacobson's novel features an aged scholar, old enough to have experienced WHAT HAPPENED, who suggests an alternative slogan for contemporary memory:

> Rather than go on perpetuating the neurasthenic concept of victimisation, Grossenberger argued, the never-forgetters would have done better carving 'I Forgive You' on their stones. In return for which, we might have forgiven them. But that chance came and went. And now who, today, is going to forgive whom for what? Only by having everyone say sorry, without reference to what they are saying sorry for, can the concept of blame be eradicated, and guilt at last can be anaesthetised.[160]

Replacing 'Never Forget' with 'I Forgive You' appears a tactic that would appeal to an author who also asked 'When Will Jews be Forgiven the Holocaust?' and indeed it seems possible it is from this point that the circumstances of the novel stem from. Forgetting the Holocaust does not seem to result in a better world, perhaps offering an answer to Zygmunt Bauman who asked what it means 'to live in a world forever pregnant with the kind of horrors that the Holocaust has come to stand for? Does the memory of the Holocaust make the world a better and safer, or a worse and more dangerous place?'[161] By forgetting but also leading it until it was too late to forgive, anti-Semitic hatred in *J* had time to fester until it resulted in a (near-) final purge.

Crucially, Jacobson's novel reminds us that for all the alternate histories, secret histories, dystopian futures, or second world fantasies that non-mimetic fiction might select as a setting for its Holocaust narratives, and despite the Holocaust now being over seventy years in our past, the issues that arise from such texts are very much contemporary to our own time. It may be tempting with all of these fictions to view the detachment from realism as a detachment from relevance, and indeed this is the dismissive attitude prevalent among certain scholars of both Holocaust studies and contemporary fictions. This book has continuously contradicted this school of thought. However, while many of the texts featured above offer new insights into the Holocaust as a historic event, and analyse our relationship to that history, *J* powerfully replaces the Holocaust as a living, contemporary issue. More specifically, *J* highlights elements of our culture and society which have failed to learn the lessons of the Holocaust, showing not only where anti-Semitic attitudes have clung on in post-war Britain, but how they still very much contain a lethal genocidal potential.

Conclusion

Perhaps more than any of the other Anglo-American texts in this book, the novels of this chapter are introspective in the sense that they are concerned less with the evils and deeds of Nazi Germany and more with the potential for those same deeds to be visited upon our shores not by invading armies but by poisonous politics. In doing so, however, they do not lose sight of the horror of the Holocaust, rather they reposition it as a repeatable, or emulatable, act which could just as easily have occurred (or yet occur) in the United Kingdom or United States. Neither nation's history is clean of acts of genocide, nor indeed of concentration camps. At the same time as highlighting the Allies moral failings in the 1930s and 1940s, these texts also universalize the Holocaust using it and the accompanying mechanisms of fascism and the Second World War to draw attention to contemporary concerns whether they be the creeping power of the state, the response of democracy to terrorism, or the rise of racism and hatred in the discourses of our politics, our media and our everyday lives.

The effect of this process has been to place the Holocaust and the circumstances which allowed it to happen in points of comparison with other atrocities and significant events, both historic and potential. These comparisons do not diminish the Holocaust, nor undermine its importance, but they do challenge the rhetoric of unapproachability and exceptionalism, re-integrating the genocide into a grim continuum of human atrocity.

The Plot Against America and *Farthing* were written in the wake of 9/11 and the shockwave which swept around the globe embroiling nations in a War on Terror both abroad and within their own borders. Sacrifices of freedom were made in the name of security, whether the acceptance of large-scale CCTV observation, or the changes to the way airports screen flyers; and texts such as Roth's and Walton's warned of the dangers should such trends continue unchecked. Their novels were written in a growing climate of fear and a period of self-reflection in which previous assumptions of unassailability were challenged; in such a climate loud populist voices grow bolder and powerful and both Roth and Walton recognized the danger therein.

Writing around a decade later, Tidhar and Jacobson's novels were both published in 2014 and their more extreme styles, relative to Roth's and Walton's, are indicative of a climate which has itself only grown more dangerous. *J* and *A Man Lies Dreaming* are both dystopian novels about the rise of the far-right, anti-Semitism and nationalist politics and it is almost impossible to look back at them now without seeing them through the lens of the events in 2016, two years later, of the election of Donald Trump in the United States and the Brexit vote in the United Kingdom. Anti-Semitic incidents in the United States increased by 57 per cent in 2017 compared with 2016, which itself was a record high for recent years, while in 2018, France and Germany reported 74 per cent and 60 per cent increases in anti-semitic attacks respectively.[162] From the murder of British MP Jo Cox in 2016 to the killing of Heather Heyer in a car attack in Charlottesville in 2017, and the deadliest anti-Semitic attack in American history when gunman Robert Gregory Bowers killed eleven in a shooting at the Tree of Life synagogue in Squirrel Hill, Pittsburgh, in 2018, the flashpoints of violence featuring the far-right have been powerful and shocking. It seems understandable why writers are turning their focus to the evils of the human past and using them to draw our attention to the dangers of the present.

By embracing the dystopian potential of the Holocaust and using it to create speculative fiction, these texts revive the nightmare of the genocide, making it more present and thus more pressing. In doing so they demonstrate that the Holocaust is now fully integrated into Anglo-American culture so that, for better or worse, it has become a set of dystopian tropes which we can readily recognize, adapt and reinterpret as context demands.

Epilogue: Further Fabulation

One generation later, it can still be said and must now be affirmed: There is no such thing as a literature of the Holocaust, nor can there be. The very expression is a contradiction in terms. Auschwitz negates any form of literature, as it defies all systems, all doctrines ... A novel about Auschwitz is not a novel, or else it is not about Auschwitz. The very attempt to write such a novel is blasphemy.[1]

Elie Wiesel was the most vocal defender of the representation of the Holocaust as unrepresentable, yet he is also one of its most prolific writers, producing both fiction and non-fiction about the genocide. However, there is a blurriness to these distinctions; Wiesel's own *Night* is normally referred to as a Holocaust memoir yet many critics have identified its fictive qualities. Ruth Franklin points out that it, 'like the stories of Tadeusz Borowski, the autobiographical work of Primo Levi, and *virtually every other important work of literature about the Holocaust* – has been understood, at different times, as *both* a novel and a memoir'.[2] There is a slippage of terminology and classification, aided by the insistence of impossibility, the reliance on highfalutin quasi-religious statements – often ironically poetic in their insistence of the futility of poetry – and made more complicated still by infamous examples of forgery.[3] A slippage which seems to support the insistence that the Holocaust truly is something different as a source material for humanity's writing, that the standard tools are no longer adequate, but that does not mean that we are without resources.

The texts I have discussed in this book are testament to the storytelling capacities of speculative fiction and its capacity to be utilized as just such a resource for attempting to explore the Holocaust's relationship with our culture, especially now more than seventy years since its end. The paradox of the Holocaust is its prolific presence in literature (fiction and non-fiction) placed against the rhetoric of unspeakability which has historically dominated surrounding discourse. Speculative fiction narratives seek to square the circle, unravelling the paradox by dislocating the Other of the Holocaust to the Other of the non-mimetic through estrangement, an Other which thanks to millennia of non-mimetic narratives we are more comfortably able to cognitively conceptualize. Fredric Jameson writes of historical fabulations that 'agency steps out of the historical record itself into the process of devising it; and new multiple or alternate strings of events rattle the bars of the national traditional and the history manuals'.[4] The Holocaust is not outside of history, despite the sentiment expressed by some supporters of exceptionalism that perhaps it should be, and so the Holocaust is not beyond the effect described by Jameson.

Wiesel also wrote that the title of his important essay 'The Holocaust as Literary Inspiration' is an impossible contradiction. 'Wouldn't that mean, then', he writes 'that Treblinka and Belzec, Ponar and Babi Yar all ended in fantasy, in words, in beauty, that it was simply a matter of literature?'[5] Wiesel equates literature with beauty, with words, crucially with fantasy; it is not that equation that he finds abhorrent, rather the translation or transmutation of the Holocaust into those things. The texts I have focused on in this book are drawn from the more realist end of speculative fiction's spectrum, but it is worth considering for a moment examples of texts which come closer to being considered fantasy.

Fantasy 'can provide a place to stand and judge the canon', writes Brian Attebery, allowing a new perspective on literary works.[6] Fantasy, and speculative fiction more widely, can also provide a new perspective on history when its narratives incorporate the historical as plot elements. However, precisely because of the grounds which see the fantastic excluded from the contemporary literary canon – that is, a misplaced notion that such fiction prizes entertainment at the expense of insight or intent, or that there is a tendency to infantilize – the application of this genre to living, and particularly traumatic, history is greeted as at best irrelevant and at worst insulting.

Magic is one of the archetypal tropes of fantasy fiction and, perhaps more than any other, its presence in a text is normally an indicator of genre to a reader. In the context of the Holocaust however the use of magic in a narrative has potentially damaging implications. Magical or supernatural Nazis, employing fantasy or horror tropes, risk aligning themselves with morally simplistic stock fantasy villains, repeating and reinforcing the concept of the Nazis as a trope: the epitome of evil. The first danger here is in classifying an entire movement by a single rationale, removing the possibility of moral complexity and the 'good Nazi'. This streamlines the narrative which may be useful for thrillers or other suspenseful fictions, but it is intellectually, cognitively and perhaps morally, unsatisfying. Roger Luckhurst comments on the long relationship between Nazis and zombies, for example. He writes:

> The zombie Nazi simply conflates two unqualified mass evils. It stays away from the 'living dead' of [Holocaust victims], but evokes them by inversion, switching victims for perpetrators. Viewers are morally freed twice over to enjoy the spectacle of (re-)killing. Nazis, after all, come in masses too.[7]

Perhaps more worrying is the use of unqualified evils to not only place Nazis on the far end of a good–evil spectrum, but to place ourselves (that is, Anglo-American readers) at the inverse position. To use the 'ultimate evil' of occult/satanic/zombie Nazis as an opportunity to present Anglo-American conduct in the Second World War, and indeed in other parts of history, as necessarily virtuous, good and even holy. Invoking black magic in the employ of the Nazis automatically also invokes the tropes of good versus evil, and thus places the conflict within a familiar but potentially damaging narrative framework. As Michael Butter writes: 'American culture uses the discourse of uniqueness and good and evil to displace and disremember the more problematic aspects of its own history.'[8] This remains true if we broaden Butter's point out to encapsulate British culture alongside American.

These problems are far more pronounced when the subject matter is the Holocaust specifically, rather than the more general threat of Nazism or the Second World War more broadly. It is likely for this reason that magic, or the supernatural, and the Holocaust are relatively infrequent partners within the sweep of Anglo-American non-mimetic fiction. There are, however, a few examples of text which employ these elements, with varying degrees of success, though they seem understudied by literary scholars even by the standards of other speculative fictions. I have already made reference to R. A. Lafferty's 'The Three Armageddons of Enniscorthy Sweeny' (1977) and Jerry Yulsman's *Elleander Morning* (1984) but the magic involved in these texts is aimed not at changing the Holocaust directly but rather altering it indirectly through a wider system of historical changes which result in totally alternate worlds. Instead I want to look for a moment at texts which focus more closely on the Holocaust elements of their fiction and yet still employ magic.

One of the most notable such texts is Lisa Goldstein's *The Red Magician* (1982). The novel is narrated from the point of view of a schoolgirl, Kicsi, in a Jewish-Yiddish village in wartime Hungary. A girl who daydreams about exotic locations such as Paris, London, Arabia, etc. For this reason, she is drawn to a stranger who visits the village, a fellow Jew named Vörös. He is well-travelled and mysterious, fulfilling all the standard criteria required for a teenage crush. He also turns out to be a magician capable of, among other things, prophesizing the future. Of course, the future he glimpses is one of darkness and destruction, an approaching all-consuming evil that will wipe the village off the face of the earth, but his warnings go largely unheeded by anyone except Kicsi.

Like the warnings of Moshe the Beadle in Elie Wiesel's *Night*, or perhaps even more appropriately the anticipatory dream-vision of Mrs Schächter, in that same book, Vörös's warnings are not only ignored, they are denigrated, downgraded and actively opposed.[9] The leader of this opposition is the village's rabbi, himself a Kabbalistic mage of some power. Thus Vörös's attempts to save the village are thwarted by the rabbi's attempts to not only preserve his power in the community, but also to isolate it from external change, even if that change presents itself as benevolent or a salvation. In this way the conflict between the magicians can be characterized as one of conflicting ideologies of youthful international dynamism versus older, more rural conservatism.

Judith Kerman, one of the few critics to give Goldstein's novel any real attention, remarks that it 'speaks directly to the ontological question of the Holocaust, which is real and what is fantasy, in several places'. 'But', she continues, 'in spite of evidently higher ambitions, *The Red Magician* fails to rise above genre fiction'.[10] The notion of rising above genre fiction is an interesting one, suggesting a higher plane of literary worth, yet Kerman is no literature snob seeking to put non-mimetic fiction in its place, instead she sees in Goldstein's novel a relatively shallow fiction lacking in the depth of character or story required to convey the intended Holocaust narrative:

> The reader consensus on which the high fantasy genre depends, in fact, is precisely that its devices are *not* real; but the reader of *The Red Magician* viscerally understands the urgency of the historic context and the actual mystery of the historic evil. This historic reality flattens out any inherent moral resonance the genre devices might have still carried, demanding that the author penetrate the genre to its deeper meanings, not only in occasional statements but in every detail and movement of the story. Unfortunately, by this standard *The Red Magician* fails. Although its characters ask some of the central ontological and moral questions, the structure and texture of the story itself do not.[11]

Kermen argues then not that fantasy is inappropriate or incapable of discussing the Holocaust, but rather that the 'historic reality' renders standard fantasy tropes as flat and that deeper, more penetrating, devices are required to produce a successful narrative. Ellen R. Weil, however, points out that the fantasy elements of *The Red Magician* are 'not only rooted in Jewish mystical tradition, but are carefully confined to events before and after the protagonist's internment in a concentration camp, which is described in a single realistic chapter in the center of the narrative'.[12] This framing of the realist section of the novel, describing the emptying of the village into cattle cars and the internment of Kicsi and the others at an unnamed camp, grounds the central reality of the Holocaust offsetting the fantastical magic of the magician and the rabbi in a peculiar and perhaps not entirely successful way.

Those fantastical sections involve the summoning of spirits, the building of a golem, visions and magical necklaces. The preservation of the concentration camp as a space devoid of magic adds to the power of the sections set in this hellish locale. Robbed both of the childhood innocence Kicsi had before she knew magic, and of the wider fantasy world Vörös has presented to her, the girl is exposed to a traumatic reality more difficult to comprehend than any fantasy magic. Just as the Holocaust experience is a lacuna or traumatic gap in the reality of victims' lives, incommunicable and unbelievable, so too does Goldstein present it as a gap in the magic of the novel; thus the fantasy deepens the contrast between the everyday pre-Holocaust and the Holocaust scenes themselves. This turn to realist mimesis, a temporary severance with speculative fiction, is perhaps reflective of the personal nature of the story for Goldstein: both of her parents were European Jews held in concentration camps; her mother was Hungarian and provided the basis for much of the novel.[13]

Ultimately the book is most powerful in how it demonstrates the fundamental shift in Kicsi's character pre- and post-Holocaust and how she struggles to find a reason to exist in a new world where she is a Holocaust survivor. She is finally successful in finding the will to live, if not the reason for her survival, but to do so she has to literally confront the long history of anti-Semitic violence. The manner in which this is done is so powerful and effective precisely because of the speculative fiction techniques used: the summoning of ghosts to speak about the terrors of the past and invoke them in the present. Similarly, the crucial role of a Holocaust survivor in overcoming these ghosts of the past speaks to the notes of hope which Vörös attempts to imbue in Kicsi, that the world will recover and the Jews will find new homes:

> 'But the wounds will heal, Kicsi. See, the land revives. And the people – already the people are finding new ways of life, learning to live again.' She saw a tracery of green spread across the land, a slow stain of healing. People greeted relatives

thought to be dead, rejoiced, moved in a great stream away from the burned lands, out toward the new lands of Palestine or America. 'That is how it has always been. And underneath it ... is a kind of joy. The joy of life.'[14]

Survivor guilt and an absence of reason to go on living are the real antagonists of *The Red Magician*; the Nazis are largely faceless figures in the background, oppressive and terrible but without character or focus, while the rabbi is shown to be a tortured figure with a much more complex morality than his status as Vörös's counterpoint might suggest. As such Kicsi's triumph, even over the supernatural spirits, is dissimilar from traditional magic fantasy novels, and while she gets a happy ending of sorts – sailing for a new life in America with her sister – it is tinged with sadness because Vörös insists he is unable to accompany her.

In presenting such an ending, Goldstein sidesteps a significant problem in combining fantasy and the Holocaust: the narrative drive of fantasy, particularly that with a young adult slant, towards a happy ending. To impose a truly happy ending on the novel would jar with the suffering which Kicsi has endured and undermine the power of the novel's Holocaust sections. In *The Red Magician* magic is used to offer perspective on the Holocaust, but not to assuage it. The fantasy is used to examine questions of survival and adaptation in a post-Holocaust environment, condensing philosophical and ethical complexities down into a narrower timeframe in a manner which feels neither rushed nor arbitrary. The second novel I would like to examine here also uses its fantasy to offer new perspectives, though overall its use of magic is less successful and more problematic with regard to the Holocaust content of the novel.

The Magicians of Night (1992) by Barbara Hambly uses fantasy to offer a particularly unique take on the Nazi programme. The sequel to a fairly typical secondary world immersive fantasy, *The Rainbow Abyss* (1991), *Magicians of Night* offers resolution of a prominent plot point but in a most unexpected manner. In *The Rainbow Abyss*, the wizard Jaldis had 'opened a Dark Well and through it ... seen into the Void which lies between all the infinite number of universes of which the Cosmos is made! And in that Void ... [he] heard a voice crying out of a world where magic had once existed, but now exists no more'.[15] At the end of the novel, Jaldis and his apprentice Rhion embark through a portal to the magic-less world, though Jaldis dies in the attempt. *The Magicians of Night* begins almost exactly where its predecessor lets off, but without his master Rhion is trapped in the strange magic-less world, inverting the standard portal fantasy narrative. He awakes in the care of strange men, the magicians of the alien planet. Unfortunately, it soon becomes clear to the reader, if not to Rhion, that the strange world is Earth, and the magicians are Nazi occultists. Thus the series title, 'Sun-Cross', takes on a new sinisterism; as Rhion describes the emblem of these strange magicians it is quickly apparent to the reader what he is looking at:

> the sun-cross wrought huge in black upon a white circle against a ground of bloody red.
> The sun-cross, Rhion noticed for the first time, was reversed, so that it turned not toward light, but toward darkness.[16]

Under their leader von Rath, these Nazi magicians, the 'Occult Bureau of the Ancestral Heritage Division of the Protection Squad', seek to harness magic in order to win the war.[17] The magicians are not all German but they are all sponsored by the SS and subscribe in varying degrees to the Nazi occultism characterized by a sense of Aryan supremacy, and an anti-modernist, theosophic obsession with symbols and mythology which is preserved in contemporary popular culture. 'Magic' one of them argues, 'is a quality of the *vril*, the mystical power inherited by the Aryan Race from the men of Atlantis whom Manu, the last [of] the Atlantean Superman, led across Europe to the secret fastnesses of Thibet.'[18]

Rhion is tricked into working with the Nazi magicians until he comes to realize that their hunger for power is dangerous and rooted in evil, including ritual human sacrifice. He begins to dig into the truth of his situation and comes to realize the extent to which von Rath has misled and manipulated him. Ultimately Rhion intuits that his best hopes for escape, and indeed survival, are not with the Nazi magicians but with the Jews and Allied forces he has been told to distrust. Karen Hellekson points out that across the two Sun-Cross novels Hambly's overarching theme is that in any world, magical or otherwise, there are those who wish to control others and cast them as less-than-human and without rights. She writes that 'wizards and Jews have much in common: both are killed with impunity in their world; neither are considered human; neither have rights. It's no coincidence that Rhion is thought to be a Jew while in Germany'.[19] Hellekson's reading is certainly supported by the text, and we can readily compare the violence unleashed on magician characters in *The Rainbow Abyss* (such as Jaldis himself who has had his throat cut to remove his voice and so has to carry a box of magic flutes which speak for him) with the glimpse of the treatment of Jews which Rhion encounters. For example, Rhion breaks his eyeglasses and is offered a selection of others until a prescription pair can be manufactured for him:

> Rhion put his hand into the box and nearly threw up with shock.
> The psychic impact was as if he'd unsuspectingly plunged his arm into acid. … Hands shaking, sweat standing cold on his face, Rhion looked back at the box. For a moment it seemed to him that those flat, folded shapes of metal and glass were the skeletons of men, stacked like cordwood for burning, sunken eyes sealed shut and mouths opened in a congealed scream of uncomprehending despair.[20]

This is clear Holocaust imagery, from the stacked masses of emaciated corpses, to the image of them burning like firewood. That Rhion alone feels the psychic connection enforces the idea of an affinity between him and the victims whose glasses these once were. This is emphasized when Rhion is told that a pair he chooses make him 'look like a damn rabbi'.[21]

Hambly's novel clearly exploits the trope of the Nazi as techno-pagan, a villain from a morally simplistic pulpish mould. Von Rath is typically devoid of moral compass; though at times he seems concerned for Rhion's well-being, as the novel progresses it becomes clear he only sees him as another tool to personal gain. When questioned about his use of human sacrifice for raising magical power, von Rath points out that 'they were not true human beings. The women were gypsies, the boy a Jew'.[22] During one encounter with Rhion near the middle of the novel the wizard looks into the SS officer's face and sees 'nothing human in von Rath's eyes', a choice of language which presents the Other as evil, echoing the Nazi's own dehumanizing language.[23] Similarly, by the novel's end, in the final explosive conflict between Rhion and a now magically empowered von Rath the latter is described as 'Lucifer ascendant in fire and shadow and rage'.[24]

Derek J. Thiess writes that popular culture transmits historical myths, such as that of the techno-pagan Nazi, without thought or recourse to its accuracy. However, he goes on to point out that 'the sf alternate history', which *Magicians of Night* can be considered to be (although I feel secret historical fantasy would be a more accurate label), 'also seeks to innovate upon that image and to problematize it. In contrast to the revisionist narrative of Nazi history, even as it is found in popular forms, the sf alternate history … trends "toward the unknown"'.[25] However I'd argue that Hambly's novels problematize the Nazi techno-pagan image far less than the straighter alternate history novels he cites.²⁶ Both by employing the techno-pagan mythos, and through evocative comparisons such as those between von Rath and Lucifer, Hambly reinforces the position of the SS magicians as being at the extreme end of a morality spectrum, simplifying the moral picture and thus reducing von Rath to a 'Dark Lord' fantasy trope.

In the context of this book, however, most worrying are the specifics of the novel's finale. Von Rath is defeated in a mystic duel resulting in a suitably gruesome demise; wreathed in a magical fire as Rhion turns his power back upon him, he screams 'like twenty men screaming, a hundred – dunked into acid, eaten by rats, rolled in fire that wouldn't die. … von Rath screaming, screaming like the damned in their long plunge to hell'.²⁷ The screaming and melting is reminiscent of the fate of the Nazis who gaze into the Ark of the Covenant in *Raiders of the Lost Ark*, one of the films Thiess highlights as doing the most to propagate the techno-pagan mythos. For the reader this hideous killing is a cathartic irony – that a torturer who inflicted such pain and suffering on those he sacrificed for magical gains should have such pain inflicted upon him by the source of that magic seems fitting. This however plays into narratalogical fantasies of justice, common to fantasy but often absent in history. An even greater problem is encountered however in the way Hambly wraps up the Holocaust elements of her novel.

In Rhion's efforts to get home he recruits a secretly Jewish tavern-maid; together they break her father, Leibnitz, something of a magician himself, out of the local concentration camp. He is being held as part of von Rath's efforts to gather all of the 'specially designated' inferior humans with magical potential that he can, in order to sacrifice them to gain power. In turning von Rath's power back on itself Rhion inadvertently causes a surge in magical power on Earth temporarily activating those with magical potential all over the world; isolated cases of magic being performed, from Siberia to Haiti, are reported through an intelligence briefing in the novel's final pages.²⁸ Another of these instances of magical prowess is featured in the report:

> The reports spoke of a massive series of escapes from concentration camps and labor camps throughout Germany: during an outbreak of inexplicable fires at Dachau … kept the guards too busy to notice the departure of eighty-seven Jews led by three of von Rath's 'specially designated' Kabbalists; unexplained quarrels amongst the guards at Buchenwald that amounted to a campwide riot during which fifty-four Polish, Jewish, and gypsy children vanished from the camp along with a 'specially designated' gypsy witch; the execution of three guards at

Gross Rosen for neglect of duty in allowing twelve Jewish and Polish occultists apparently to cut the wires literally under their noses and walk out; and others; many others[29]

While satisfying on the level of fantasy, imposing a happy ending of this nature upon the Holocaust is seriously problematic, and made more so by the references to real camps such as Dachau and Buchenwald rather than fictitious camps such as Kegenwald which feature more prominently in the novel. Such moments diminish the horrifying reality of the Holocaust, sacrificed in pursuit of a more satisfyingly upbeat ending one must imagine, recalling the 'sweetening or sugar-coating' of the Holocaust which Gary Weissman identifies in some post-war efforts to experience or understand the genocide.[30] The reported escape of the anonymous captives is damaging to the novel's representation of the Holocaust in a manner not applicable to the happy ending of Rhion arriving home, or Leibnitz and his daughter being admitted to the United Kingdom as refugees, because while those represent the closure of character arcs, the escapes are an otherwise superfluous aside which serves no narrative function other than to make a happier ending for the novel.[31] As a Second World War magical fantasy or occult thriller, along the lines of Dennis Wheatley's *They Used Dark Forces* (1964) or Katherine Kurtz's *Lammas Night* (1983), *The Magicians of Night* would be a fairly typical but enjoyable adventure. However, by explicitly connecting the narrative to that of the Holocaust it centres itself within a different critical sphere, one more honest about the implications of Nazi rule, but also one less forgiving of artistic license.

Overall, Hambly's novel is less successful than Goldstein's *The Red Magician* in its intertwining of magical fantasy and the Holocaust. A significant factor in this is *The Magicians of Night* taking magic within the confines of the concentration camp in a significant manner, something which *The Red Magician* at most alludes to but largely avoids. There is perhaps actually more magic in Goldstein's novel than in Hambly's, which contains a lot of talking about magic, but it is the context of the magic juxtaposed with the Holocaust narrative which is Hambly's biggest failing. Certainly, both novels demonstrate that magic and the Holocaust need not be mutually exclusive in the narrative as a whole, and indeed can successfully engage commentary with the trauma through their speculative fictions.

Similarly, Jane Yolen's two Holocaust novels employ fantasy in vastly different manners. *The Devil's Arithmetic* (1988), a highly successful young adult novel, adapted for screen in 1999, features a young protagonist who inexplicably time travels from her family's Passover Seder in modern New York to a Polish village in 1942 where she is absorbed into the life of Chaya, a girl who is caught up in the Holocaust. Despite the dislocation of the modern American teenager into the young Polish girl's body, as the novel progresses the distinction between Hannah and Chaya becomes ever more diminished until there is only the faintest trace of Hannah's memories in Chaya's mind. Ultimately Chaya is killed in the camp and Hannah is transported back to the present, with no time lost, but now fully imbued with an appreciation of the horrors her grandparents survived. While the time travel is definitely fantastic in nature, it plays little role beyond providing the plot device to combine modern and Holocaust narratives.

The fantasy is even less prominent (to the point of absence) in Yolen's other novel, *Briar Rose* (1992). The novel, ostensibly for adults but again popular with older teens, is not actually a speculative fiction Holocaust narrative at all, despite receiving a positive reception – including genre specific award recognition – from the SF community.[32] Indeed, Gary K. Wolfe references its inclusion on the 1993 World Fantasy Award shortlist as evidence of fantasy as a genre beginning to evaporate into broader literature; he describes the novel as being 'meticulous in its historical realism'.[33] It is, however, an interesting example of a non-mimetic narrative being employed to talk powerfully and poignantly about the Holocaust, atrocity and personal trauma. The difference being that, unlike the other texts in this book, the non-mimesis is entirely intra-textual – that is, between fictional characters within the novel rather than directly between author and reader. The novel centres on a young journalist, Rebecca, and her relationship with her grandmother Gemma. When Gemma dies, Rebecca is drawn to the mystery of Gemma's past and her journey to America, particularly because of Gemma's life-long repetition of an unusual and seemingly personally adapted version of the Briar Rose fairy tale. Through a journey to Poland and conversations with locals, who are often reluctant to talk to her, Rebecca learns that Gemma is a survivor of the Chelmno extermination camp, and that the fairy tale maps over her life.[34] Thus the fairy tale, rather than an instance of non-mimesis in the text, is revealed to be, as Vandana Saxena writes, 'a medium to narrate events that defy the teller's understanding and comprehension and hence the conventional modes of narration'.[35] In other words, the non-mimetic narrative framework of the fairy tale is used to transmit the untransmittable traumatic rupture of the Holocaust from the grandmother to a future generation.

While both Yolen's novels are remarkable instances of the Holocaust in fiction, the actual relevance of the non-mimetic elements of their fiction, while fascinating in different ways, is far less than some other fantasy texts.[36] In addition to this, Yolen's texts have already attracted significant critical attention, at least relative to other fantasy texts which engage with the Holocaust. So in the interest of restraining the scope of this book[37] an alternative candidate could be a text such as Joseph Skibell's *A Blessing on the Moon* (1997) which draws on Talmudic fables, Eastern European and Yiddish mythology, and fantasy to create a non-mimetic rendering of the author's great-grandfather Chaim Skibelski, having him die in a mass grave but crawl out of it nonetheless to tell his story, accompanied by his also-dead rabbi who has taken the form of a talking crow. A fascinatingly strange novel, which S. Lillian Kremer labels 'a novel of magic realism'.[38]

Discussing magic-realist narratives, Jenni Adams notes: 'Given the frequent (antirealist) theorization of the Holocaust as a traumatic event resistant to narrative integration, the magical … can be read as a dramatization of the event's traumatic dimension – the irruption of unreality functioning as a symbolic substitution for the unknowable and unnarratable historical extremity.'[39] For Adams the estrangement effect of magic within magic realism allows the texts of her study to integrate with the unknowable and unnarratable discourse of the Holocaust while still offering texts which contribute to our understanding and remembrance of the genocide. Whether magic realism, explicit magic fantasy or more subtly non-realist alternate histories or dystopias, I have shown how speculative fiction as a whole has an extensive set of tools with which we can approach a narration of the Holocaust's impact in Anglo-American culture.

Conclusion

Shoshana Felman, in explicit contradiction to the rhetoric of unrepresenatability, writes that the Holocaust 'does not kill the possibility of art – on the contrary, it requires it for its transmission, for its realization in our consciousness as witnesses'.[40] Felman argues that Holocaust art is not only possible but that it is necessary. The recent passing of Elie Wiesel, as the research for this book was being completed, reminds us that this becomes a more pressing point as we approach the modern day; as the day on which not a single survivor, resistor, perpetrator, bystander or collaborator is left to tell us their story first-hand is fast approaching.[41]

In the face of this other absence, the following sentiment from Hilda Schiff becomes all the more important. Schiff begins the editor's introduction to her anthology *Holocaust Poetry* with the statement that 'the Holocaust was a unique epoch in the experience of mankind'.[42] The poems in the collection are, she writes, 'a fundamental aid to historical understanding' and as with any literature of a period, they are an 'integral part of that period', allowing us 'to understand historical events and experiences better than the bare facts alone can do because they enable us to absorb them inwardly. In involving ourselves in the authentic literature of the Holocaust, we come as close as we can to entering psychologically into those unique events as they were actually felt by those individuals who experienced them'.[43] Of course it would be a horrendous undertaking to truly experience the feeling of the Holocaust's events personally; we nonetheless strive for something like an empathic understanding.

Rightly so, the Holocaust remains an emotive and powerful issue, and in speculative fiction representations there remains the risk of trivializing the atrocity. This risk is, however, no greater than that faced by realist fiction and this book has provided a rebuttal to any accusation that speculative fiction narratives are somehow intrinsically less serious, more playful, or have a lower capacity for dealing with difficult and complex issues. Nonetheless, because of the particular tools and tropes available to the author of speculative fiction, there may be the temptation to provide some manner of closure or redemption which jars uncomfortably with the Holocaust narrative, neither constructively critiquing it nor complying with it. The use of magic to rescue camp prisoners in *Magicians of Night* without serious consequence or thought of implications, for example. However, again this is a risk no more applicable than the dangers mimetic fiction faces in over-sentimentalizing the Holocaust, or over-sensationalizing the evil of individual perpetrators, and so on.

While I have endeavoured in these pages to give a wide overview of the multiplicity of speculative fiction works which have engaged with the Holocaust I have not been comprehensive in my survey. There remains much work to be done, not the least on the texts which originate in languages other than English. Nonetheless in this book I have attempted to demonstrate that speculative fiction in its alternative approach to the Holocaust, less burdened by the critical discourses associated with realism, brings a much-needed diversity to the literature of trauma and genocide. A process of unravelling the problem of having a surfeit of memory (a symptom of a culture saturated with imagery) while simultaneously being denied direct access to that memory.[44] While largely unrecognized as a set by scholars in these fields, these texts provide a vital modification of existing paradigms enabling a reinvigoration of existing narratives (and a reorganization – potentially bringing undernourished narratives such as those of women or homosexuals closer to the fore), ensuring the narratives of the Holocaust remain active and fluid rather than ossified within history books. Susan Sontag expressed similar concerns with relation to photography, writing about a developing 'pseudofamiliarity with the horrible [which] reinforces alienation, making one less able to react in real life', as repetition of images and material receive diminishing returns of shock from the audience.[45]

The Otherness of the Holocaust is, at its root, the Otherness of trauma. Indeed, as Ruth Leys writes, the Holocaust contributes vastly to our understanding of trauma, while in turn it benefits from an improved awareness of conditions such as post-traumatic stress disorder, meaning that 'the Holocaust now appears, retroactively so to speak ... to have been *the* crucial trauma of the century'.[46] Some commentators, as already shown, would argue that due to its scale, extremity, intention and results, the Holocaust is exceptional versus all other traumas, even other genocides, and thus is incomparable to them. Many of the fictions I've discussed have the effect of to some degree repudiating this; they reinsert the Holocaust into a chronology of human trauma and genocide, placing it alongside other atrocities fictional or historical, personal or global, implicitly or explicitly, inviting comparative examinations which have the effect of making the event remarkable but comparable.

The danger of considering the Holocaust as trauma is expressed by Robert Eaglestone who worries that 'if it is invoked with all the rest of the analytical and therapeutic tools, trauma theory will overcode the accounts of the Holocaust with a discourse of healing analysis or therapy, and so pass over both the epistemological and ethical impossibility of comprehending the survivors' testimony by seeming to grasp and resolve it.'[47] Attempts to 'resolve' the Holocaust is particularly troubling were it to come from, as those in the book, a collection of Anglo-American writers, many of whom are not Jewish and have no direct connection to the genocide. Eaglestone's concerns are powerful and valid, however they play little role here. As we have seen, speculative fiction commonly does not seek to resolve the trauma of the Holocaust because it does not attempt to 'grasp' it. It makes no overtures to an accurate representation, and though it may strive for something approaching realism within its non-realist world, the rejection of the real world thus renders impossible any attempt to apply any sort of 'healing analysis' to actual survivors or employ 'therapeutic tools' on the historical Holocaust.

Yet, I do not argue that speculative fiction is somehow better for conveying the trauma of the Holocaust than more realist modes of fiction. Rather I have tried to demonstrate that speculative fiction offers a complementary method of interpretation, one which allows us to approach the problem of Holocaust representation from a different direction, providing new ways of speaking about silence, and alternate approaches to giving voice to the voiceless. Speculative fiction does not decode the uninterpretable elements of traumatic experience, rather it offers new insights while maintaining its Otherness. I do, however, strongly argue that these texts are as deserving of critical attention and appreciation as anything from the realist canon of Holocaust fiction and would suggest that excluding them has less to do with preserving the sanctity of the genocide and more to do with a genre-snobbery that demeans the subject material far more than the manner in which it is handled in the texts referenced in this book. If there is value in the literature of trauma because of its effect upon the reader, a generating of empathy and understanding in an attempt to bring us closer empathically to the victims of trauma and genocide, then I suggest that all of the tools of literature should be employed in this effort, not merely those that are mimetic or realist, nor just those considered 'literary'.

Notes

Introduction: Fictionalizing the Holocaust

1. Alvin H. Rosenfeld, *A Double Dying: Reflections on Holocaust Literature* (Indianapolis: Indiana University Press, 1988), 12.
2. Elie Wiesel, 'The Holocaust as Literary Inspiration', in *Dimensions of the Holocaust*, ed. Elie Wiesel et al. (Evanston, IL: Northwestern University Press, 1977), 5–19.
3. Robert, Eaglestone, *The Holocaust and the Postmodern* (Oxford: Oxford University Press, 2009), 2.
4. Veronica Hollinger, 'Cybernetic Deconstructions: Cyberpunk and Postmodernism', in *Science Fiction Criticism: An Anthology of Essential Writings*, ed. Rob Latham (London: Bloomsbury, 2017), 43.
5. Peter Novick, *The Holocaust and Collective Memory* (London: Bloomsbury, 2000), 2.
6. Caroline Sharples and Olaf Jensen, 'Introduction', in *Britain and the Holocaust: Remembering and Representing War and Genocide*, ed. Caroline Sharples and Olaf Jensen (Houndmills: Palgrave, 2013), 2. Emphasis in original.
7. The influence of writers outside of the Anglo-American sphere cannot be discounted, not least the likes of Jorge Luis Borges or Franz Kafka, but also of course the survivors themselves who often published first in their native languages.
8. Harold Bloom, 'Introduction', in *Literature of the Holocaust*, ed. Harold Bloom (Broomall, PA: Chelsea House, 2004), 1.
9. Rosenfeld, *A Double Dying*, 8.
10. Elie Wiesel, 'Why I Write', in *From the Kingdom of Mercy* (New York: Summit, 1990), 9.
11. Saul Friedländer, *Reflections of Nazism: An Essay on Kitsch and Death*, trans. Thomas Weyr (New York: Harper & Row, 1984), 80–1. Emphasis mine.
12. Adorno, Theodor W., 'Culture, Criticism and Society', in *Prisms*, trans. Samuel Weber and Shierry Weber (Cambridge, MA: MIT Press, 1981), 34.
13. Raul Hilberg, Cynthia Ozick, Aharon Appelfeld, and Saul Friedländer, 'Roundtable Discussion', in *Writing and the Holocaust*, ed. Berel Lang (New York: Holmes & Meier, 1988), 284.
14. Ruth Franklin, *A Thousand Darknesses: Lies and Truth in Holocaust Fiction* (Oxford: Oxford University Press, 2011), 19.

15 See: *Negative Dialectics* (1966).
16 Bloom, 'Introduction', 1.
17 Paul Celan, 'Speech on the Occasion of Receiving the Literature Prize of the Free Hanseatic City of Bremen', in *Collected Prose*, trans. Rosmarie Waldrop (Riverdale-on-Hudson, NY: The Sheep Meadow Press, 1986), 34.
18 Jean-François Lyotard, *The Differend: Phrases in Dispute*, trans. Georges Van Den Abbeele (Minneapolis: University of Minnesota Press, 1998), 57.
19 Lyotard, *The Differend*, 93. In response to Lyotard's tool-destroying earthquake analogy, Geoffrey Hartman insists that 'the after-shocks *are* measureable; we are deep into the process of creating new instruments to record and express what happened'. Geoffrey H. Hartman, *The Longest Shadow: In the Aftermath of the Holocaust* (Bloomington, 1996), 1.
20 George Steiner, 'Preface', in *Language and Silence: Essays on Language, Literature, and the Inhuman* (Harmondsworth: Peregrine, 1979), 15.
21 James T. Fussell, 'A Crime Without A Name', *Prevent Genocide International*, accessed 1 May 2016, http://www.preventgenocide.org/genocide/crimewithoutaname.htm.
22 Adam Jones, *Genocide: A Comprehensive Introduction*, 2nd edn (London: Routledge, 2011), 8–15. The etymology of 'Holocaust' comes from the Ancient Greek *holokauston*, meaning 'whole burnt', though it earns its capitalization through its association with the genocide in Europe at the hands of the Nazis, though not without controversy or debate. For an excellent overview of the history of the naming of the Holocaust, *Churbn*, or *Sho'ah*, and the associated debates see: 'Names of the Holocaust: Meaning and Consequences', chapter five of James Young, *Writing and Rewriting the Holocaust* (Bloomington: Indiana University Press, 1988), 83–98.
23 Berel Lang, 'Holocaust Genres and the Turn to History', in *The Holocaust and the Text: Speaking the Unspeakable*, ed. Andrew Leak and George Paizis (London: Palgrave, 2000), 18. Emphasis in original.
24 Berel Lang, 'Introduction', in *Writing and the Holocaust*, ed. Berel Lang (New York: Holmes & Meier, 1988), 3. Emphasis in original.
25 Raul Hilberg, 'I Was Not There', in *Writing and the Holocaust*, ed. Berel Lang (New York: Holmes & Meier, 1988), 17.
26 Friedländer, *Reflections of Nazism*, 93.
27 Novick, *The Holocaust and Collective Memory*, 333.
28 See: Steven T. Katz, *The Holocaust in Historical Context, Volume 1: The Holocaust and Mass Death before the Modern Age* (Oxford: Oxford University Press, 1994).
29 The roots of the *Porajmos* run almost as deeply as those of the Holocaust. For example in 1937 Heinrich Himmler published a polemic called 'On Combating the Gypsy Plague'. See: Ian Hancock, 'Responses to the Porrajmos: The Romani

Holocaust', in *Is the Holocaust Unique? Perspectives of Comparative Genocide*, ed. Alan S. Rosenbaum (Cumnor Hill: Westview, 1996), 39–64.

30 Isabel Fonseca, *Bury Me Standing: The Gypsies and their Journey* (London: Vintage, 2006), 274.

31 Although it's worth noting that even the notion of Jewishness in this context is not a simple definition as the victims of the Holocaust included those who fit the Nazi's definitions of 'Jew' rather than whether individuals personally identified as such, or indeed would have been identifiable as such by other Jews. Jean Améry is one well-known case in point. Améry (1912–1978), born Hanns Chaim Mayer, was half-Jewish, but on his father's side, excluding him from orthodox matrilineality, he was raised in the Catholic faith of his mother. See: Irène Heidelberger-Leonard, *The Philosopher of Auschwitz: Jean Améry and Living with the Holocaust* (London: I.B. Tauris, 2000).

32 Timothy Snyder, *Black Earth: The Holocaust as History and Warning* (London: Vintage, 2015), 232.

33 Michael Rothberg, *Traumatic Realism* (Minneapolis, MN: Minnesota University Press, 2000), 106.

34 Slavoj Žižek, *For They Know Not What They Do: Enjoyment as a Political Factor* (London: Verso, 1991), 272.

35 Here my argument bears some resemblance to Sidra DeKoven Ezrahi's proposal of Auschwitz as the 'terminus of a *centripetal* imagination, wholly transcendent and therefore wholly unrepresentable' seen in Borowski, Lanzmann and Wilkomirski, versus the '*centrifugal* narrative, on the other hand, [which] provides an infinity of mobile points of departure and access'. Ezrahi praises the latter for prompting 'a new moral discourse'. Though our selections of texts are radically different (there are no alternate histories in Ezrahi's essay on alternative history), there is a parallel in how I conceive of speculative fiction as providing alternative points of access. Sidra DeKovan Ezrahi, *Impossible Images: Contemporary Art after the Holocaust*, ed. Shelley Hornstein, Laura Levitt, and Laurence J. Silverstein (New York: New York University Press, 2003), 124, 122. Emphases in original.

36 Giorgio Agamben, *Remnants of Auschwitz: The Witness and the Archive*, trans. Daniel Heller-Roazen (New York: Zone Books, 1999), 12.

37 Rothberg, *Traumatic Realism*, 99–106.

38 Elie Wiesel, 'Art and the Holocaust: Trivializing Memory', trans. Iver Peterson, *The New York Times*, 11 June 1989, accessed 20 August 2016, http://www.nytimes.com/1989/06/11/movies/art-and-the-holocaust-trivializing-memory.html.

39 David Rousset, *The Other Kingdom*, trans. Ramon Guthrie (New York: Reynal & Hitchcock, 1947), 40.

40 Rousset, *The Other Kingdom*, 72, 172.

41 The evocation of Jarry's proto-surreal *Ubu Roi* (1896) and particularly the works of Kafka is echoed by later writers on the Holocaust. Harold Bloom refers to Kafka's 'uncanny prophecies', while George Steiner asserts that 'Kafka heard the name Buchenwald in the word *birchwood*'. Bloom, 'Introduction', 1; George Steiner, 'Silence and the Poet', in *Language and Silence: Essays on Language, Literature, and the Inhuman* (Harmondsworth: Peregrine, 1979), 72. Langer points out that Steiner makes a strange oversight as 'Buchenwald' literally translates to 'beech wood'. 'He may have been thinking of Birkenau (Birken = birch trees)'. Lawrence L. Langer, *The Holocaust and the Literary Imagination* (New Haven: Yale University Press, 1975), 18. Although it is possible Steiner is himself making reference to, or recalling, Rousset.

42 Kingsley Amis, *New Maps of Hell* (London: Four Square, 1963), 116.

43 Darko Suvin, *Metamorphoses of Science Fiction: On the Poetics and History of a Literary Genre*, ed. Gerry Canavan (Bern: Peter Lang, 2016), 15.

44 Bertolt Brecht, 'A Short Organum for the Theatre', in *Brecht on Theatre: The Development of an Aesthetic*, trans. John Willett (London: Methuen, 1964), 192.

45 Gerry Canavan, 'The Suvin Effect', in Darko Suvin, *Metamorphoses of Science Fiction: On the Poetics and History of a Literary Genre*, ed. Gerry Canavan (Bern: Peter Lang, 2016), xviii.

46 Ray Bradbury, 'Day After Tomorrow: Why Science Fiction?' *The Nation*, 2 May 1953, 367.

47 Seo-Young Chu, *Do Metaphors Dream of Literal Sheep: A Science-Fictional Theory of Representation* (Cambridge: Harvard University Press, 2010), 74.

48 Paradoxically, while alternate history comes to us through utopian writing, Andrew Milner suggests that science fiction (at least in the form of the nineteenth-century novel) 'insofar as it had been an adaptation of any pre-existing form' adapted 'not so much the utopia as the *historical novel*'. Andrew Milner, 'Utopia and Science Fiction Revisited', in *Red Planets: Marxism and Science Fiction*, ed. Mark Bould and China Miéville (London: Pluto Press, 2009), 224. Emphasis mine.

49 Suvin, *Metamorphoses of Science Fiction*, 79.

50 Katz, *The Holocaust in Historical Context*, 3.

51 Zoë Vania Waxman, *Writing the Holocaust: Identity, Testimony, Representation* (Oxford: Oxford University Press, 2006), 186.

52 Szymon Laks, *Music of Another World*, trans. Chester A. Kisiel (Evanston, IL: Northwestern University Press, 1989), 7.

53 See: Daniel H. Magilow, Elizabeth Bridges, and Kristin T. Vander Lugt, eds., *Nazisploitation!: The Nazi Image in Low-Brow Cinema and Culture* (London: Continuum, 2012).

Chapter 1

1. Adolf Hitler, *Mein Kampf*, trans. Ralph Manheim (London: Hutchinson, 1990), 283.
2. Hitler, *Mein Kampf*, 307.
3. David Aaronovitch, *Voodoo Histories: How Conspiracy Theory Has Shaped Modern History* (London: Vintage, 2010), 40.
4. Primo Levi, *The Drowned and the Saved*, trans. Raymond Rosenthal (London: Abacus, 2010), 145.
5. Levi, *The Drowned and the Saved*, 147.
6. Hitler, *Mein Kampf*, 302.
7. Katharine Burdekin, *Swastika Night* (New York: Feminist Press, 1985), 72.
8. Burdekin, *Swastika Night*, 66.
9. James J. Barnes and Patience P. Barnes, *Hitler's Mein Kampf in Britain and America: A Publishing History 1930–39* (Cambridge: Cambridge University Press, 1980), 1.
10. Chris Morgan notes that 'the first major work of this period was *The Gas War of 1940* by "Miles" (1931), which included some accurate forecasts – except, that is, for the gas'. Chris Morgan, *The Shapes of Futures Past: The Story of Prediction* (Exeter: Webb and Bower, 1980), 71.
11. Burdekin, *Swastika Night*, 70.
12. Burdekin, *Swastika Night*, 182.
13. Daphne Patai, 'Introduction', in Katharine Burdekin, *Swastika Night* (New York: Feminist Press, 1985), v.
14. Burdekin, *Swastika Night*, 12.
15. Burdekin, *Swastika Night*, 70.
16. Gavriel D. Rosenfeld, *The World Hitler Never Made* (Cambridge: Cambridge University Press, 2005), 37.
17. No mention is made of others selected for slaughter by the Nazis such as the Roma and Sinti, nor does it refer to how the Nazis treat other races in their global empire which presumably encompasses all of Africa and Western Asia, nor does Burdekin touch on the persecution of those with disabilities or homosexuals, indeed instead she extrapolates the homoeroticism inherent in Nazi fascism to create a normalization of paedophilic homosexuality.
18. Burdekin, *Swastika Night*, 157.
19. Primo Levi, *If This Is a Man*, trans. Stuart Woolf (London: Abacus, 2010), 37–8.
20. Carlo Pagetti describes Burdekin's positioning of women in the text as being akin to that of Swift's Yahoos. Carlo Pagetti, 'In the Year of Our Lord Hitler 720: Katharine Burdekin's *Swastika Night*', *Science Fiction Studies*, 52 (1990), 361.
21. Robert Crossley, 'Dystopian Nights', *Science Fiction Studies*, 14, no. 1 (1987), 93–8, 93.

22 Patai, 'Introduction', xii.
23 George Orwell, quoted in L. J. Hurst, 'Anywhere but Stoke Poges', *Vector*, 148 (1989), 14.
24 Note that while the methods of controlling history vary between the novels, they are consistent with the regimes that the authors were commentating on: the Nazis tried to destroy records and physical evidence of their atrocities, even before it was clear they would lose the war, while Stalin's soviet regime (the principle foundation of Orwell's state of Oceania) famously doctored documents and even photographs to remove evidence of people who had fallen out of favour such as Leon Trotsky or Nikolai Yezhov.
25 Andy Croft, 'World Without End Foisted Upon the Future – Some Antecedents of Nineteen Eighty-Four', in *Inside the Myth: Orwell, Views from the Left*, ed. Christopher Norris (London, 1984), 209.
26 Orwell commented on the rationing in 1944 quoting a pamphlet by Stanley Urwin, 'Publishing in Peace and War', which lists 22,000 tons of paper as the amount permitted to go to the publishing of books versus 250,000 tons for newspapers and 100,000 for the government's stationary office. He wrote that 'paper for books is so short that even the most hackneyed "classic" is liable to be out of print, many schools are short of textbooks, new writers get no chance to start and even established writers have to expect a gap of a year or two years between finishing a book and seeing it published'. George Orwell, 'As I Please', *Tribune*, 20 October 1944.
27 Douglas Brown and Christopher Serpell, *If Hitler Comes: A Cautionary Tale* (London: Faber and Faber, 2010), 9–10.
28 Brown and Serpell, *If Hitler Comes*, 7.
29 Brown and Serpell, *If Hitler Comes*, 91–3.
30 Collaboration remains a theme of some alternate history after the war. Notable examples include Len Deighton's *SS-GB* (1978) and Owen Sheers *Resistance* (2007), both narratives set in a United Kingdom occupied by Nazi Germany. The main character of Deighton's novel is a detective superintendent of the London Metropolitan Police who is attempting to balance his duty to keep citizens safe with his moral duty to resist the Nazis. In *The Resistance* a group of men leave their Welsh valley to join the resistance; the novel centres on the wives left behind and their relationships with the German soldiers who occupy the valley in the men's absence. Each of these texts challenges the simplified narratives of resistance and collaboration, recognizing the complexity of individuals' lived experiences.
31 Noël Coward, *The Letters of Noël Coward*, ed. Barry Day (London: Vintage, 2009), 506.

32 Michael Billington, 'Lifting the Curtain', *The Guardian*, 24 October 2007, accessed 20 February 2018, https://www.theguardian.com/stage/2007/oct/24/theatre1.
33 Noël Coward, *Peace in Our Time* (London: William Heinemann, 1947), 31–2.
34 W. A. Darlington, 'Review of *Peace in Our Time*', *Daily Telegraph*, 21 July 1947. Quoted in Rosenfeld, *The World Hitler Never Made*, 50.
35 Andrew Roberts, 'Andrew Roberts on "If Hitler Comes"', *Faber Finds*, accessed 20 August 2012, www.faber.co.uk/article/2009/11/if-hitler-comes-andrew-roberts-review/. Coward himself remarked in a letter to a friend in the previous year: 'If I had really cared about press notices, I would have shot myself in the Twenties.'
36 Coward, *The Letters of Noël Coward*, 530.
37 Quoted in Sheridan Morley, 'Introduction', in Noël Coward, *Collected Plays: Volume Seven* (London: Bloomsbury Methuen, 1999), xi.
38 Neil Levi and Michael Rothberg, 'Theory and the Holocaust', in *The Holocaust: Theoretical Readings*, ed. Neil Levi and Michael Rothberg (Edinburgh: Edinburgh University Press, 2003), 6.
39 Philippe Sands, 'Primo Levi's *If This Is a Man* at 70', *The Guardian*, 22 April 2017, accessed 20 February 2019, https://www.theguardian.com/books/2017/apr/22/primo-levi-auschwitz-if-this-is-a-man-memoir-70-years. The book re-entered print in 1958 and was translated into English, French and German in the following two years. Since then it has assumed its rightful place as an essential text of the twentieth century.
40 Translated as Liana Millu, *Smoke Over Birkenau*, trans. Lynne Sharon Schwartz. Schwartz's translation earned the book the PEN Renato Poggioli translation award in 1991.
41 Sarban, *The Sound of His Horn* (Floyd, VA: Black Curtain Press, 2013), 52.
42 John Wyndham, 'Roar of Rockets', *John o'London's Weekly*, 63 (2 April 1954), 333–4.
43 Quoted in David Ketterer, 'Introduction: A Ground-Breaking Cloned Nazi Thriller', in John Wyndham, *A Plan for Chaos* (Liverpool: Liverpool University Press, 2009).
44 Mark Valentine, *Time, A Falconer: A Study of Sarban* (Tartarus, 2010), 74.
45 Sarban, *The Sound of His Horn*, 92.
46 Sarban, *The Sound of His Horn*, 118.
47 Sarban, *The Sound of His Horn*, 56–7.
48 In just one such example, Jean Améry wrote of his experiences that his captors 'had tortured me and turned me into a bug, as dark powers had done to the protagonist of Kafka's *The Metamorphosis*'. See: Jean Améry, 'Resentments', in *The Holocaust: Theoretical Readings*, ed. Neil Levi and Michael Rothberg (Edinburgh: Edinburgh University Press, 2003), 36–44 (p. 37).
49 For more on the Holocaust represented in comics see: Glyn Morgan, 'Speaking the Unspeakable and Seeing the Unseeable: The Role of Fantastika in Visualizing the

Holocaust, or, More Than Just *Maus*', *The Luminary*, 6 (2015), http://www.lancaster.ac.uk/luminary/issue6/issue6article3.htm. For an examination of French comics in particular, see: Didier Pasamonik and Joël Kotek (eds.), *Shoah et Bande Dessinée: L'image au service de la mémoire* (Paris: Denoël Graphic, 2017), produced in association with the Mémorial de la Shoah in Paris.

50 Sarban, *The Sound of His Horn*, 81.
51 C. S. Forester, 'Introduction', in *The Nightmare* (Los Angeles: Pinnacle, 1979), vii.
52 'wandering, adj.'. OED Online. June 2013. Oxford University Press. 15 August 2013, accessed 13 July 2016, http://www.oed.com /view/Entry/225442?result=1&rskey= TkOHBl&.
53 William Wordsworth, 'Song for the Wandering Jew', in William Wordsworth and Samuel Taylor Coleridge, *Lyrical Ballads, 1798 and 1802*, ed. Fiona Stafford (Oxford: Oxford University Press, 2013), 284.
54 Alberto Manguel, 'The Exile's Library', *The Guardian*, 21 February 2009, accessed 24 August 2017, http://www.theguardian.com/books/2009/feb/21/wandering-jew-history).
55 Joseph Gaer, *The Legend of the Wandering Jew* (New York: Mentor, 1961), 152.
56 Michael Young, *The Trial of Adolf Hitler* (New York: Dutton, 1944), 151.
57 C. S. Forester, 'The Wandering Gentile', in *Nightmares* (Los Angeles: Pinnacle, 1979), 228.
58 Forester, 'The Wandering Gentile', 230.
59 Forester, 'The Wandering Gentile', 230.
60 Rosenfeld, *The World Hitler Never Made*, 208.
61 Forester, 'The Wandering Gentile', 233.
62 Forester, 'The Wandering Gentile', 237.
63 Forester, 'The Wandering Gentile', 237.
64 C. M. Kornbluth, 'Two Dooms', in *Hitler Victorious*, ed. Gregory Benford and Martin H. Greenberg (London: Grafton, 1988), 27.
65 Kornbluth, 'Two Dooms', 42.
66 David Cesarani, 'Challenging the "Myth of Silence": Postwar Response to the Destruction of European Jewry', in *After the Holocaust: Challenging the Myth of Silence*, ed. David Cesarani and Eric J. Sundquist (Abingdon: Routledge, 2012), 30.
67 There are of course outliers; Cesarani and Sundquist's collection contains essays detailing many and varied examples of Holocaust testimony, documentary and fiction in the immediate post-war era. This is in addition to well-known and well-publicized incidents such as the Nuremberg Trials themselves; the publication, translation and adaptation of Anne Frank's *Diary of a Young Girl* (published in Dutch in 1947, in English in 1952, adapted as a radio play in 1952, for stage in 1955,

with the first film adaptation in 1959) is another example, as is the publication in French of Elie Wiesel's own *Night* (Fr. *La Nuit*, 1958; English translation in 1960), although this was itself a heavily adapted version of a little known earlier text published in Yiddish, *Un di Velt Hot Geshvign* (1956).

68 Roskies and Diamant's four phases are 'Wartime Writing, 1938–45'; 'Communal Memory, 1945–60'; 'Provisional Memory, 1960–85'; and 'Authorized Memory, 1985–Present'. The events which mark these changes for them are the Eichmann Trial in 1961 and the Bitburg controversy in 1985. See: Roskies and Diamant, *Holocaust Literature*.

69 Rosenfeld, *The World Hitler Never Made*, 46.

70 Orville Prescott, 'Book of the Times', *The New York Times*, 17 October 1960, 27.

71 Deborah Lipstadt, 'America and the Memory of the Holocaust', *Modern Judaism* 16, no. 3 (1996), 204.

72 Harry J. Stern, '5 Million Jews Would Have Perished If Hitler Had Won War, Shirer Says', *The Canadian Jewish Chronicle*, 15 December 1961, 9.

73 William L. Shirer, 'If Hitler Had Won World War II', *Look*, 25, no. 26 (1961), 28–9. Emphasis in original.

74 Shirer, 'If Hitler Had Won World War II', 29.

75 Shirer, 'If Hitler Had Won World War II', 42.

76 As an indication of the raw emotion this event touched upon, the BBC reported that at the military ceremony 'a British band played the German national anthem – better known as "Deutschland ueber Alles". A French band had refused to play the music because of its Nazi connotations'. BBC News, 'On This Day: 1955: West Germany Accepted into Nato', *BBC News*, 9 May 2008, accessed 20 August 2016, http://news.bbc.co.uk/onthisday/hi/dates/stories/may/9/newsid_2519000/2519979.stm.

77 Novick, *The Holocaust and Collective Memory*, 1–2.

78 S. Lillian Kremer, *Witness Through the Imagination: Jewish American Holocaust Literature* (Detroit: Wayne State University Press, 1989), 16.

79 Leslie Epstein, 'Writing about the Holocaust', in *Writing and the Holocaust*, ed. Berel Lang (New York: Holmes & Meier, 1988), 261. Emphasis in original.

Chapter 2

1 Genocide abroad and in colonies before the Holocaust was considerably less shocking to European and American sensibilities, and the half-hearted efforts to prevent genocide subsequently in Cambodia, Rwanda, the Congo and elsewhere suggest too little has changed. For more on colonial genocides

see: David Olusoga and Casper Erichsen, *The Kaiser's Holocaust: Germany's Forgotten Genocide and the Colonial Roots of the Holocaust* (London: Faber & Faber, 2010) and Mike Davis, *Late Victorian Holocausts: El Niño Famines and the Making of the Third World* (London: Verso, 2017). An essential source for more general research on genocide, including both pre- and post-Holocaust, is Jones, *Genocide*.

2 An argument can be made that Harris's novel *Archangel* (1998) is a 'secret history' novel, a related genre to alternate history. Secret histories are narratives which are written around established historical facts, not directly contradicting them (although often giving alternative explanations for them), and so are less sustained exercises in speculative fictionalization than the alternate history or science fiction novel which requires the construction of entire new worlds.

3 Walter Benjamin, 'On the Concept of History', in *Walter Benjamin Selected Writings, Volume 4, 1938–1940*, ed. Howard Eiland and Michael W. Jennings, trans. Edmund Jephcott et al. (Cambridge, MA: Harvard University Press, 2003), 391.

4 Kathleen Singles, *Alternate History: Playing with Contingency and Necessity* (Berlin: De Gruyter, 2013), 148.

5 George Orwell, *Nineteen Eighty-Four* (London: Penguin, 2004), 280.

6 Philip K. Dick, *The Man in the High Castle* (London: Penguin Classics, 2001), 66.

7 Dick, *The Man in the High Castle*, 69.

8 Pamela Sargent, 'Science Fiction, Historical Fiction, and Alternate History', *Bulletin of Science Fiction Writers of America* (Fall, 1995), 5.

9 Dick, *The Man in the High Castle*, 67.

10 Dick, *The Man in the High Castle*, 17.

11 Dick, *The Man in the High Castle*, 29.

12 Dick, *The Man in the High Castle*, 19.

13 Guy Saville, 'A is for Apocalypse Now', *AfrikaReichTrilogy*, 24 July 2011, accessed 1 September 2016, http://afrikareichtrilogy.blogspot.co.uk/2011/07/is-for-apocalypse-now.html.

14 Guy Saville, *The Afrika Reich* (London: Hodder & Stoughton, 2011), 13–14.

15 Dick, *The Man in the High Castle*, 217.

16 Dick, *The Man in the High Castle*, 222–3.

17 Dick, *The Man in the High Castle*, 223.

18 Philip K. Dick, *The Exegesis of Philip K. Dick*, ed. Pamela Jackson and Jonathan Lethem (New York: Houghton Mifflin Harcourt, 2011), 510. Ellipsis in original.

19 Howard Zinn, *A People's History of the United States* (New York: Harper Perennial, 2015), 416; Hugh Brogan, *The Penguin History of the USA*, 2nd edn (New York: Penguin, 1999), 568.

20 Howard Canaan, 'Metafiction and the Gnostic Quest in *The Man in the High Castle*: Dick's Alternate History Classic after Four Decades', in *Classic and

Iconoclastic Alternate History Science Fiction, ed. Edgar L. Chapman and Carl B. Yorke (Lewiston, NY: Edwin Mellen Press, 2003), 104.

21 Dick, *The Man in the High Castle*, 247.
22 ' … and I've been sorry ever since because when it came time to resolve the novel at the end, the *I Ching* didn't know what to do. It got me through most of the book. Every time they cast a hexagram I actually cast four of them and got something and assigned it to them and they proceeded on the basis of the advice given. But then when it came time to close down the novel the *I Ching* had no more to say. And so there's no real ending on it. I like to regard it as an open ending. It will segue into a sequel sometime.' Philip K. Dick and Mike Hodel, 'Hour 25: A Talk with Philip K. Dick', *Philip K. Dick Fans*, accessed 29 September 2016 (http://www.philipkdickfans.com/literary-criticism/interviews/hour-25-a-talk-with-philip-k-dick/).
23 Philip K. Dick, 'Biographical Material on Hawthorne Abendsen', in *The Shifting Realities of Philip K. Dick: Selected Literary and Philosophical Writings*, ed. Lawrence Sutin (New York: Vintage, 1995), 118. The piece forms part of fragments of a sequel to *The Man in the High Castle* which Dick never completed.
24 'That was me. That was me. Horrible, he said, horrible. Evil is like cement. Evil is a pun, concrete cement, you see. What he's thinking, his thoughts are all jumbled up.' Dick and Hodel, 'Hour 25'.
25 Dick, *The Man in the High Castle*, 238.
26 John Rieder, 'The Metafictive World of *The Man in the High Castle*: Hermeneutics, Ethics, and Political Ideology', *Science Fiction Studies*, 15, no. 2 (1988), 217.
27 Philip K. Dick, 'Naziism and the High Castle', in *The Shifting Realities of Philip K. Dick: Selected Literary and Philosophical Writings*, ed. Lawrence Sutin (New York: Vintage, 1995), 118. The essay was originally published in the science fiction fanzine *Niekas* in 1964 in response to a review of *The Man in the High Castle* by Poul Anderson that had been printed in an earlier issue.
28 Dick and Hodel, 'Hour 25'.
29 Karen Hellekson, *The Alternate History: Refiguring Historical Time* (Kent, OH: The Kent State University Press, 2001), 70.
30 Dick, *The Man in the High Castle*, 45–6.
31 Canaan, 'Metafiction and the Gnostic Quest in *The Man in the High Castle*', 101.
32 Laks, *Music of Another World*, 79.
33 Robert Harris, *Fatherland* (London: Arrow, 1993), 5.
34 Harris, *Fatherland*, 11.
35 The similarities between March/Charlie and Winston/Julia do not end at catalysing. For instance, one of their first meaningful rendezvous is in Großer Tiergarten because 'even the Gestapo had yet to devise a means of bugging a park' (Harris, *Fatherland*, 169), an echo of the first private meeting in Orwell's novel: in the countryside outside of the city, amid a grove of 'small ashes … none of them

thicker than one's wrist. ... nothing big enough to hide a mike in' (Orwell, *Nineteen Eighty-Four*, 125). It is unusual to find a modern dystopia which has not been influenced on some level by Orwell, but for Harris *Nineteen Eighty-Four* seems to have been a particularly dominant touchstone.

36 Harris, *Fatherland*, 209. The reference to 'special trains' masking the true numbers of the dead is itself a clear reference to the Holocaust.
37 Harris, *Fatherland*, 209–10.
38 Harris, *Fatherland*, 38.
39 Harris, *Fatherland*, 211–12.
40 Steve Blankenship, 'The Aftermath of the Katyn Massacre: Silent as the Grave', *World History Bulletin*, 27, no. 1 (2001), 64.
41 Dariusz Tołczyk, 'Katyn: The Long Cover-Up', *New Criterion*, 28, no. 9 (2010), 6.
42 Using the Katyn Forest Massacre as his only named atrocity also allows Harris to indirectly invoke the unpalatable memory of the blind eye British and American leaders had to undertake when dealing with Stalin as an ally throughout the Second World War but especially after the massacre came to light in 1943.
43 Harris, *Fatherland*, 38.
44 M. Keith Booker, *Dystopian Literature: A Theory and Research Guide* (Westport, CT: Greenwood Press, 1994), 167–8.
45 Harris, *Fatherland*, 385–6.
46 Jerome de Groot, *The Historical Novel*, The New Critical Idiom (Abingdon: Routledge, 2010), 172.
47 Sara Anelli, 'Counterfactual Holocausts: Robert Harris' *Fatherland* and Martin Amis' *Time's Arrow*', *Textus*, 20 (2007), 419.
48 Harris, *Fatherland*, 208.
49 Harris, *Fatherland*, 327.
50 George Winthrop-Young, 'The Third Reich in Alternate History: Aspects of a Genre-Specific Depiction of Nazi Culture', *The Journal of Popular Culture*, 39, no. 5 (2006), 894.
51 Hellekson, *The Alternate History*, 5.
52 Rosenfeld, *The World Hitler Never Made*, 83.
53 Rosenfeld, *The World Hitler Never Made*, 83.
54 Harris, *Fatherland*, 95. Emphasis in original.
55 Harris, *Fatherland*, 364.
56 Harris, *Fatherland*, 382. Ellipsis in original.
57 Timoth Melley, *Empire of Conspiracy: The Culture of Paranoia in Postwar America* (Ithaca, NY: Cornell University Press, 2000), 150.
58 John Scaggs, *Crime Fiction*, The New Critical Idiom (Abingdon: Routledge, 2008), 120.

59 Aaronovitch, *Voodoo Histories*, 342. Hoaxes can be considered a form of conspiracy and Harris is certainly familiar with those, having written *Selling Hitler* (1986) about the infamous Hitler diary hoax.
60 Michael Markun, *Culture of Conspiracy: Apocalyptic Visions in Contemporary America* (Berkeley: University of California Press, 2003), 4.
61 Melley, *Empire of Conspiracy*, 137.
62 Harris, *Fatherland*, 201–2.
63 Harris, *Fatherland*, 108.
64 Harris, *Fatherland*, 46, 198.
65 Robert Harris et al., 'Voices of Europe: Need for Germany Far Outweighs Any Fears', *The New York Times*, 29 September 1992, accessed 28 August 2014, http://www.nytimes.com/1992/09/29/world/voices-of-europe-need-for-germany-far-outweighs-any-fears.html.
66 Amy Walker, 'Do Mention the War: The Politicians Comparing Brexit to WWII', *The Guardian*, 4 February 2019, accessed 10 March 2019, https://www.theguardian.com/politics/2019/feb/04/do-mention-the-war-the-politicians-comparing-brexit-to-wwii.
67 Declan Conlon, 'Obsession with World War Played Role in Brexit, Says Harris', *The Irish Times*, 29 September 2017, accessed 10 March 2019, https://www.irishtimes.com/news/politics/obsession-with-world-war-played-role-in-brexit-says-harris-1.3238736.
68 Stephen Fry, *Making History* (London: Arrow, 2004), 11.
69 Fry, *Making History*, 89.
70 Fry, *Making History*, 91.
71 Fry, *Making History*, 89.
72 Fry, *Making History*, 8.
73 Peter Osbourne, 'Small-Scale Victories, Large-Scale Defeats: Walter Benjamin's Politics of Time', in *Walter Benjamin's Philosophy: Destruction and Experience*, ed. Andrew Benjamin and Peter Osbourne (London: Routledge, 1994), 90.
74 Niall Ferguson, 'Virtual History: Towards a "Chaotic" Theory of the Past', in *Virtual Histories: Alternatives and Counterfactuals*, ed. Niall Ferguson (London: Picador, 1997), 3.
75 Andrew Roberts, 'Introduction', in *What Might Have Been*, ed. Andrew Roberts (London: Phoenix, 2005), 9.
76 Richard J. Evans, *Altered Pasts: Counterfactuals in History* (London: Little Brown, 2013), 128.
77 Evans, *Altered Pasts*, 129.
78 Fry, *Making History*, 52.
79 Fry, *Making History*, 53.

80 The university is actually such a well-known centre for scientific animal testing that they dedicate some pages on their website to its explanation and justification: 'Animal Research', *University of Cambridge*, accessed 10 March 2019 https://www.cam.ac.uk/research/research-at-cambridge/animal-research.
81 Fry, *Making History*, 212.
82 Fry, *Making History*, 53.
83 Fry, *Making History*, 188. Emphasis in the original.
84 Perhaps suggesting that alternate history, the blending of history with science fiction in the form of literature, is the best of all.
85 Fry, *Making History*, 147.
86 Fry, *Making History*, 153.
87 Fry, *Making History*, 381.
88 Fry, *Making History*, 380.
89 Fry, *Making History*, 356–5.
90 Fry, *Making History*, 381–6.
91 All quotes: Fry, *Making History*, 361–2.
92 Fry, *Making History*, 384.
93 Fry, *Making History*, 384.
94 Fry, *Making History*, 385.
95 Fry, *Making History*, 574.
96 Rosenfeld, *The World Hitler Never Made*, 303.
97 Zygmunt Bauman, *Modernity and the Holocaust* (Ithaca, NY: Cornell University Press, 1989), 7.
98 Goldhagen, *Hitler's Willing Executioners*, chapter three.
99 Goldhagen, *Hitler's Willing Executioners*, 419.
100 Lilian Friedberg, 'Dare to Compare: Americanizing the Holocaust', in *The Holocaust: Theoretical Readings*, ed. Neil Levi and Michael Rothberg (Edinburgh: Edinburgh University Press, 2003), 469.
101 In part, Goldhagen's book is a response to this instinct within history; his work begins as a rebuttal of the idea that the exterminatory actions of the Holocaust can only be blamed on the SS and not the more general Wehrmacht.
102 Hellekson, *The Alternate History*, 16.
103 Hellekson, *The Alternate History*, 33.
104 Michiko Kakutani, 'Books of the Times: Plotting to Erase Hitler from History', *New York Times*, 21 April 1998, accessed 28 September 2016, http://www.nytimes.com/1998/04/21/books/books-of-the-times-plotting-to-erase-hitler-from-history.html.
105 Stephen Fry, 'Interview: Stephen Fry', *AV Club*, 22 September 2004, accessed 15 July 2015, http://www.avclub.com/article/stephen-fry-13891.

106 Fry, 'Interview'.
107 Dominick LaCapra, 'Representing the Holocaust: Reflections on the Historians' Debate', in *Probing the Limits of Representation: Nazism and the 'Final Solution'*, ed. Saul Friedlander (Cambridge, MA: Harvard University Press, 1992), 111.
108 Susan Neiman, *Evil in Modern Thought: An Alternative History of Philosophy* (Princeton: Princeton University Press, 2015), 252.

Chapter 3

1 See: Gerald Steinacher, *Nazis on the Run: How Hitler's Henchmen Fled Justice* (Oxford: Oxford University Press, 2011).
2 Michael R. Beschloss, *The Conquerors: Roosevelt, Truman and the Destruction of Hitler's Germany, 1941–1945* (New York: Simon & Schuster, 2002), 256.
3 The title of this chapter borrows of course from Primo Levi's *The Drowned and the Saved*.
4 Simon Wiesenthal, *The Murderers Among Us: The Simon Wiesenthal Memoirs* (New York: McGraw Hill, 1967), 86–7.
5 ODESSA, or *Organisation der ehemaligen SS-Angehörigen* (Organisation of former SS members), was a hypothesized group who may have been helping Nazis flee to and maintain new identities in new locations. While some groups did aid Nazis in their flight, there is no evidence of such a secret underground network existing. Nonetheless the term has been popularized by writers of fiction, notably Frederick Forsyth in his bestselling thriller *The Odessa File* (1972).
6 *Raiders of the Lost Ark*, dir. Steven Spielberg (Paramount Pictures, 1981). Although, at least *Raiders of the Lost Ark* also alludes to the murky practices of the US government as they shut out the hero at the film's conclusion telling him the Ark is no longer his concern and will instead be studied by anonymous 'top men' (Although the final shot depicting the Ark being deposited in a warehouse of identical-looking pine boxes suggests a tendency towards inefficient bureaucracy which somewhat tempers the audience's distrust of the US government, if not Jones's). Doctor Jones's next encounter with the Nazis, in *The Last Crusade*, dir. Steven Spielberg (Paramount Pictures, 1989), set in 1938 features Nazis who are even more archetypal in their pursuit of occult power (in this case the Holy Grail); they even have an Austrian castle as a base of operations. At the film's climax, Jones and his friends once more foil the Nazis and literally ride off into the sunset. Earlier in the film we see a book burning in Berlin, which even features a brief appearance of Hitler himself, but we are discouraged from dwelling too long on

the implications of this scene, and certainly are not meant to consider what other crimes the Nazis are conducting in 1938 (referred to as 'The Fateful Year') while the hero makes his triumphant exit.

7 Max Radin, *The Day of Reckoning* (New York: Knopf, 1943); Young, *The Trial of Adolf Hitler*.
8 Rosenfeld, *The World Hitler Never Made*, 345.
9 Jesse Bier, Letter from Bier to Gavriel D. Rosenfeld, 10 August 2001. Quoted in Rosenfeld, *The World Hitler Never Made*, 479. Ellipsis in original.
10 Michael Butter, *The Epitome of Evil: Hitler in American Fiction 1939–2002* (New York: Palgrave, 2009), 122–30.
11 Barry Malzberg, 'Hitler at Nuremberg', in *By Any Other Fame*, ed. Mike Resnick and Martin Greenberg (New York: Daw, 1994), 296–302.
12 David Charnay, *Operation Lucifer: The Chase, Capture, and Trial of Adolf Hitler* (Calabasas, CA: Squire General Limited, 2001).
13 Ira Levin, *The Boys from Brazil* (London: Corsair, 2011), 223.
14 Levin, *The Boys from Brazil*, 229.
15 Levin, *The Boys from Brazil*, 237–8.
16 Levin, *The Boys from Brazil*, 251.
17 Levin, *The Boys from Brazil*, 252. Emphasis in original.
18 Levin, *The Boys from Brazil*, 252.
19 Levin, *The Boys from Brazil*, 254–5.
20 Israeli Attorney General Gideon Hausner asked the question repeatedly in his examination of survivors as part of the Eichmann Trial. David G. Roskies and Naomi Diamant, *Holocaust Literature: A History and Guide* (Waltham, MA: Brandeis University Press, 2012), 128.
21 Levi, *The Drowned and the Saved*, 122. See: pages 122–36, particularly 128–31 in which Levi specifically addresses the question 'why didn't you rebel?'
22 Levin, *The Boys from Brazil*, 258.
23 Butter, *The Epitome of Evil*, 14.
24 Butter, *The Epitome of Evil*, 101.
25 Gavriel D. Rosenfeld, *Hi Hitler!* (Cambridge: Cambridge University Press, 2015), 239.
26 George Steiner, *The Portage to San Cristobal of A.H.* (New York: Simon and Schuster, 1981), 7.
27 Lovecraft makes reference to a 'Him Who is not to be Named' (see: 'The Whisper in Darkness', and others). Rowling's Voldemort is referred to by the moniker 'He Who Must Not Be Named' for much of the series (*Harry Potter*, 1997–2007). Voldemort himself is a Hitler-figure, Rowling readily adopting the language and methodology of fascism in his actions and those of his loyal 'Death Eaters'; in the

recent play *Harry Potter and the Cursed Child* (2016) an alternate world is created (a 'Voldemort Wins' take on the Hitler Wins trope) and 'mudblood death camps' for wizards of impure lineage, and 'the torture, the burning alive of those that oppose' Voldemort are mentioned (part two, III, iii, 184).

28 Steiner, *The Portage to San Cristobal of A.H.*, 44–6.
29 Efraim Sicher, 'The Burden of Memory', in *Breaking Crystal: Writing and Memory after Auschwitz*, ed. Efraim Sicher (Chicago: University of Illinois Press, 1998), 69.
30 Steiner, *The Portage to San Cristobal of A.H.*, 167–8.
31 Steiner, *The Portage to San Cristobal of A.H.*, 168. For Steiner's admiration of Solzhenitsyn see for example: George Steiner, 'In Exile Wherever He Goes', *The New York Times*, 1 March 1998, accessed 20 August 2016, https://www.nytimes.com/books/98/03/01/reviews/980301.01steinet.html in which he refers to him as 'not only the world's most famous writer but a spiritual guide, a prophet, an exemplar unrivalled since Voltaire or Tolstoy'.
32 Steiner, *The Portage to San Cristobal of A.H.*, 168.
33 Steiner, *The Portage to San Cristobal of A.H.*, 169.
34 Norman Finkelstein, *The Ritual of New Creation: Jewish Tradition and Contemporary Literature* (Albany: State University of New York Press, 1992), 115.
35 Steiner, *The Portage to San Cristobal of A.H.*, 169–70. Emphasis in original.
36 Rosenfeld, *The World Hitler Never Made*, 229.
37 Finkelstein, *The Ritual of New Creation*, 115–16.
38 Sicher, 'The Burden of Memory', 70.
39 Sicher, 'The Burden of Memory', gives extensive references and quotations detailing the controversy with commentators offering both criticism and defence of Steiner's novel. In particular see: pages 69–70.
40 Steiner, *The Portage to San Cristobal of A.H.*, 170.
41 Rosenfeld, *The World Hitler Never Made*, 229.
42 Steiner, *The Portage to San Cristobal of A.H.*, 229.
43 Steiner, *The Portage to San Cristobal of A.H.*, 96.
44 Steiner, *The Portage to San Cristobal of A.H.*, 65.
45 S. Lillian Kremer, *Witness through the Imagination*, 333–4.
46 Evans, *Altered Pasts*, 118.
47 Oskar Gröning was ninety-three when he was sentenced, in 2015, of facilitating mass murder. In 2017 Huber Zafke was ninety-six years old when charges against him were dropped as a result of his increasingly severe dementia. These examples form part of the group of cases which are generally called 'the last Nazi trials', a list of which can be found in the Jewish Virtual Library ('The Last Nazi Trials', accessed 14 March 2019, https://www.jewishvirtuallibrary.org/modern-nazi-trials). I point out the advanced ages of these individuals not to elicit sympathy or pass any sort

of judgement on the trials, but rather to underline that the era of Nazi Trials, much like the era of the survivors themselves, is coming to an end.

48 Alvin H. Rosenfeld, 'Popularization and Memory: The Case of Anne Frank', in *Lessons and Legacies: The Meaning of the Holocaust in a Changing World*, ed. Peter Hayes (Evanston, IL: Northwestern University Press, 1991), 244.

49 Naomi Alderman, 'Anne Frank and So On', *Jewish Quarterly*, last updated 9 April 2013, accessed 20 August 2016, http://jewishquarterly.org/2013/01/anne-frank/.

50 Lawrence L. Langer, *Using and Abusing the Holocaust* (Bloomington: Indiana University Press, 2006), 18–19.

51 Philip Roth, *Ghost Writer* (London: Vintage, 2005), 170–1.

52 In a more overt moment of speculative fiction, Roth's short story '"I Always Wanted You to Admire My Fasting"; or, Looking at Kafka' (1975) Roth portrays an alternate history with one change which sees Franz Kafka survive the tuberculosis that killed him in 1924 and instead emigrate as a refugee to the United States where we encounter him, unpublished, teaching Hebrew to a young Philip Roth. Roth of course has another novel which is a far more typical example of speculative fiction, and I deal with *The Plot Against America* (2004) in Chapter 4 of this book.

53 Roth, *Ghost Writer*, 16.

54 George Steiner, quoted in Kremer, *Witness Through the Imagination*, 324.

55 Henri Raczymow, 'Memory Shot Through with Holes', in *The Holocaust: Theoretical Readings*, ed. Neil Levi and Michael Rothberg (Edinburgh: Edinburgh University Press, 2003), 414.

56 Shalom Auslander, *Hope: A Tragedy* (London: Picador, 2012), 39.

57 Ruth Wisse quoted in Samuel Freedman, *Jew vs. Jew: The Struggle for the Soul of American Jewry* (New York: Simon & Schuster, 2000), 344.

58 Auslander, *Hope: A Tragedy*, 325. Emphasis in original.

59 Emily Miller Budick, *The Subject of Holocaust Fiction* (Bloomington: Indiana University Press, 2015), 28.

60 Nathan Englander, 'What We Talk About When We Talk About Anne Frank', in *What We Talk About When We Talk About Anne Frank* (London: Phoenix, 2013), 3–32.

61 Yareth Rosen, 'That Great Big Jewish Alaska', *Moment*, 5 January 2012, accessed 20 August 2016, http://www.momentmag.com/that-great-big-jewish-alaska/.

62 *Fairbanks Daily News-Miner*, 3 October 1939, 2.; Other editorials in the *Daily News-Miner*, and reports in other places, tended to worry firstly that the German-Jewish were the wrong kind of people for Alaskan life (Scandinavian types are often cited as more desirable), and secondly that they would arrive penniless and without skills or means to support themselves. There was, however, some support for the bill in Alaska from others: one woman, a 'long-time resident' wrote to the

paper saying 'Let the German-Jew refugees come to Alaska if they want to. Alaska is a big country. Give them a chance.' *Fairbanks Daily News-Miner*, 21 November 1938, 7. All sources quoted in Gerald S. Berman, 'Reaction to the Resettlement of World War II Refugees in Alaska', *Jewish Social Studies*, 44, no. 3–4 (1982), 271–82.

63 United States Congress, Senate, Committee on Territories and Insular Affairs, *Settlement and Development of Alaska: Hearings Before a Subcommittee, Seventy-Sixth Congress, Third Session, on S.3577, a Bill to Provide for the Settlement and Development of Alaska. May 13, 15, and 18, 1940* (Washington, DC: U.S. Government Printing Office, 1940), 231.

64 Michael Chabon, *The Yiddish Policemen's Union* (London: Harper Perennial, 2008), 27.

65 Chabon, *The Yiddish Policemen's Union*, 28.

66 Chabon, *The Yiddish Policemen's Union*, 28.

67 Thus, on a linguistic level at least, Chabon does undo the Holocaust.

68 Chabon, *The Yiddish Policemen's Union*, 30.

69 Chabon, *The Yiddish Policemen's Union*, 31.

70 Chabon, *The Yiddish Policemen's Union*, 77–8.

71 Chabon, *The Yiddish Policemen's Union*, 32.

72 Chabon, *The Yiddish Policemen's Union*, 78.

73 Elie Wiesel, *Night*, trans. Marion Wiesel (London: Penguin, 2008), 34.

74 See: Richard L. Rubenstein, *After Auschwitz: History, Theology and Contemporary Judaism* (Baltimore: Johns Hopkins University Press, 1992).

75 Thane Rosenbaum, *The Golems of Gotham* (New York: Perennial, 2003), 3.

76 Chabon, *The Yiddish Policemen's Union*, 99.

77 Chabon, *The Yiddish Policemen's Union*, 43.

78 Sarah Phillips Casteel, 'Jews among the Indians: The Fantasy of Indigenization in Mordecai Richler's and Michael Chabon's Northern Narratives', *Contemporary Literature*, 50, no. 4 (2009), 799.

79 Rachel Rubinstein, *Members of the Tribe: Native America in the Jewish Imagination* (Texas: Wayne State University Press, 2010), 172.

80 Chabon, *The Yiddish Policemen's Union*, 316.

81 The Nazis employed the false flag Gleiwitz Incident to justify the invasion of Poland, and most notably of all the burning of the Reichstag which, although a subject of continued debate, was certainly used by the Nazi Party as a propaganda tool and rallying cry in a manner similar to Chabon's burning temples.

82 Helene Meyers, *Reading Michael Chabon* (Santa Barbara: Greenwood, 2010), 73.

83 Chabon, *The Yiddish Policemen's Union*, 277.

84 Chabon, *The Yiddish Policemen's Union*, 401.

85 Jon Wiener, 'Arctic Jews: An Interview with Michael Chabon', *Dissent*, 14 April 2007, accessed 20 August 2016, http://www.dissentmagazine.org/online_articles/arctic-jews-an-interview-with-michael-chabon.

86 Northeastern News, 'The Amazing Adventures of Michael Chabon', *News @ Northeastern*, 6 April 2012, accessed 20 August 2016, http://www.northeastern.edu/news/2012/04/chabon/.

87 Michael Chabon, 'Imaginary Homelands', in *Maps & Legends: Reading and Writing Along the Borderlands* (London: Fourth Estate, 2010), 163.

88 Chabon, 'Imaginary Homelands', 165.

89 This is attested to by the popularity of this combination, not least in several novels I refer to in this book, including those by Tidhar, Harris and Walton.

90 Lavie Tidhar, 'Uganda', in *Hebrewpunk* (Clacton-on-Sea: Apex, 2007), 52–99. The scheme was also the subject for Adam Rovner's travel guide to the fictional nation of 'New Judea': 'What If the Jewish State Had Been Established in East Africa?' which was joint winner of the 2016 Sideways Award for best short-form alternate history. Adam Rovner, 'What If the Jewish State Had Been Established in East Africa?' in *What Ifs of Jewish History: From Abraham to Zionism*, ed. Gavriel D. Rosenfeld (Cambridge: Cambridge University Press, 2016), 165–86.

91 Lavie Tidhar, *Unholy Land* (San Francisco: Tachyon, 2018), ii–iii.

92 Tirosh is also a more thinly-veiled stand-in for the author than usual, being like Tidhar a writer who 'won a small award a few years back, for a weird political novel called *Osama*'. Although in a typical twist of Tidhar humour unfortunately no one in the new reality knows anything about the book or even who it's named after, asking if Al-Qaeda are a band (110).

93 Tidhar, *Unholy Land*, 118–19.

94 Tidhar, *Unholy Land*, 24.

95 Tidhar, *Unholy Land*, 179–80.

96 Tidhar, *Unholy Land*, 180.

97 Norman Spinrad, *Science Fiction in the Real World* (Carbondale: Southern Illinois University Press, 1990), 158.

98 Norman Spinrad, *The Iron Dream* (St Albans: Panther, 1974), 255.

99 R. A. Lafferty, 'The Three Armageddons of Enniscorthy Sweeny', in *Apocalypses* (Los Angeles: Pinnacle, 1977), 281–9. There is some confusion as to the date of Armageddon I since the First World War began in 1914, but a conversation between Sweeny and a very much alive (though troubled) Prince Franz Ferdinand of Austria (p. 236) makes explicit that the subject matter of this opera relates to the assassination of the then archduke and the international ramifications of this act. Armageddon III is, of course, in the future relative to the date of the novella's original publication.

100 I am forced to agree with the note of surprise in Lisa Tuttle's introduction to the recent SF Masterworks edition of the novel in which she reports that the book 'even won Germany's Kurd-LaBwitz Preis [the premier science fiction literary award in Germany], despite its rather chilling view of the German national character'. Lisa Tuttle, 'Introduction', in Jerry Yulsman, *Elleander Morning* (London: Gollancz, 2015), 1.

101 Elana Gomel, *Postmodern Science Fiction and Temporal Imagination* (London: Bloomsbury, 2010), 105.

Chapter 4

1 Philip Roth, *The Plot Against America* (London: Vintage, 2005), 1.
2 Roth, *The Plot Against America*, 54.
3 Alexander Nazaryan, 'Getting Close to Fascism with Sinclair Lewis's "It Can't Happen Here"', *The New Yorker*, 19 October 2016, accessed 10 March 2019, https://www.newyorker.com/culture/culture-desk/getting-close-to-fascism-with-sinclair-lewiss-it-cant-happen-here.
4 When Donald Trump won the Presidential election in 2016 the book apparently sold out on Amazon.com within a week. See: Beverly Gage, 'Reading the Classic Novel That Predicted Trump', *New York Times*, 17 January 2017, accessed 9 March 2019, https://www.nytimes.com/2017/01/17/books/review/classic-novel-that-predicted-trump-sinclair-lewis-it-cant-happen-here.html.
5 Philip Roth, *American Pastoral* (London: Vintage, 1998), 287.
6 Stefanie Boese, '"Those Two Years": Alternate History and Autobiography in Philip Roth's *The Plot Against America*', *Studies in American Fiction*, 41, no. 2 (2014), 276.
7 Roth, *The Plot Against America*, 1.
8 'America First Group to Quit', *The Telegraph-Herald* (Dubuque, IA), 12 December 1941, accessed 16 November 2018, https://news.google.com/newspapers?id=hFxFAAAAIBAJ&sjid=ELwMAAAAIBAJ&pg=3259,4276685&hl=en. Emphasis mine.
9 see the Roth short story: '"I Always Wanted You to Admire My Fasting"; or, Looking at Kafka' (1975)?
10 Joe Kubert, *Yossel: April 19, 1943* (New York: DC Comics, 2003).
11 Roth, *The Plot Against America*, 385–90.
12 Roth, *The Plot Against America*, 205.
13 Roth, *The Plot Against America*, 8.
14 Roth, *The Plot Against America*, 206.
15 Roth, *The Plot Against America*, 241.

16 Roth, *The Plot Against America*, 309.
17 Roth, *The Plot Against America*, 310.
18 Roth, *The Plot Against America*, 316.
19 Roth, *The Plot Against America*, 345.
20 David Brauner, *Philip Roth* (Manchester: Manchester University Press, 2007), 207.
21 Rosenfeld, *The World Hitler Never Made*, 155.
22 Rosenfeld, *The World Hitler Never Made*, 155.
23 Roth, *The Plot Against America*, 7.
24 Roth, *The Plot Against America*, 11.
25 Gabriel Brownstein, 'Fight or Flight', *The Village Voice*, 21 September 2004, accessed 7 February 2016, http://www.villagevoice.com/arts/fight-or-flight-7139189.
26 Michael Schaub, '*The Plot Against America* by Philip Roth', *Bookslut*, October 2004, accessed 10 February 2019, http://www.bookslut.com/fiction/2004_10_003275.php.
27 Michael Wood, 'Just Folks', *London Review of Books*, 26, no. 21, 4 November 2004, accessed 7 February 2019, http://www.lrb.co.uk/v26/n21/michael-wood/just-folks.
28 Dan Shiffman, '*The Plot Against America* and History Post-9/11', *Philip Roth Studies*, 5, no. 1 (2009), 62.
29 Brett Ashley Kaplan, *Jewish Anxiety and the Novels of Philip Roth* (London: Bloomsbury, 2015), 152.
30 Catherine Gallagher, *Telling It Like It Wasn't: The Counterfactual Imagination in History and Fiction* (Chicago: Chicago University Press, 2018), 274.
31 Philip Roth, 'The Story Behind "The Plot Against America,"' *New York Times*, 19 September 2004, accessed 7 February 2015, http://www.nytimes.com/2004/09/19/books/review/19ROTHL.html.
32 Roth, *The Plot Against America*, 371.
33 Ian R. MacLeod, 'Summer Isles', in *Breathmoss and Other Exhalations* (Urbana, IL: Golden Gryphon Press, 2004), 235–309. The novella is an abridged version of a novel of the same title which was later published in 2005 in a limited run.
34 Roy Thomas, *Superman: War of the Worlds*, illus. Michael Lark (New York: DC Comics, 1999), 63.
35 Edward VIII is referenced in both *The Plot Against America* and Jo Walton's Small Change Trilogy; a side-note in the former, and a more important plot point by the third book of the latter. He is also referenced as having been restored to the throne in Harris's *Fatherland*. He is even the main focus of some alternate history narratives, most prominently perhaps, D. J. Taylor's *The Windsor Faction* (2013) which won the Sidewise Award for best long-form alternate history.
36 Albert Speer, *Inside the Third Reich* (New York: Macmillan, 1970), 118.

37 Walters, *The Leader*, 387.
38 Walters, *The Leader*, 396, 387.
39 Walters, *The Leader*, 39.
40 Jo Walton, 'A Pit in Dothan: Josephine Tey's *Brat Farrar*', *Tor.com*, 10 September 2010, accessed 3 February 2016, http://www.tor.com/2010/09/10/a-pit-in-dothan-josephine-teys-brat-farrar/.
41 Jo Walton, *Farthing* (New York: Tor, 2006), 110.
42 Walton, *Farthing*, 16.
43 Walton, *Farthing*, 17.
44 Walton, *Farthing*, 13.
45 Walton, *Farthing*, 47.
46 Walton, *Farthing*, 23.
47 Walton herself describes the novel as a 'cosy mystery' in Farah Mendlesohn, 'Jo Walton in Conversation with Farah Mendlesohn', *Vector*, 276 (2014), 11.
48 Jo Walton, 'The Small Change Series', accessed 6 February 2016, http://www.jowaltonbooks.com/books/the-small-change-series/.
49 Jo Walton, 'Who Survives Catastrophe?' *Foundation*, 93 (2005), 35.
50 Though Walton tried to keep us interested in the detective fiction plot by adding an element of 'how-dunnit', albeit not creating a true inverted detective novel, by adding peculiar elements to the murder such as the body being daubed in blood-red lipstick rather than actual blood.
51 Walton, *Farthing*, 245.
52 Walton, *Farthing*, 228.
53 Walton, *Farthing*, 244. The *sic* here refers to an internal inconsistency in the text.
54 Walton, *Farthing*, 246.
55 Walton, *Farthing*, 247, 286. Dan Hartland takes issue with the comparison, pointing out that the Reichstag and James Thirkie are not equatable symbols; the former 'was a symbol of the German nation' while the latter 'is merely a politician, however successful'. See: Dan Hartland, '*Farthing* by Jo Walton', *Strange Horizons*, 23 October 2006, accessed 10 March 2019, http://strangehorizons.com/non-fiction/reviews/farthing-by-jo-walton/.
56 Hartland, '*Farthing* by Jo Walton'; see also Paul Kincaid, '*Farthing*', New York Review of Science Fiction, 223, 19, no. 7 (2007), 10.
57 Walton, *Farthing*, 232.
58 Walton, *Farthing*, 233.
59 Walton, *Farthing*, 233.
60 Hartland, '*Farthing* by Jo Walton'.
61 Walton references the trilogy by both names in her acknowledgements for the third book *Half a Crown* (New York: Tor, 2008).

62 Mendlesohn, 'Jo Walton in Conversation with Farah Mendlesohn', 11; See also: James Bacon, '*Farthing* by Jo Walton', *Vector*, 256 (2008): 37–8, who describes the novel as 'a very gentle read' (37) while also noting that: 'The anti-Semitic attitudes that play a part in the story are well thought through. Britain in the 1930s had more anti-Semitic feelings than people would like to admit and Walton brings this home' (38).

63 Jo Walton, *Half a Crown* (New York: Tor, 2008), 19.

64 John Clute, '*Half a Crown* by Jo Walton', *Strange Horizons*, 15 December 2008, accessed 10 March 2019, http://strangehorizons.com/non-fiction/reviews/half-a-crown-by-jo-walton/.

65 J. G. Stinson, '*Farthing*', *The New York Review of Science Fiction*, 226 (2007), 7.

66 Clute, '*Half a Crown* by Jo Walton'. Emphasis in original. This view is echoed in *The Encyclopedia of Science Fiction* entry on Walton, also authored by Clute, which describes the world of the novels as 'a Dystopia that seems frozen shut'. Accessed 10 March 2019, http://www.sf-encyclopedia.com/entry/walton_jo.

67 Clute, '*Half a Crown* by Jo Walton'.

68 Joan Gordon, '*Half a Crown* by Jo Walton', *The New York Review of Science Fiction*, 247 (2009), 13.

69 Pastor Martin Niemöller's speech and poems, of which there are numerous versions, are frequently employed as a warning against political apathy. 'First They Came for the Jews', in *Holocaust Poetry*, ed. Hilda Schiff (London: Fount, 1995), 9.

70 Walton, *Half a Crown*, 314.

71 Clute, '*Half a Crown* by Jo Walton'; note that Clute refers to the address as being delivered over radio rather than television, while presumably it would have been broadcast on both; the evidence in the novel is only for television (we see the broadcast from Carmichael's point of view); had it been radio the parallels with First Lady Lindbergh's broadcast in *The Plot Against America* would have been all the more considerable, and perhaps memory of the latter is confusing Clute's recollection.

72 Clute, '*Half a Crown* by Jo Walton'.

73 E. H. Carr, *What Is History?* (Middlesex: Penguin, 1968), 97. Carr dismissively refers to these as part of 'what I may call the "might-have-been" school of thought – or rather emotion' (96). Such accusations of having a lack of seriousness are reflected in debates around speculative fiction more widely as not being serious literature, and can perhaps explain the alternate history genre's obsession with author notes in which the writers cite their historical sources, a far rarer occurrence in other forms of speculative fiction.

74 Clute, '*Half a Crown* by Jo Walton'.

75 Walton, *Farthing*, 300. Paul Kincaid also suggests the use of Rudolph Hess's flight to Britain as a point of departure could be a nod to Christopher Priest's *The Seperation* (London: Gollancz, 2002) which along with Roth's novel he considers 'the two most intriguing and significant alternate histories of recent years'. Kincaid, 'Farthing', 10.

76 Jack Deighton, '*Farthing* by Jo Walton', 7 December 2015, accessed 9 February 2016, http://jackdeighton.co.uk/2015/12/07/farthing-by-jo-walton/. Worth noting here is C. J. Sansom's *Dominion* (London: Mantle, 2012), another alternate history novel about fascism arising in the United Kingdom which uses a similar idea as Walton's of peace with Germany allowing fascism to flourish. Unlike Walton, however, Sansom makes use of Mosley and by 1952, the year in which the novel is set, Mosley is home secretary under Prime Minister Lord Beaverbrook and has created a paramilitary 'auxillary police' out of his British Union of Fascist Blackshirts.

77 Walton in Mendlesohn, 'Jo Walton in Conversation with Farah Mendlesohn', 11. Ellipsis in original.

78 Walton, 'The Small Change Series'.

79 Walton, *Farthing*, 5.

80 Stinson, 'Farthing', 7.

81 Kincaid, 'Farthing', 11.

82 Cory Doctorow, '*Farthing*: Heart-Rending Alternate History about British-Reich Peace', *BoingBoing*, 20 June 2006, accessed 20 September 2016, http://boingboing.net/2006/06/20/farthing-heartrendin.html.

83 Hartland, '*Farthing* by Jo Walton'.

84 Rosenfeld, *The World Hitler Never Made*, 35.

85 Lavie Tidhar, *A Man Lies Dreaming* (London: Hodder, 2014), 1.

86 Tidhar, *A Man Lies Dreaming*, 3.

87 Judith R. Baskin, *The Cambridge Dictionary of Judaism and Jewish Culture* (Cambridge: Cambridge University Press, 2011), defines *shund* as 'melodramatic and sentimental depictions of Jewish American immigrant life' (183). The word literally means 'trash' (157). The Anglo-American equivalent would be 'pulp'.

88 Baskin, *Cambridge Dictionary of Judaism*, 600.

89 Lavie Tidhar in Glyn Morgan, 'An Interview with Lavie Tidhar', *Glyn-Morgan.blogspot*, 8 April 2015, accessed 20 August 2016, http://glyn-morgan.blogspot.co.uk/2015/04/interview-with-lavie-tidhar.html.

90 Tidhar, *A Man Lies Dreaming*, 31.

91 Tidhar, *A Man Lies Dreaming*, 38.

92 Tidhar, *A Man Lies Dreaming*, 156.

93 Tidhar, *A Man Lies Dreaming*, 156.

94 Dinur/Ka-Tzetnik was asked at the trial why he'd written under a pseudonym. He replied: 'It was not a pen name. I do not regard myself as a writer and a composer of literary material. This is a chronicle of the planet of Auschwitz. I was there for about two years. Time there was not like it is here on earth. Every fraction of a minute there passed on a different scale of time. And the inhabitants of this planet had no names, they had no parents nor did they have children. There they did not dress in the way we dress here; they were not born there and they did not give birth; they breathed according to different laws of nature; they did not live – nor did they die – according to the laws of this world. ... I believe with perfect faith that, just as in astrology the stars influence our destiny, so does this planet of the ashes, Auschwitz, stand in opposition to our planet earth, and influences it.' Yehiel Dinur, *The Trial of Adolf Eichmann: Record of Proceedings in the District Court of Jerusalem*, 9 vols (Jerusalem: State of Israel Ministry of Justice, 1992–1995), III (1993), 1237. The original testimony was given in Hebrew. Hannah Arendt provides an alternative translation of this image as 'the star of ashes at Auschwitz is there facing our planet, radiating toward our planet'. Hannah Arendt, *Eichmann in Jerusalem: A Report on the Banality of Evil* (London: Penguin, 2006), 224.

95 Nora Levin, *The Holocaust: The Destruction of European Jewry, 1933–1945* (New York: T. Y. Crowell, 1968), xii.

96 I refer of course to the opening line of L. P. Hartley's *The Go-Between* (1953) which has become a proverb in its own right: 'The past is a foreign country: they do things differently there.'

97 Arthur A. Cohen, 'Thinking the Tremendum: Some Theological Implications of the Death Camps', in *An Arthur A. Cohen Reader: Selected Fiction and Writings on Judaism, Theology, Literature, and Culture*, ed. David Stern and Paul Mendes-Flohr (Detroit: Wayne State University Press, 1998), 234–49 (pp. 234–5).

98 Orwell, *Nineteen Eighty-Four*, 42–3.

99 Wiesel, 'The Holocaust as Literary Inspiration', 7.

100 Elie Wiesel, quoted in Terrence Des Pres, 'The Authority of Silence in Elie Wiesel's Art', in *Writing in to the World: Essays, 1973–1987* (New York: Viking, 1991), 27.

101 Hayden White, *The Content of the Form: Narrative Discourse and Historical Representation* (Baltimore: Johns Hopkins University Press, 1987), 4.

102 Levi, *If This is a Man and The Truce*, 129.

103 Tidhar in Morgan, 'Interview with Lavie Tidhar'.

104 Tidhar in Morgan, 'Interview with Lavie Tidhar'.

105 Tidhar in Morgan, 'Interview with Lavie Tidhar'. Emphases in original.

106 Tidhar, *A Man Lies Dreaming*, 34.

107 *Ilsa, She Wolf of the SS*, dir. Don Edmonds (New York: Cambist Films, 1975). For essays on a wide selection of aspects of Nazisploitation see: Daniel H. Magilow,

Kristin T. Vander Lugt, and Elizabeth Bridges, eds, *Nazisploitation!: The Nazi Image in Low-Brow Cinema and Culture* (London: Continuum, 2012).

108 Tidhar, *A Man Lies Dreaming*, 87–8, 90. Note that this quote demonstrates the shifting narratorial position. It begins as an extract from Wolf's diary, and within the first ellipsis there is a shift back to a scene with Shomer in Auschwitz, before we rejoin Wolf but this time from a third-person perspective.

109 Tidhar, *A Man Lies Dreaming*, 99.

110 Tidhar, *A Man Lies Dreaming*, 120.

111 Tidhar, *A Man Lies Dreaming*, 97.

112 Tidhar, *A Man Lies Dreaming*, 239.

113 See: Rosenfeld, *The World Hitler Never Made*, and Rosenfeld, *Hi Hitler! How the Nazi Past Is Being Normalized in Contemporary Culture*.

114 Tidhar, *A Man Lies Dreaming*, 240.

115 Tidhar, *A Man Lies Dreaming*, 241.

116 Himmelfarb rejected structural interpretations of the Holocaust's history, preferring the 'great men' model; in the essay he wrote that 'Antisemitism was a necessary condition for the Holocaust, it was not a sufficient condition. Hitler was needed. Hitler murdered the Jews because he wanted to murder them.' Milton Himmelfarb, 'No Hitler, No Holocaust', *Commentary* (March 1984), 37.

117 Tidhar, *A Man Lies Dreaming*, 138.

118 Tidhar, *A Man Lies Dreaming*, 248.

119 Tidhar, *A Man Lies Dreaming*, 249.

120 Tidhar, *A Man Lies Dreaming*, 250.

121 Tidhar, *A Man Lies Dreaming*, 260.

122 Tidhar, *A Man Lies Dreaming*, 261.

123 Tidhar in Morgan, 'Interview with Lavie Tidhar'.

124 Young, *Writing and Rewriting the Holocaust*, 15.

125 Norman Finkelstein, *The Holocaust Industry*, 2nd edn (London: Verso, 2003), 8.

126 Maximillian Edwards, 'A Man Lies Dreaming by Lavie Tidhar', *Strange Horizons*, 12 January 2015, accessed 10 March 2019, http://strangehorizons.com/non-fiction/reviews/a-man-lies-dreaming-by-lavie-tidhar/.

127 Howard Jacobson, *J* (London: Jonathan Cape, 2014), 13.

128 Jacobson, *J*, 46.

129 Jacobson, *J*, 19. Ellipsis in original.

130 The word kapo is itself a piece of the lexicon of the Holocaust. A word with no clear etymology it describes a prisoner who was in charge of a block of prisoners. These were normally criminal-class prisoners, never Jews, and had privileges above those of normal camp internees.

131 Levi, *The Drowned and the Saved*, 72.

132 Jane Yolen, *The Devil's Arithmetic* (New York: Puffin, 1990), 128. Emphasis in original.
133 Andrea Reiter, *Narrating the Holocaust*, trans. Patrick Camiller (London: Continuum, 2000), 99, 101.
134 Levi, *The Drowned and the Saved*, 76, 78.
135 Jacobson, *J*, 78.
136 Jacobson admits Port Reuben is a version of Port Isaac in Cornwall, 'which is, of course, already a Jewish name'. He lived there with his second wife, Rosalin Sadler, in the late seventies and early eighties, running a gift shop which sold Welsh love spoons. See: John Walsh, '"I write about male sexual obsession… fortunately none of my three wives has mistaken fiction for fact": Howard Jacobson on Sex, Religion and Anti-Semitism', *Daily Mail*, 8 August 2015, accessed 25 February 2016, http://www.dailymail.co.uk/home/event/article-3186946/Howard-Jacobson-write-male-sexual-obsession-fortunately-none-three-wives-mistaken-fiction-fact.html.
137 Jacobson, *J*, vii. An all-destructive wolf is likely a reference to Hitler and his *nom de guerre* (as seen in Tidhar's *A Man Lies Dreaming*).
138 Patricia Waugh, *Metafiction: The Theory and Practice of Self-Conscious Fiction* (London: Methuen, 1984), 2.
139 Jacobson, *J*, 211.
140 Jacobson, *J*, 206.
141 Jacobson, *J*, 206.
142 Jacobson, *J*, 199.
143 Jacobson, *J*, 203.
144 Howard Jacobson, *When Will Jews Be Forgiven the Holocaust* (Amazon Singles, 2014), Kindle.
145 Howard Jacobson, 'Let's See the "criticism" of Israel of What It Really Is', *The Independent*, 18 February 2009, accessed 20 September 2016, http://www.independent.co.uk/voices/commentators/howard-jacobson/howard-jacobson-letrsquos-see-the-criticism-of-israel-for-what-it-really-is-1624827.html.
146 Jacobson, 'Let's See the "criticism" of Israel of What It Really Is'.
147 Jacobson, *J*, 87.
148 Jacobson, *J*, 110.
149 I refer to the title of Jacobson's novel as *J* but its more accurate title is a unique symbol: a letter J which has been twice struck through. It occurs throughout the novel and is signified by the protagonist Kevern (and before him, his father) running two fingers over their lips as they say words beginning with the letter.
150 Ruth Gilbert, 'Reality Gaps: Negotiating the Boundaries of British-Jewish Identities in Contemporary Fiction', in *Boundaries, Identities and Belonging in Modern Judaism*, ed. Maria Diemling and Larry Ray (Abingdon: Routledge, 2016), 115.

151 Sigmund Freud, *Moses and Monotheism: Three Essays*, in *The Standard Edition of the Complete Psychological Work of Sigmund Freud*, trans. and ed. James Strachey, vol. 23 (London: The Hogarth Press, 1964), 91–2.
152 Jacobson, *When Will Jews Be Forgiven the Holocaust?* Emphases in original.
153 Jacques Maritain, *The Range of Reason*, The Jacques Maritain Centre, accessed 29 September 2016, https://www3.nd.edu/~maritain/jmc/etext/range10.htm.
154 Jacobson, *When Will Jews Be Forgiven the Holocaust?* Emphases in original.
155 Jacobson, *J*, 253.
156 Jacobson, *J*, 304.
157 Jacobson, *J*, 116.
158 Jacobson, *J*, 119.
159 Jacobson, *J*, 34–5.
160 Jacobson, *J*, 35.
161 Zygmunt Bauman, 'Categorical Murder, or: How to Remember the Holocaust', in *Re-presenting the Shoah for the 21st Century*, ed. Ronit Lentin (New York: Berghahn, 2004), 27.
162 See: Hugo Bachega, 'The Threat of Rising Anti-Semitism', *BBC News*, 2 November 2018, accessed 10 March 2019, https://www.bbc.co.uk/news/world-us-canada-46 038438 and Jon Henley, 'Antisemitism Rising Sharply Across Europe, Latest Figures Show', *The Guardian*, 15 February 2019, accessed 10 March 2019, https://www.theguardian.com/news/2019/feb/15/antisemitism-rising-sharply-ac ross-europe-latest-figures-show.

Epilogue: Further Fabulation

1 Wiesel, 'For Some Measure of Humility' (1975); quoted in Rosenfeld, *A Double Dying*, 14. Wiesel returns to many themes, expressions and motifs regularly throughout his writings; the idea that 'a novel about Auschwitz is not a novel, or else not about Auschwitz' finds its earliest expression (to my knowledge) in this quote, but its more famous form comes from 'The Holocaust as Literary Inspiration': 'A novel about Treblinka is either not a novel or not about Treblinka'; less commonly quoted is the next sentence which continues, 'A novel about Majdanek is about blasphemy. *Is* blasphemy' (7. Emphasis in original).
2 Franklin, *A Thousand Darknesses*, 9. Emphasis in original.
3 History is always littered with forgeries and mistaken sources, the Hitler Diaries for example, but the most infamous with regard to the Holocaust is probably Binjamin Wilkomirski's *Fragments* (1995) which garnered near universal praise for its extraordinary honesty and powerful truth-telling across mainstream media

and from noted Holocaust historians and scholars, winning the United States' National Jewish Book Award, and the French Prix Memoire de la Shoah, among other plaudits. In 1998 it was exposed as a fake; the debate about its literary value and what we can learn from the experience of its perceived authenticity is a fascinating but still undeveloped area for study. That said, see: Lawrence Langer's chapter 'Fragments of Memory: A Myth of Past Time' in his *Using and Abusing the Holocaust* (Bloomington: Indiana University Press, 2006), pages 48–63, for one such exploration. Sue Vice also touches on the book in the conclusion to her monograph *Holocaust Fiction* (Abingdon: Routledge, 2000), 164–5.

4 Fredric Jameson, *Postmodernism, or the Cultural Logic of Late Capitalism* (Durham, NC: Duke University Press, 1997), 369.
5 Wiesel, 'The Holocaust as Literary Inspiration', 7.
6 Brian Attebery, *Strategies of Fantasy* (Bloomington: Indiana University Press, 1992), ix.
7 Roger Luckhurst, *Zombies: A Cultural History* (London: Reaktion, 2015), 116.
8 Butter, *The Epitome of Evil*, 16.
9 Wiesel, *Night*. Moshe the Bard, as a foreigner, is deported before the rest of young Elie's village, survives a mass shooting in the forest and returns to warn the villagers but they ignore what they see as his attempts to extract pity or money from them, others think him simply mad (6–7); Mrs Schächter sees fire and flame devouring her and fellow Jews as they are transported in cattle trucks; she loudly screams her visions, pointing towards Auschwitz; the other Jews in her cattle truck pity her and assume she has gone mad from the heat, dehydration and stress of the situation (24–6).
10 Judith B. Kerman, 'Uses of the Fantastic in Literature of the Holocaust', in *The Fantastic in Holocaust Literature and Film*, ed. Judith B. Kerman and John Edgar Browning (Jefferson, NC: McFarland, 2015), 17.
11 Kerman, 'Uses of the Fantastic in Literature of the Holocaust', 18.
12 Ellen R. Weil, 'The Door to Lilith's Cave: Memory and Imagination in Jane Yolen's Holocaust Novels', in *The Fantastic in Holocaust Literature and Film*, ed. Judith B. Kerman and John Edgar Browning (Jefferson, NC: McFarland, 2015), 115.
13 Earl Ingersoll and Nancy Kress, 'Seeing the Magic in Everyday Life: A Conversation with Lisa Goldstein', *SFRA Newsletter*, 184 (1991), 8.
14 Goldstein, *The Red Magician*, 127–8.
15 Barbara Hambly, *The Rainbow Abyss* (New York: Del Rey, 1991), 4.
16 Barbara Hambly, *The Magicians of Night* (New York: Del Rey, 1992), 7.
17 Hambly, *The Magicians of Night*, 7–8.
18 Hambly, *The Magicians of Night*, 48. Emphasis in original. 'Vril' is a reference to an alleged secret society which actually finds its roots in the 1871 novel *The Coming*

Race by English novelist Edward Bulwer-Lytton, though some pseudoscientists considered it to be revealing of some deeper spiritual truth. Also worth noting here is that Himmler did actually sanction at least one expedition to Tibet in 1938.

19 Karen Hellekson, 'Rhion's Adventures Continue', *SFRA Review*, 201 (1992), 45–6 (p. 46).
20 Hambly, *The Magicians of Night*, 94.
21 Hambly, *The Magicians of Night*, 96.
22 Hambly, *The Magicians of Night*, 131.
23 Hambly, *The Magicians of Night*, 176.
24 Hambly, *The Magicians of Night*, 329.
25 Derek J. Thiess, *Relativism, Alternate History, and the Forgetful Reader* (Lanham, MD: Lexington, 2015), 92.
26 In particular Thiess refers to two novels already discussed in previous chapters: Philip K. Dick's *The Man in the High Castle* and Robert Harris's *Fatherland*.
27 Hambly, *The Magicians of Night*, 336.
28 Hambly, *The Magicians of Night*, 349.
29 Hambly, *The Magicians of Night*, 348.
30 Gary Weissman, *Fantasies of Witnessing: Postwar Efforts to Experience the Holocaust* (Ithaca, NY: Cornell University, 2004), 12.
31 Hambly herself expresses an awareness of this danger in the author's note which functions as an afterword to the novel which is tinged with anxiety about the subject matter with which she is dealing:

> What I *did* want to do was to do justice to those topics [the Holocaust, the SS, occultism, etc.] … where they touched upon my own piece of magical fantasy, without being led too far astray. This I hope I have accomplished – I certainly did the best I could. … To those who lost family and loved ones in the disasters of those years, who might feel that I have trivialized of their deaths by turning the whole thing into background for what is, basically, entertainment, I apologize sincerely. I lost no one – my mother's family left Poland years before, and it could be justly argued that I operate from a position of ignorance.
>
> My intention is, as it has always been, strictly to entertain – but in doing so, at least I have tried not to gloss over facts, or do violence to the truth as I could learn it. I hope that I have succeeded on both counts.
>
> (pages 355–6, emphasis in original)

32 Like *The Devil's Arithmetic*, *Briar Rose* was nominated for a Nebula Award by the Science Fiction and Fantasy Writers of America. It was also nominated for, and won, the Mythopoeic Award for Adult Literature.

33 Gary K. Wolfe, *Evaporating Genres: Essays on Fantastic Literature* (Middletown, CT: Wesleyan University Press, 2011), 33.
34 In reality there were no known female survivors of Chelmno which leads Wolfe to remark of the novel that 'At its most fantasy, it's a very minimalist alternate history'. Wolfe, *Evaporating Genres*, 33.
35 Vandana Saxena, 'Mother Goose Tales: Integrational Storytelling and the Holocaust in Jane Yolen's Briar Rose and Peter Rushforth's Kindergarten', in *The Fantastic in Holocaust Literature and Film*, ed. Judith B. Kerman and John Edgar Browning (Jefferson, NC: McFarland, 2015), 123.
36 Yolen's *Mapping the Bones* (2018) again returns to the Holocaust drawing on the tale of Hansel and Gretl as a fairy-tale touchstone, although it is explicitly a children's book. It uses the evocative power of the oven in Holocaust imagery to connect the older tale with a story of Jewish children trying to survive in Nazi-occupied Poland.
37 For examples of the more extensive scholarship regarding Yolen's novels see: Ellen R. Weil, Vandana Saxena, and Carol A. Senf's chapters in *The Fantastic in Holocaust Literature and Film*, ed. Kerman and Browning. It is significant that three of the four chapters in the part of this work dedicated to 'The Holocaust and Fantasy Literature' deal either heavily or exclusively with Yolen's work. Among other sources see also: Elizabeth R. Baer, 'A Postmodern Fairy Tale of the Holocaust: Jane Yolen's "Briar Rose"', *Studies in American Jewish Literature (1981–)*, 24 (2003), 145–52.
38 S. Lillian Kremer, 'The Holocaust in English-Language Literatures', in *Literature of the Holocaust*, ed. Alan Rosen (Cambridge: Cambridge University Press, 2013), 147.
39 Jenni Adams, *Magic Realism in Holocaust Literature: Troping the Traumatic Real* (Houndmills: Palgrave, 2011), 37.
40 Shoshana Felman, 'In an Era of Testimony: Claude Lanzmann's *Shoah*', *Yale French Studies*, 79 (1991), 41.
41 See: Peter Hayes and John K. Roth, eds, *The Oxford Handbook of Holocaust Studies* (Oxford: Oxford University Press, 2010), 6. Hayes and Roth refer to this issue as a contemporary concern for Holocaust studies as an academic discipline, referring to these labels as 'protagonists'.
42 Hilda Schiff, 'Introduction', in *Holocaust Poetry* (London: Fount, 1995), xi.
43 Schiff, 'Introduction', xii.
44 The surfeit of memory is Charles S. Maier's term. See: Charles S. Maier, 'A Surfeit of Memory? Reflections on History, Melancholy, and Denial', *History and Memory*, 5 (1992), 136–1.
45 Susan Sontag, *On Photography* (Harmondsworth: Penguin, 1977), 41.
46 Ruth Leys, *Trauma: A Genealogy* (Chicago: University of Chicago Press, 2000), 15. Emphasis in original.
47 Robert Eaglestone, *The Holocaust and the Postmodern* (Oxford: Oxford University Press, 2009), 33.

Bibliography

Aaronovitch, David. *Voodoo Histories: How Conspiracy Theory Has Shaped Modern History*. London: Vintage, 2010.
Adams, Jenni. *Magic Realism in Holocaust Literature: Troping the Traumatic Real*. Houndmills: Palgrave, 2011.
Adorno, Theodor W. 'Culture, Criticism and Society'. In *Prisms*. Translated by Samuel Weber and Shierry Weber, 17–34. Cambridge, MA: MIT Press, 1981.
Adorno, Theodor W. *Negative Dialectics*. Translated by E. B. Ashton. London: Routledge, 1973.
Agamben, Giorgio. *Remnants of Auschwitz: The Witness and the Archive*. Translated by Daniel Heller-Roazen. New York: Zone Books, 1999.
Alderman, Naomi. 'Anne Frank and So On'. *Jewish Quarterly*. Last updated 9 April 2013. Accessed 20 August 2016. http://jewishquarterly.org/2013/01/anne-frank/.
Allhoff, Fred. *Lightning in the Night*. 1940. Englewood Cliffs, NJ: Prentice-Hall, 1979.
'America First Group To Quit'. *The Telegraph-Herald (Dubuque, IA)*, 12 December 1941. Accessed 16 November 2018. https://news.google.com/newspapers?id=hFxFAAA AIBAJ&sjid=ELwMAAAAIBAJ&pg=3259,4276685&hl=en.
Améry, Jean. 'Resentments'. In *The Holocaust: Theoretical Readings*. Edited by Neil Levi and Michael Rothberg, 36–44. Edinburgh: Edinburgh University Press, 2003.
Amis, Kingsley. *New Maps of Hell*. London: Four Square, 1963.
Anelli, Sara. 'Counterfactual Holocausts: Robert Harris' *Fatherland* and Martin Amis' *Time's Arrow*'. *Textus* 20 (2007): 407–32.
'Animal Research'. University of Cambridge. Accessed 10 March 2019. https://www.cam.ac.uk/research/research-at-cambridge/animal-research.
Arendt, Hannah. *Eichmann in Jerusalem: A Report on the Banality of Evil*. London: Penguin, 2006.
Attebery, Brian. *Strategies of Fantasy*. Bloomington: Indiana University Press, 1992.
Auden, W. H. 'Refugee Blues'. In *Collected Poems*. London: Faber and Faber, 2004.
Auslander, Shalom. *Hope: A Tragedy*. London: Picador, 2012.
Bachega, Hugo. 'The Threat of Rising Anti-Semitism'. *BBC News*, 2 November 2018. Accessed 10 March 2019. https://www.bbc.co.uk/news/world-us-canada-46038438.
Bacon, James. '*Farthing* by Jo Walton'. *Vector* 256 (2008): 37–8.
Baer, Elizabeth R. 'A Postmodern Fairy Tale of the Holocaust: Jane Yolen's "Briar Rose"'. *Studies in American Jewish Literature (1981–)* 24 (2003): 145–52.

Barnes, James J. and Patience P. Barnes. *Hitler's Mein Kampf in Britain and America: A Publishing History 1930–39.* Cambridge: Cambridge University Press, 1980.

Baskin, Judith R. *The Cambridge Dictionary of Judaism and Jewish Culture.* Cambridge: Cambridge University Press, 2011.

Bauman, Zygmunt. 'Categorical Murder, or: How to Remember the Holocaust'. In *Re-Presenting the Shoah for the 21st Century.* Edited by Ronit Lentin, 25–39. New York: Berghahn, 2004.

Bauman, Zygmunt. *Modernity and the Holocaust.* Ithaca, NY: Cornell University Press, 1989.

BBC News. 'On This Day: 1955: West Germany Accepted into Nato'. *BBC News*, 9 May 2008. Accessed 20 August 2016. http://news.bbc.co.uk/onthisday/hi/dates/stories/may/9/newsid_2519000/2519979.stm.

Benjamin, Walter. 'On the Concept of History'. In *Walter Benjamin Selected Writings, Volume 4, 1938–1940.* Edited by Howard Eiland and Michael W. Jennings. Translated by Edmund Jephcott, et al. , 399–411. Cambridge, MA: Harvard University Press, 2003.

Berman, Gerald S. 'Reaction to the Resettlement of World War II Refugees in Alaska'. *Jewish Social Studies* 44, nos. 3–4 (1982): 271–82.

Beschloss, Michael R. *The Conquerors: Roosevelt, Truman and the Destruction of Hitler's Germany, 1941–1945.* New York: Simon & Schuster, 2002.

Bier, Jesse. 'Father and Son'. In *A Hole in the Lead Apron and Six Other Stories*, 186–99. New York: Harcourt, 1964.

Billington, Michael. 'Lifting the Curtain'. *The Guardian*, 24 October 2007. Accessed 20 February 2018. https://www.theguardian.com/stage/2007/oct/24/theatre1.

Blankenship, Steve. 'The Aftermath of the Katyn Massacre: Silent as the Grave'. *World History Bulletin* 27, no. 1 (2001): 64–71.

Bloom, Harold. 'Introduction'. In *Literature of the Holocaust.* Edited by Harold Bloom. Broomall, PA: Chelsea House, 2004.

Boese, Stefanie. '"Those Two Years": Alternate History and Autobiography in Philip Roth's The Plot Against America'. *Studies in American Fiction* 41, no. 2 (2014): 271–2.

Booker, M. Keith. *Dystopian Literature: A Theory and Research Guide.* Westport, CT: Greenwood Press, 1994.

Bradbury, Ray. 'Day After Tomorrow: Why Science Fiction?' *The Nation*, 2 May 1953, 364–7.

Brauner, David. *Philip Roth.* Manchester: Manchester University Press, 2007.

Brecht, Bertolt. 'A Short Organum for the Theatre'. In *Brecht on Theatre: The Development of an Aesthetic.* Translated by John Willett, 179–205. London: Methuen, 1964.

Brogan, Hugh. *The Penguin History of the USA.* 2nd edition. New York: Penguin, 1999.

Brown, Douglas and Christopher Serpell. *If Hitler Comes: A Cautionary Tale.* London: Faber and Faber, 2010.

Brownstein, Gabriel. 'Fight or Flight'. *The Village Voice*, 21 September 2004. Accessed 7 February 2016. http://www.villagevoice.com/arts/fight-or-flight-7139189.

Budick, Emily Miller. *The Subject of Holocaust Fiction*. Bloomington: Indiana University Press, 2015.

Burdekin, Katharine. *Swastika Night*. New York: The Feminist Press, 1985.

Butter, Michael. *The Epitome of Evil: Hitler in American Fiction 1939–2002*. New York: Palgrave, 2009.

Canaan, Howard. 'Metafiction and the Gnostic Quest in *The Man in the High Castle*: Dick's Alternate History Classic after Four Decades'. In *Classic and Iconoclastic Alternate History Science Fiction*. Edited by Edgar L. Chapman and Carl B. Yorke, 93–122. Lewiston, NY: Edwin Mellen Press, 2003.

Canavan, Gerry. 'The Suvin Effect'. In Darko Suvin, *Metamorphoses of Science Fiction: On the Poetics and History of a Literary Genre*. Edited by Gerry Canavan, xi–xxxvi. Bern: Peter Lang, 2016.

Casteel, Sarah Philips. 'Jews among the Indians: The Fantasy of Indigenization in Mordecai Richler's and Michael Chabon's Northern Narratives'. *Contemporary Literature* 50, no. 4 (2009): 775–810.

Celan, Paul. 'Speech on the Occasion of Receiving the Literature Prize of the Free Hanseatic City of Bremen'. In *Collected Prose*. Translated by Rosmarie Waldrop, 33–6. Riverdale-on-Hudson, NY: The Sheep Meadow Press, 1986.

Cesarani, David. 'Challenging the "Myth of Silence": Postwar Response to the Destruction of European Jewry'. In *After the Holocaust: Challenging the Myth of Silence*. Edited by David Cesarani and Eric J. Sundquist, 1–38. Abingdon: Routledge, 2012.

Cesarani, David and Eric J. Sundquist, Editors. *After the Holocaust: Challenging the Myth of Silence*. Abingdon: Routledge, 2012.

Chabon, Michael. 'Imaginary Homelands'. In *Maps & Legends: Reading and Writing Along the Borderlands*, 157–79. London: Fourth Estate, 2010.

Chabon, Michael. *The Yiddish Policemen's Union*. London: Harper Perennial, 2008.

Charnay, David. *Operation Lucifer: The Chase, Capture, and Trial of Adolf Hitler*. Calabasas, CA: Squire General Limited, 2001.

Chu, Seo-Young. *Do Metaphors Dream of Literal Sheep: A Science-Fictional Theory of Representation*. Cambridge: Harvard University Press, 2010.

Clute, John. '*Half a Crown* by Jo Walton'. *Strange Horizons*, 15 December 2008. Accessed 10 March 2019. http://strangehorizons.com/non-fiction/reviews/half-a-crown-by-jo-walton/.

Clute, John, 'Jo Walton'. *The Encyclopedia of Science Fiction*. Last modified 3 September 2018. Accessed 10 March 2019. http://www.sf-encyclopedia.com/entry/walton_jo.

Cohen, Arthur A. 'Thinking the Tremendum: Some Theological Implications of the Death Camps'. In *An Arthur A. Cohen Reader: Selected Fiction and Writings on*

Judaism, Theology, Literature, and Culture. Edited by David Stern and Paul Mendes-Flohr, 234–49. Detroit: Wayne State University Press, 1998.

Cole, Stephen and Justin Richard. *Doctor Who: The Shadow in the Glass.* London: BBC Books, 2001.

Conlon, Declan. 'Obsession with World War Played Role in Brexit, Says Harris'. *The Irish Times*, 29 September 2017. Accessed 10 March 2019. https://www.irishtimes.com/news/politics/obsession-with-world-war-played-role-in-brexit-says-harris-1.3238736.

Coward, Noël. *The Letters of Noël Coward.* Edited by Barry Day. London: Vintage, 2009.

Coward, Noël. *Peace in Our Time.* London: William Heinemann, 1947.

Croft, Andy. 'World Without End Foisted Upon the Future – Some Antecedents of Nineteen Eighty-Four'. In *Inside the Myth: Orwell, Views from the Left.* Edited by Christopher Norris, 183–216. London: 1984.

Robert Crossley. 'Dystopian Nights'. *Science Fiction Studies* 14, no. 1 (1987): 93–8.

Dahl, Roald. *The BFG.* London: Jonathan Cape, 1982.

Davis, Mike. *Late Victorian Holocausts: El Niño Famines and the Making of the Third World.* London: Verso, 2017.

de Groot, Jerome. *The Historical Novel: The New Critical Idiom.* Abingdon: Routledge, 2010.

Deighton, Jack. '*Farthing* by Jo Walton', 7 December 2015. Accessed 9 February 2016. http://jackdeighton.co.uk/2015/12/07/farthing-by-jo-walton/.

Deighton, Len. *SS-GB.* London: Jonathan Cape, 1978.

Des Pres, Terrence. 'The Authority of Silence in Elie Wiesel's Art'. In *Writing in to the World: Essays, 1973–1987*, 25–32. New York: Viking, 1991.

Dick, Philip K. 'Biographical Material on Hawthorne Abendsen'. In *The Shifting Realities of Philip K. Dick: Selected Literary and Philosophical Writings.* Edited by Lawrence Sutin, 118. New York: Vintage, 1995.

Dick, Philip K. *The Exegesis of Philip K. Dick.* Edited by Pamela Jackson and Jonathan Lethem. New York: Houghton Mifflin Harcourt, 2011.

Dick, Philip K. *The Man in the High Castle.* London: Penguin, 2001.

Dick, Philip K. 'Naziism and the High Castle'. In *The Shifting Realities of Philip K. Dick: Selected Literary and Philosophical Writings.* Edited by Lawrence Sutin, 112–18. New York: Vintage, 1995.

Dick, Philip K. and Mike Hodel. 'Hour 25: A Talk with Philip K. Dick'. *Philip K. Dick Fans.* Accessed 29 September 2016. http://www.philipkdickfans.com/literary-criticism/interviews/hour-25-a-talk-with-philip-k-dick/.

Doctorow, Cory. '*Farthing*: Heart-Rending Alternate History about British-Reich Peace'. *BoingBoing*, 20 June 2006. Accessed 20 September 2016. http://boingboing.net/2006/06/20/farthing-heartrendin.html.

Eaglestone, Robert. *The Holocaust and the Postmodern.* Oxford: Oxford University Press, 2009.

Edwards, Maximillian. 'A Man Lies Dreaming by Lavie Tidhar'. *Strange Horizons*, 12 January 2015. Accessed 10 March 2019. http://strangehorizons.com/non-fiction/reviews/a-man-lies-dreaming-by-lavie-tidhar/.
Englander, Nathan. 'What We Talk About When We Talk About Anne Frank'. In *What We Talk About When We Talk About Anne Frank*, 3–32. London: Phoenix, 2013.
Epstein, Leslie. 'Writing about the Holocaust'. In *Writing and the Holocaust*. Edited by Berel Lang, 261–70. New York: Holmes & Meier, 1988.
Evans, Richard J. *Altered Pasts: Counterfactuals in History*. London: Little Brown, 2013.
Ezrahi, Sidra DeKovan. 'Racism and Ethics: Constructing Alternative History'. In *Impossible Images: Contemporary Art after the Holocaust*. Edited by Shelley Hornstein, Laura Levitt, and Laurence J. Silverstein, 118–28. New York: New York University Press, 2003.
Felman, Shoshana. 'In an Era of Testimony: Claude Lanzmann's *Shoah*'. *Yale French Studies* 79 (1991): 39–81.
Ferguson, Niall. 'Virtual History: Towards a "Chaotic" Theory of the Past'. In *Virtual Histories: Alternatives and Counterfactuals*. Edited by Niall Ferguson, 1–90. London: Picador, 1997.
Finkelstein, Norman. *The Holocaust Industry*. 2nd edition. London: Verso, 2003.
Finkelstein, Norman. *The Ritual of New Creation: Jewish Tradition and Contemporary Literature*. Albany: State University of New York Press, 1992.
Fonseca, Isabel. *Bury Me Standing: The Gypsies and their Journey*. 1995. Reprinted with an afterword. London: Vintage, 2006.
Forester, C. S. 'Introduction'. In *The Nightmare*, vii–viii. Los Angeles: Pinnacle, 1979.
Forester, C. S. 'The Wandering Gentile'. In *Nightmares*, 225–46. Los Angeles: Pinnacle, 1979.
Freedman, Samuel. *Jew vs. Jew: The Struggle for the Soul of American Jewry*. New York: Simon & Schuster, 2000.
Freud, Sigmund. *Moses and Monotheism: Three Essays*. In *The Standard Edition of the Complete Psychological Work of Sigmund Freud*. Translated and edited by James Strachey. Volume 23. London: The Hogarth Press, 1964.
Friedberg, Lilian. 'Dare to Compare: Americanizing the Holocaust'. In *The Holocaust: Theoretical Readings*. Edited by Neil Levi and Michael Rothberg, 468–73. Edinburgh: Edinburgh University Press, 2003.
Friedländer, Saul. *Reflections of Nazism: An Essay on Kitsch and Death*. Translated by Thomas Weyr. New York: Harper & Row, 1984.
Franklin, Ruth. *A Thousand Darknesses: Lies and Truth in Holocaust Fiction*. Oxford: Oxford University Press, 2011.
Fry, Stephen. 'Interview: Stephen Fry'. *AV Club*, 22 September 2004. Accessed 15 July 2015. http://www.avclub.com/article/stephen-fry-13891.
Fry, Stephen. *Making History*. London: Arrow, 2004.

Fussell, James T. 'A Crime Without A Name'. *Prevent Genocide International*. Accessed 1 May 2016. http://www.preventgenocide.org/genocide/crimewithoutaname.htm.

Gaer, Joseph. *The Legend of the Wandering Jew*. New York: Mentor, 1961.

Gage, Beverly. 'Reading the Classic Novel that Predicted Trump'. *New York Times*, 17 January 2017. Accessed 9 March 2019. https://www.newyorker.com/culture/culture-desk/getting-close-to-fascism-with-sinclair-lewiss-it-cant-happen-here.

Gallagher, Catherine. *Telling It Like It Wasn't: The Counterfactual Imagination in History and Fiction*. Chicago: Chicago University Press, 2018.

Gilbert, Ruth. 'Reality Gaps: Negotiating the Boundaries of British-Jewish Identities in Contemporary Fiction'. In *Boundaries, Identities and Belonging in Modern Judaism*. Edited by Maria Diemling and Larry Ray, 107–20. Abingdon: Routledge, 2016.

Goldhagen, Daniel Jonah. *Hitler's Willing Executioners*. London: Vintage, 1996.

Gomel, Elana. *Postmodern Science Fiction and Temporal Imagination*. London: Bloomsbury, 2010.

Gordon, Joan. '*Half a Crown* by Jo Walton'. *The New York Review of Science Fiction* 247 (2009): 12–13.

Hambly, Barbara. *The Magicians of Night*. New York: Del Rey, 1992.

Hambly, Barbara. *The Rainbow Abyss*. New York: Del Rey, 1991.

Hancock, Ian. 'Responses to the Porrajmos: The Romani Holocaust'. In *Is the Holocaust Unique? Perspectives of Comparative Genocide*. Edited by Alan S. Rosenbaum, 39–64. Cumnor Hill: Westview, 1996.

Harris, Robert. *Fatherland*. London: Arrow Books, 1993.

Harris, Robert. *Selling Hitler*. London: Faber & Faber, 1986.

Harris, Robert, et al. 'Voices of Europe: Need for Germany Far Outweighs Any Fears'. *The New York Times*, 29 September 1992. Accessed 28 August 2014. http://www.nytimes.com/1992/09/29/world/voices-of-europe-need-for-germany-far-outweighs-any-fears.html.

Hartland, Dan. '*Farthing* by Jo Walton'. *Strange Horizons*, 23 October 2006. Accessed 10 March 2019. http://strangehorizons.com/non-fiction/reviews/farthing-by-jo-walton/.

Hartley, L. P. *The Go-Between*. London: Penguin, 2004.

Hartman, Geoffrey H. *The Longest Shadow: In the Aftermath of the Holocaust*. Bloomington: Indiana University Press, 1996.

Hayes, Peter and John K. Roth, Editors. *The Oxford Handbook of Holocaust Studies*. Oxford: Oxford University Press, 2010.

Heidelberger-Leonard, Irène. *The Philosopher of Auschwitz: Jean Améry and Living with the Holocaust*. London: I.B. Tauris, 2000.

Hellekson, Karen. *The Alternate History: Refiguring Historical Time*. Kent, OH: The Kent State University Press, 2001.

Hellekson, Karen. 'Rhion's Adventures Continue'. *SFRA Review* 201 (1992): 45–6.

Henley, Jon. 'Antisemitism Rising Sharply Across Europe, Latest Figures Show'. *The Guardian*, 15 February 2019. Accessed 10 March 2019. https://www.theguardian.com/news/2019/feb/15/antisemitism-rising-sharply-across-europe-latest-figures-show.

Hilberg, Raul. 'I Was Not There'. In *Writing and the Holocaust*. Edited by Berel Lang, 17–25. New York: Holmes & Meier, 1988.

Hilberg, Raul, Cynthia Ozick, Aharon Appelfeld and Saul Friedländer. 'Roundtable Discussion'. In *Writing and the Holocaust*. Edited by Berel Lang, 273–89. New York: Holmes & Meier, 1988.

Himmelfarb, Milton. 'No Hitler, No Holocaust'. *Commentary*, March 1984: 37–43.

Hitler, Adolf. *Mein Kampf*. Translated by Ralph Manheim. London: Hutchinson, 1990.

Hollinger, Veronica. 'Cybernetic Deconstructions: Cyberpunk and Postmodernism'. In *Science Fiction Criticism: An Anthology of Essential Writings*. Edited by Rob Latham, 43–58. London: Bloomsbury, 2017.

Hurst, L. J. 'Anywhere but Stoke Poges'. *Vector* 148 (1989): 14.

Ilsa, She Wolf of the SS. Directed by Don Edmonds. New York: Cambist Films, 1975.

Ingersoll, Earl and Nancy Kress. 'Seeing the Magic in Everyday Life: A Conversation with Lisa Goldstein'. *SFRA Newsletter* 184 (1991): 7–19.

Ishiguro, Kazuo. *The Remains of the Day*, 1989.

Jacobson, Howard. *J*. London: Jonathan Cape, 2014.

Jacobson, Howard. 'Let's See the "criticism" of Israel of What It Really Is'. *The Independent*, 18 February 2009. Accessed 20 September 2016. http://www.independent.co.uk/voices/commentators/howard-jacobson/howard-jacobson-letrsquos-see-the-criticism-of-israel-for-what-it-really-is-1624827.html.

Jacobson, Howard. *When Will Jews Be Forgiven the Holocaust*. Amazon Singles, 2014. Kindle.

Jameson, Fredric. *Postmodernism, or the Cultural Logic of Late Capitalism*. Durham, NC: Duke University Press, 1997.

Jewish Virtual Library. 'The Last Nazi Trials'. Accessed 14 March 2019. https://www.jewishvirtuallibrary.org/modern-nazi-trials.

Jones, Adam. *Genocide: A Comprehensive Introduction*. 2nd edition. London: Routledge, 2011.

Kakutani, Michiko. 'Books of the Times: Plotting to Erase Hitler From History'. *New York Times*, 21 April 1998. Accessed 28 September 2016. http://www.nytimes.com/1998/04/21/books/books-of-the-times-plotting-to-erase-hitler-from-history.html.

Kaplan, Brett Ashley. *Jewish Anxiety and the Novels of Philip Roth*. London: Bloomsbury, 2015.

Katz, Steven T. *The Holocaust in Historical Context, Volume 1: The Holocaust and Mass Death before the Modern Age*. Oxford: Oxford University Press, 1994.

Kedward, H. R. *Fascism in Western Europe 1900–1945*. London: Blackie & Son, 1969.

Kerman, Judith B. 'Uses of the Fantastic in Literature of the Holocaust'. In *The Fantastic in Holocaust Literature and Film*. Edited by Judith B. Kerman and John Edgar Browning, 13–24. Jefferson, NC: McFarland, 2015.

Ketterer, David. 'Introduction: A Ground-Breaking Cloned Nazi Thriller'. In John Wyndham, *A Plan for Chaos*. Liverpool: Liverpool University Press, 2009.

Kincaid, Paul. 'Farthing'. *New York Review of Science Fiction* 223, no. 19.7 (2007): 10–11.

Kornbluth, C. M. 'Two Dooms'. In *Hitler Victorious*. Edited by Gregory Benford and Martin H. Greenberg, 21–82. London: Grafton, 1988.

Kremer, S. Lillian. 'The Holocaust in English-Language Literatures'. In *Literature of the Holocaust*. Edited by Alan Rosen, 131–49. Cambridge: Cambridge University Press, 2013.

Kremer, S. Lillian. *Witness Through the Imagination: Jewish American Holocaust Literature*. Detroit: Wayne State University Press, 1989.

Kubert, Joe. *Yossel: April 19, 1943*. New York: DC Comics, 2003.

LaCapra, Dominick. 'Representing the Holocaust: Reflections on the Historians' Debate'. In *Probing the Limits of Representation: Nazism and the 'Final Solution'*. Edited by Saul Friedlander, 108–27. Cambridge, MA: Harvard University Press, 1992.

Lafferty, R. A. 'The Three Armageddons of Enniscorthy Sweeny'. In *Apocalypses*, 189–374. Los Angeles: Pinnacle, 1977.

Laks, Szymon. *Music of Another World*. Translated by Chester A. Kisiel. Evanston, IL: Northwestern University Press, 1989.

Lang, Berel. 'Holocaust Genres and the Turn to History'. In *The Holocaust and the Text: Speaking the Unspeakable*. Edited by Andrew Leak and George Paizis, 17–31. London: Palgrave, 2000.

Lang, Berel. 'Introduction'. In *Writing and the Holocaust*. Edited by Berel Lang, 1–15. New York: Holmes & Meier, 1988.

Langer, Lawrence L. *The Holocaust and the Literary Imagination*. New Haven: Yale University Press, 1975.

Langer, Lawrence L. *Using and Abusing the Holocaust*. Bloomington: Indiana University Press, 2006.

The Last Crusade. Directed by Steven Spielberg. Paramount Pictures, 1989.

Levi, Neil and Michael Rothberg. 'Theory and the Holocaust'. In *The Holocaust: Theoretical Readings*. Edited by Neil Levi and Michael Rothberg, 1–22. Edinburgh: Edinburgh University Press, 2003.

Levi, Primo. *The Drowned and the Saved*. Translated by Raymond Rosenthal. London: Abacus, 2010.

Levi, Primo. *If This Is a Man*. Translated by Stuart Woolf. London: Abacus, 2010.

Levin, Ira. *The Boys from Brazil*. London: Corsair, 2011.

Levin, Nora. *The Holocaust: The Destruction of European Jewry, 1933–1945*. New York: T. Y. Crowell, 1968.

Lewis, Sinclair. *It Can't Happen Here*. 1935. New York: Signet Classic, 1993.

Leys, Ruth. *Trauma: A Genealogy*. Chicago: University of Chicago Press, 2000.

Lipstadt, Deborah. 'America and the Memory of the Holocaust'. *Modern Judaism* 16, no. 3 (1996): 195–294.

London, Jack. *Iron Heel*. 1907. Reprinted with notes and introduction. London: Penguin, 2007.

Lovecraft, H. P., 'The Whisper in Darkness'. In *Necronomicon: The Best Weird Tales of H.P. Lovecraft*. Edited by Stephen Jones, 298–349. London: Gollancz, 2008.

Luckhurst, Roger. *Zombies: A Cultural History*. London: Reaktion, 2015.

Lyotard, Jean-François. *The Differend: Phrases in Dispute*. Translated by Georges Van Den Abbeele. Minneapolis: University of Minnesota Press, 1998.

MacLeod, Ian R. 'Summer Isles'. In *Breathmoss and Other Exhalations*, 235–309. Urbana, IL: Golden Gryphon Press, 2004.

Magilow, Daniel H., Elizabeth Bridges and Kristin T. Vander Lugt, Editors. *Nazisploitation!: The Nazi Image in Low-Brow Cinema and Culture*. London: Continuum, 2012.

Maier, Charles S. 'A Surfeit of Memory? Reflections on History, Melancholy, and Denial'. *History and Memory* 5 (1992): 136–51.

Malzberg, Barry. 'Hitler at Nuremberg'. In *By Any Other Fame*. Edited by Mike Resnick and Martin Greenberg, 196–302. New York: Daw, 1994.

Manguel, Alberto. 'The Exile's Library'. *The Guardian*, 21 February 2009. Accessed 24 August 2017. http://www.theguardian.com/books/2009/feb/21/wandering-jew-history.

Maritain, Jacques. *The Range of Reason: The Jacques Maritain Centre*. Accessed 29 September 2016. https://www3.nd.edu/~maritain/jmc/etext/range10.htm.

Markun, Michael. *Culture of Conspiracy: Apocalyptic Visions in Contemporary America*. Berkeley: University of California Press, 2003.

Melley, Timoth. *Empire of Conspiracy: The Culture of Paranoia in Postwar America*. Ithaca, NY: Cornell University Press, 2000.

Mendlesohn, Farah. 'Jo Walton in Conversation with Farah Mendlesohn'. *Vector* 276 (2014): 4–11.

Meyers, Helene. *Reading Michael Chabon*. Santa Barbara: Greenwood, 2010.

Millu, Liana. *Smoke Over Birkenau*. Translated by Lynne Sharon Schwartz. Evanston, IL: Northwestern University Press, 1998.

Milner, Andrew. 'Utopia and Science Fiction Revisited'. In *Red Planets: Marxism and Science Fiction*. Edited by Mark Bould and China Miéville, 213–30. London: Pluto Press, 2009.

Morgan, Chris. *The Shapes of Futures Past: The Story of Prediction*. Exeter: Webb and Bower, 1980.

Morgan, Glyn. 'An Interview with Lavie Tidhar'. *Glyn-Morgan.blogspot*, 8 April 2015. Accessed 20 August 2016. http://glyn-morgan.blogspot.co.uk/2015/04/interview-with-lavie-tidhar.html.

Morgan, Glyn. 'Speaking the Unspeakable and Seeing the Unseeable: The Role of Fantastika in Visualizing the Holocaust, or, More Than Just *Maus*'. *The Luminary* 6 (2015): http://www.lancaster.ac.uk/luminary/issue6/issue6article3.htm.

Morley, Sheridan. 'Introduction'. In Noël Coward, *Collected Plays: Volume Seven*. London: Bloomsbury Methuen, 1999.

Nazaryan, Alexander. 'Getting Close to Fascism with Sinclair Lewis's "It Can't Happen Here"'. *The New Yorker*, 19 October 2016. Accessed 10 March 2019. https://www.newyorker.com/culture/culture-desk/getting-close-to-fascism-with-sinclair-lewiss-it-cant-happen-here.

Neiman, Susan. *Evil in Modern Thought: An Alternative History of Philosophy*. Princeton: Princeton University Press, 2015.

Niemöller, Martin. 'First They Came for the Jews'. In *Holocaust Poetry*. Edited by Hilda Schiff, 9. London: Fount, 1995.

Northeastern News. 'The Amazing Adventures of Michael Chabon'. *News @ Northeastern*, 6 April 2012. Accessed 20 August 2016. http://www.northeastern.edu/news/2012/04/chabon/.

Novick, Peter. *The Holocaust and Collective Memory*. London: Bloomsbury, 2000.

Olusoga, David and Casper Erichsen. *The Kaiser's Holocaust: Germany's Forgotten Genocide and the Colonial Roots of the Holocaust*. London: Faber & Faber, 2010.

Orwell, George. 'As I Please'. *Tribune*, 20 October 1944.

Orwell, George. *Nineteen Eighty-Four*. London: Penguin, 2000.

Osbourne, Peter. 'Small-Scale Victories, Large-Scale Defeats: Walter Benjamin's Politics of Time'. In *Walter Benjamin's Philosophy: Destruction and Experience*. Edited by Andrew Benjamin and Peter Osbourne, 59–109. London: Routledge, 1994.

Pagetti, Carlo. 'In the Year of Our Lord Hitler 720: Katharine Burdekin's *Swastika Night*'. *Science Fiction Studies* 52 (1990): 360–269.

Pasamonik, Didier and Joël Kotek. Editors. *Shoah et Bande Dessinée: L'image au service de la mémoire*. Paris: Denoël Graphic, 2017.

Patai, Daphne. 'Introduction'. In Katharine Burdekin, *Swastika Night*, iii–xv. New York: Feminist Press, 1985.

Prescott, Orville. 'Book of the Times'. *The New York Times*, 17 October 1960, 27.

Raczymow, Henri. 'Memory Shot Through With Holes'. In *The Holocaust: Theoretical Readings*. Edited by Neil Levi and Michael Rothberg, 410–15. Edinburgh: Edinburgh University Press, 2003.

Radin, Max. *The Day of Reckoning*. New York: Knopf, 1943.

Raiders of the Lost Ark. Directed by Steven Spielberg. Paramount Pictures, 1981.

Reiter, Andrea. *Narrating the Holocaust*. Translated by Patrick Camiller. London: Continuum, 2000.

Rieder, John. 'The Metafictive World of *The Man in the High Castle*: Hermeneutics, Ethics, and Political Ideology'. *Science Fiction Studies* 15, no. 2 (1988): 214–25.

Roberts, Andrew. 'Andrew Roberts on "If Hitler Comes"'. *Faber Finds*. Accessed 20 August 2012. www.faber.co.uk/article/2009/11/if-hitler-comes-andrew-roberts-review/.

Roberts, Andrew. 'Introduction'. In *What Might Have Been*. Edited by Andrew Roberts, 1–14. London: Phoenix, 2005.

Rosen, Yareth. 'That Great Big Jewish Alaska'. *Moment* 5 January 2012. Accessed 20 August 2016. http://www.momentmag.com/that-great-big-jewish-alaska/.

Rosenbaum, Thane. *The Golems of Gotham*. New York: Perennial, 2003.

Rosenfeld, Alvin H. *A Double Dying: Reflections on Holocaust Literature*. Indianapolis: Indiana University Press, 1988.

Rosenfeld, Alvin H. 'Popularization and Memory: The Case of Anne Frank'. In *Lessons and Legacies: The Meaning of the Holocaust in a Changing World*. Edited by Peter Hayes, 243. Evanston, IL: Northwestern University Press, 1991.

Rosenfeld, Gavriel D. *Hi Hitler! How the Nazi Past Is Being Normalized in Contemporary Culture*. Cambridge: Cambridge University Press, 2015.

Rosenfeld, Gavriel D. *The World Hitler Never Made: Alternate History and the Memory of Nazism*. Cambridge: Cambridge University Press, 2005.

Roskies David G. and Naomi Diamant. *Holocaust Literature: A History and Guide*. Waltham, MA: Brandeis University Press, 2012.

Roth, Philip. *American Pastoral*. London: Vintage, 1998.

Roth, Philip. *Ghost Writer*. London: Vintage, 2005.

Roth, Philip. '"I Always Wanted You to Admire My Fasting"; or, Looking at Kafka'. In *Kafkaesque: Stories Inspired by Franz Kafka*. Edited by James Patrick Kelly and John Kessel, 231–43. San Francisco: Tachyon, 2011.

Roth, Philip. *The Plot Against America*. London: Vintage, 2005.

Roth, Philip. 'The Story Behind "The Plot Against America"'. *New York Times*, 19 September 2004. Accessed 7 February 2015. http://www.nytimes.com/2004/09/19/books/review/19ROTHL.html.

Rothberg, Michael. *Traumatic Realism*. Minneapolis, MN: Minnesota University Press, 2000.

Rousset, David. *The Other Kingdom*. Translated by Ramon Guthrie. New York: Reynal & Hitchcock, 1947.

Rovner, Adam. 'What if the Jewish State Had Been Established in East Africa?' In *What Ifs of Jewish History: From Abraham to Zionism*. Edited by Gavriel D. Rosenfeld, 165–86. Cambridge: Cambridge University Press, 2016.

Rowling, J. K., John Tiffany and Jack Thorne. *Harry Potter and the Cursed Child Parts One and Two*. London: Little Brown, 2016.

Rubinstein, Rachel. *Members of the Tribe: Native America in the Jewish Imagination*. Texas: Wayne State University Press, 2010.

Rubenstein, Richard L. *After Auschwitz: History, Theology and Contemporary Judaism*. Baltimore: Johns Hopkins University Press, 1992.

Sands, Philippe. 'Primo Levi's *If This Is a Man* at 70'. *The Guardian*, 22 April 2017. Accessed 20 February 2019. https://www.theguardian.com/books/2017/apr/22/primo-levi-auschwitz-if-this-is-a-man-memoir-70-years.
Sansom, C. J. *Dominion*. London: Pan Macmillan, 2012.
Sarban. *The Sound of His Horn*. Floyd, VA: Black Curtain Press, 2013.
Sargent, Pamela. 'Science Fiction, Historical Fiction, and Alternate History'. *Bulletin of Science Fiction Writers of America*, Fall 1995, 3–7.
Saville, Guy. 'A Is for Apocalypse Now'. *AfrikaReichTrilogy*, 24 July 2011. Accessed 1 September 2016. http://afrikareichtrilogy.blogspot.co.uk/2011/07/is-for-apocalypse-now.html.
Saville, Guy. *The Afrika Reich*. London: Hodder & Stoughton, 2011.
Saxena, Vandana. 'Mother Goose Tales: Integrational Storytelling and the Holocaust in Jane Yolen's Briar Rose and Peter Rushforth's Kindergarten'. In *The Fantastic in Holocaust Literature and Film*. Edited by Judith B. Kerman and John Edgar Browning, 122–36. Jefferson, NC: McFarland, 2015.
Scaggs, John. *Crime Fiction: The New Critical Idiom*. Abingdon: Routledge, 2008.
Schaub, Michael. '*The Plot Against America* by Philip Roth'. *Bookslut*, October 2004. Accessed 10 February 2019. http://www.bookslut.com/fiction/2004_10_003275.php.
Schiff, Hilda. 'Introduction'. In *Holocaust Poetry*. Edited by Hilda Schiff. London: Fount, 1995.
Sheers, Owen. *The Resistance*. London: Faber & Faber: 2007.
Shiffman, Dan. '*The Plot Against America* and History Post-9/11'. *Philip Roth Studies* 5, no. 1 (2009): 61–150.
Shirer, William L. 'If Hitler Had Won World War II'. *Look* 25, no. 26 (1961): 27–44.
Sicher, Efraim. 'The Burden of Memory'. In *Breaking Crystal: Writing and Memory After Auschwitz*. Edited by Efraim Sicher, 19–88. Chicago: University of Illinois Press, 1998.
Singles, Kathleen. *Alternate History: Playing with Contingency and Necessity*. Berlin: De Gruyter, 2013.
Skibell, Joseph. *A Blessing on the Moon*. Chapel Hill, NC: Algonquin, 2010.
Snyder, Timothy. *Black Earth: The Holocaust as History and Warning*. London: Vintage, 2015.
Sontag, Susan. *On Photography*. Harmondsworth: Penguin, 1977.
Speer, Albert. *Inside the Third Reich*. New York: Macmillan, 1970.
Spinrad, Norman. *The Iron Dream*. St Albans: Panther, 1974.
Spinrad, Norman. *Science Fiction in the Real World*. Carbondale: Southern Illinois University Press, 1990.
Steinacher, Gerald. *Nazis on the Run: How Hitler's Henchmen Fled Justice*. Oxford: Oxford University Press, 2011.
Steiner, George. *The Portage to San Cristobal of A.H.* New York: Simon and Schuster, 1981.

Steiner, George. 'Preface'. In *Language and Silence: Essays on Language, Literature, and the Inhuman*, 13–17. Harmondsworth: Peregrine, 1979.

Steiner, George. 'In Exile Wherever He Goes'. *The New York Times*, 1 March 1998. Accessed 20 August 2016. https://www.nytimes.com/books/98/03/01/reviews/980 301.01steinet.html.

Steiner, George. 'Silence and the Poet'. In *Language and Silence: Essays on Language, Literature, and the Inhuman*, 57–76. Harmondsworth: Peregrine, 1979.

Stern, Harry J. '5 Million Jews Would Have Perished If Hitler Had Won War, Shirer Says'. *The Canadian Jewish Chronicle*, 15 December 1961, 9.

Stinson, J. G. 'Farthing'. *The New York Review of Science Fiction* 226 (2007): 7.

Suvin, Darko. *Metamorphoses of Science Fiction: On the Poetics and History of a Literary Genre*. Edited by Gerry Canavan. Bern: Peter Lang, 2016.

Taylor, D. J. *The Windsor Faction*. London: Chatto & Windus, 2013.

Thiess, Derek J. *Relativism, Alternate History, and the Forgetful Reader*. Lanham, MD: Lexington, 2015.

Thomas, D. M. *The White Hotel*. London: Gollancz, 1981.

Thomas, Dylan. *Under Milk Wood*. London: Phoenix, 2000.

Thomas, Roy. *Superman: War of the Worlds*. Illustrated by Michael Lark. New York: DC Comics, 1999.

Tidhar, Lavie. *A Man Lies Dreaming*. London: Hodder, 2014.

Tidhar, Lavie. 'Uganda'. *Hebrewpunk*, 52–99. Clacton-on-Sea: Apex, 2007.

Tidhar, Lavie. *Unholy Land*. San Francisco: Tachyon, 2018.

Tołczyk, Dariusz. 'Katyn: The Long Cover-Up'. *New Criterion* 28, no. 9 (2010): 4–9.

Tuttle, Lisa. 'Introduction'. In Jerry Yulsman. *Elleander Morning*, 1–2. London: Gollancz, 2015.

United States Congress, Senate, Committee on Territories and Insular Affairs. *Settlement and Development of Alaska: Hearings Before a Subcommittee, Seventy-Sixth Congress, Third Session, on S.3577, a Bill to Provide for the Settlement and Development of Alaska*. May 13, 15, and 18, 1940. Washington, DC: U.S. Government Printing Office, 1940.

Valentine, Mark. *Time, A Falconer: A Study of Sarban*. Tartarus: 2010.

Vice, Sue. *Holocaust Fiction*. Abingdon: Routledge, 2000.

Walker, Amy. 'Do Mention the War: The Politicians Comparing Brexit to WWII'. *The Guardian*, 4 February 2019. Accessed 10 March 2019. https://www.theguardian.com/politics/2019/feb/04/do-mention-the-war-the-politicians-comparing-brexit-to-wwii.

Walsh, John. '"I write about male sexual obsession... fortunately none of my three wives has mistaken fiction for fact": Howard Jacobson on Sex, Religion and Anti-Semitism'. *Daily Mail*, 8 August 2015. Accessed 25 February 2016. http://www.dailymail.co.uk/home/event/article-3186946/Howard-Jacobson-write-male-sexual-obsession-fortunately-none-three-wives-mistaken-fiction-fact.html.

Walters, Guy. *The Leader*. London: Headline, 2004.

Walton, Jo. 'A Pit in Dothan: Josephine Tey's *Brat Farrar*'. *Tor.com*, 10 September 2010. Accessed 3 February 2016. http://www.tor.com/2010/09/10/a-pit-in-dothan-josephine-teys-brat-farrar/.

Walton, Jo. *Farthing*. New York: Tor, 2006.

Walton, Jo. Ha'*Penny*. New York: Tor, 2007.

Walton, Jo. *Half a Crown*. New York: Tor, 2008.

Walton, Jo. 'The Small Change Series'. Accessed 6 February 2016. http://www.jowaltonbooks.com/books/the-small-change-series/.

Walton, Jo. 'Who Survives Catastrophe?' *Foundation* 93 (2005): 34–9.

Waugh, Patricia. *Metafiction: The Theory and Practice of Self-Conscious Fiction*. London: Methuen, 1984.

Waxman, Zoë Vania. *Writing the Holocaust: Identity, Testimony, Representation*. Oxford: Oxford University Press, 2006.

Weil, Ellen R. 'The Door to Lilith's Cave: Memory and Imagination in Jane Yolen's Holocaust Novels'. In *The Fantastic in Holocaust Literature and Film*. Edited by Judith B. Kerman and John Edgar Browning, 111–21. Jefferson, NC: McFarland, 2015.

Weissman, Gary. *Fantasies of Witnessing: Postwar Efforts to Experience the Holocaust*. Ithaca, NY: Cornell University, 2004.

Wiener, Jon. 'Arctic Jews: An Interview with Michael Chabon'. *Dissent*, 14 April 2007. Accessed 20 August 2016. http://www.dissentmagazine.org/online_articles/arctic-jews-an-interview-with-michael-chabon.

Wiesel, Elie. 'Art and the Holocaust: Trivializing Memory'. Translated by Iver Peterson. *The New York Times*, 11 June 1989. Accessed 20 August 2016. http://www.nytimes.com/1989/06/11/movies/art-and-the-holocaust-trivializing-memory.html.

Wiesel, Elie. 'The Holocaust as Literary Inspiration'. In *Dimensions of the Holocaust*. Edited by Elie Wiesel et al., 5–19. Evanston, IL: Northwestern University Press, 1977.

Wiesel, Elie. *Night*. Translated by Marion Wiesel. London: Penguin, 2008.

Wiesel, Elie. 'Why I Write'. In *From the Kingdom of Mercy*, 9–20. New York: Summit, 1990.

Wiesenthal, Simon. *The Murderers Among Us: The Simon Wiesenthal Memoirs*. New York: McGraw Hill, 1967.

Winthrop-Young, George. 'The Third Reich in Alternate History: Aspects of a Genre-Specific Depiction of Nazi Culture'. *The Journal of Popular Culture* 39, no. 5 (2006): 878–96.

Wolfe, Gary K. *Evaporating Genres: Essays on Fantastic Literature*. Middletown, CT: Wesleyan University Press, 2011.

Wood, Michael. 'Just Folks'. *London Review of Books* 26, no. 21, 4 November 2004. Accessed 7 February 2019. http://www.lrb.co.uk/v26/n21/michael-wood/just-folks.

Wordsworth, William. 'Song for the Wandering Jew'. In *William Wordsworth and Samuel Taylor Coleridge, Lyrical Ballads, 1798 and 1802*. Edited by Fiona Stafford, 284. Oxford: Oxford University Press, 2013.

Wyndham, John. *A Plan for Chaos*. Liverpool: Liverpool University Press, 2009.
Wyndham, John. 'Roar of Rockets'. *John o'London's Weekly* 63 (2 April 1954): 333–4.
Yolen, Jane. *Briar Rose*. New York: Tor, 2002.
Yolen, Jane. *The Devil's Arithmetic*. New York: Puffin, 1990.
Yolen, Jane. *Mapping the Bones*. New York: Philomel, 2018.
Young, James. *Writing and Rewriting the Holocaust: Narrative and the Consequences of Interpretation*. Bloomington: Indiana University Press, 1988.
Young, Michael. *The Trial of Adolf Hitler*. New York: Dutton, 1944.
Yulsman, Jerry. *Elleander Morning*. London: Orbit, 1985.
Zinn, Howard. *A People's History of the United States*. New York: Harper Perennial, 2015.
Žižek, Slavoj. *For They Know Not What They Do: Enjoyment as a Political Factor*. London: Verso, 1991.

Index

11 September Terrorist Attacks   17, 101, 109–10, 121–2, 144

Aaronovitch, David   20, 57
Adams, Jenni   158
Adorno, Theodor   5, 64
Aesop   136
Agamben, Giorgio   10
Alaskan Settlement Act   89
Alderman, Naomi   85
Allhoff, Fred   39, 108
alternate history   11–14
    history of   12, 48n
Amis, Kingsley   11
Amis, Martin   129
anti-Semitism   11, 18–9, 34, 64–6, 95, 98, 100–2, 106–8, 117, 119, 121–2, 128, 133, 138–43, 151–3
    post-war rises   144
Arendt, Hannah   84, 130, 188n
Attebery, Brian   148
Auden, W. H.   116
Auschwitz   6–7, 10, 13, 19, 24, 39, 50, 52, 56, 62, 68, 91, 100, 117, 124, 129, 130–3, 135–6, 138, 147, 165n
    medical experiments in   62, 72, 76
    Metonym for Holocaust   8, 126
    'Planet Auschwitz'   90, 125–7, 188n
    writing poetry after   5 (*see also* poetry)
Auslander, Shalom   17, 72, 84–8

Barnes, James J.   21
Battle of Dorking, The   22
Bauman, Zygmunt   65, 66, 143
Belzec   8, 148
Benjamin, Walter   2, 42, 60, 64
Bergen-Belsen   84
Berlin Wall   38
Bier, Jesse   74–5
Birkenau   30, 56, 166n
Bloom, Harold   4, 6, 166n

Book of Changes. See I Ching
Bormann, Martin   43, 48, 130
Borowski, Tadeusz   125, 147, 165n
Bowers, Robert Gregory   144
Boys from Brazil, The (1978 film)   75, 79. *See also* Levin, Ira
Bradbury, Ray   12
Braun, Eva   22, 34, 36, 71, 75
Brecht, Bertolt   11
Brexit   18, 58–9, 144
Buchenwald   10, 128, 155–6, 166n
Budick, Emily Miller   88
Bulwer-Lytton, Edward   193n
Burdekin, Katharine   2, 14, 21–5, 30, 33, 118
Bush, George W.   101, 108–10
Butter, Michael   149

Calvo, Edmond-François   32
Canavan, Gerry   12
Carlyle, Thomas   16, 60–5
Carr, E. H.   119
Celan, Paul   6
Cesarani, David   38
Chabon, Michael   16, 17, 72, 88–97
Chandler, Raymond   17, 123
Charnay, David   75
Chelmno   8, 157, 194n
chess   90–1, 94
Christians   7, 21, 23, 34, 140–2
Christie, Agatha   115
Churchill, Caryl   139
Churchill, Winston   7, 24, 28, 51, 61, 107, 112–13, 115
Clute, John   118–20, 186n
Cohen, Arthur A.   126
Conrad, Joseph   80–1
Constantine, Murray. *See* Burdekin, Katharine
counterfactualism   38, 53–4, 60, 66, 83, 104–5, 119, 128–9
Coward, Noël   27–9

Cox, Jo 144
Crossley, Robert 24

Dachau 155–6
Dahl, Roald 119
Deighton, Len 168n
Derrida, Jacques 2
detective fiction 89–95, 97, 101, 114–18, 123, 128
Dick, Philip K. 15–16, 36, 38, 42–50, 68, 173n
    Exegesis 46
Dickens, Charles 120
Dimond, Anthony J. 89
Dinur, Yehiel. See Ka-Tzetnik
Doctorow, Cory 121
Doctor Who: The Shadow in the Glass 74

Eaglestone, Robert 160
Easterman, Dennis 103
Edward VIII, King (Duke of Windsor) 111–13, 119, 184n
Eichmann, Adolf 16, 74, 130
    Trial of 15, 39–40, 75, 83, 125, 171n, 178n, 188n
Elizabeth II, Queen 119
Englander, Nathan 88
Evans, Richard J. 60–1, 83
evil 6, 11, 15, 18, 28, 37, 49, 52–3, 57, 77–8, 80, 92, 109, 115, 118, 143, 145, 153–4, 159
    absolute or epitome of 41–2, 55, 59, 68–9, 76, 78, 87, 148–50
    banality 84, 130
Ezrahi, Sidra DeKoven 165n

fairy tale 119, 157, 194n
fantasy 1, 11–12, 33, 48, 75, 78–9, 86, 124–5, 130–3, 148–58
    historical 14, 38, 154
Felman, Shoshana 158
Ferguson, Niall 60
Finkelstein, Norman 81–2, 132
First World War, The 7, 27, 37, 98, 111, 112, 129, 182n
Forester, C. S. 14, 33
Frank, Anne 17, 72, 84–9, 98, 104, 170n
Franklin, Ruth 5, 147
Freud, Sigmund
    and *durcharbeiten* or 'working through' 1
    Moses and Monotheism 140
    and *Nachträgichkeit* or 'afterwardsness' 29
Friedländer, Saul 5, 7
Fry, Stephen 16, 38, 42, 59–69, 119, 122
    Moab is My Washpot 67

Gallagher, Catherine 110
genocide
    'crime without a name' 7
    Other than the Holocaust 8, 9, 81, 87, 122, 143, 160
Ghetto 8–9, 40, 51, 92, 127
Goebbels, Joseph 37, 130
Goldhagen, Daniel Jonah 16, 65–7, 122
Goldstein, Lisa 149–52, 156
golem 151
Gomel, Elana 99
graphic novels and comic books 32, 85, 105, 111, 170n
Great Depression 63, 98, 112
Gröning, Oskar 179n
Gross Rosen 156
Gypsies. See Romani and Sinti

Hambly, Barbara 152–9
Hammett, Dashiell 17
hardboiled crime 17, 95. See also Chandler, Raymond; detective fiction
Harris, Robert 15–16, 42, 50–9, 68
    Archangel 172n
Hartland, Dan 121, 185n
Hartman, Geoffrey 164n
Hellekson, Karen 49, 55, 66–7, 153
Hess, Rudolph 113, 130, 187n
Heydrich, Reinhard 52, 54, 57, 130
Heyer, Heather 144
Hilberg, Raul 7
Himmelfarb, Milton 130
Himmler, Heinrich 39, 71, 130
Historians' Debate (*Historikerstreit*) 68
history
    backward-facing angel of 60
    'great men' models of 16, 65, 189n
    social concepts of historicity 43–4
Hitler, Adolf 5, 16, 30, 34, 35, 59, 66, 87, 98, 102, 113, 133

assassination of 26, 99
  clone 76–8
  Mein Kampf 19–21
  Never Born 63–5
  On trial 34, 74–5, 79, 81–3, 88, 98
  as Private Eye 123–32
Hitzinger, Heinrich 71
Holocaust, the
  in Africa 44–6, 50, 167n
  as another universe 2, 10, 131
  denial of 54, 68, 99
  as earthquake 2, 6, 164n
  and language 2, 4, 6, 26, 125–6, 135–6
  non-Jewish victims 8, 10, 94, 165n
    (*see also* Romani and Sinti)
  other names for the Holocaust 90, 164n
  and poetry 5–6, 91, 118, 147, 159
  post-survivor era 3, 9, 13–14, 101, 158, 159
  uniqueness 1, 8, 15–16, 87, 100, 149, 159
  in the United States 39
homosexuality 8, 9, 16, 65, 94, 111, 115, 160, 167n
humour 17, 40, 67, 128, 133

I, James Blunt 24
I Ching 47–9, 173n
Ickes, Harold 89
If Hitler Comes: A Cautionary Tale.
  See *Loss of Eden*
Ilsa, She Wolf of the SS 128
Indiana Jones and the Raiders of the Lost Ark 74, 155, 177n
Ishiguro, Kazuo 116
Islamophobia 121–2. See also Muslims
Israel 3, 15, 40, 45, 79, 82, 88, 93–7, 114, 138, 139

Jacobson, Howard 17, 102, 132–44
  'When Will Jews be Forgiven the Holocaust?' 138, 140, 143
Jameson, Fredric 148
Jews. *See also* anti-Semitism; Israel; rabbi; Yiddish
  dehumanisation of 19, 23, 31–2, 134–5, 154

Wandering Jew, the 33–6
Jones, Diana Wynne 33

Kafka, Franz 10–11, 163n, 166n, 180n
Katyn Forest Massacre 52–3, 68
Katz, Steven T. 8
Ka-Tzetnik 124–5, 127, 188n
Kerman, Judith 150
Kincaid, Paul 121
Koch, Edward "Ed" 85
Koch, Ilse 128
Kornbluth, Cyril M. 33, 36–7
Kremer, S. Lillian 40, 83, 158
Kristallnacht 19, 134
Kubert, Jo 105
Ku Klux Klan 103, 106, 109
Kurtz, Katherine 156

LaCapra, Dominick 68
Lafferty, R. A. 98–9, 149
Laks, Szymon 13, 50
Lang, Berel 7
Langer, Lawrence 85, 166n, 192n
Lanzmann, Claude 165n
Leibniz, Gottfried 37
Levi, Primo 20, 29–30, 77, 124–7, 135–6, 147
Levin, Ira 16, 72–9
Levin, Nora 125
Levinas, Emmanuel 2
Lewis, Sinclair 103
Leys, Ruth 160
Lindbergh, Charles 101–10, 120, 133
Lisbon Earthquake (1755) 6, 37
London, Jack 102
Loss of Eden 25–6
Luckhurst, Roger 149
Luther, Martin 66
Lyotard, Jean-François 6. See also Holocaust, as earthquake

MacLeod, Ian R. 111
magic 148–59
Majdanek 8, 56, 191n
Malzberg, Barry 75
Maritain, Jacques 140
Mengele, Josef 16, 72–8, 125
Millu, Liana 30
Milner, Andrew 166n

Mimetic. *See* realism
Mitford Sisters   118
Moby Dick   136
Mosley, Oswald   111–13, 120, 129–30, 133, 187n
Muslims   9, 93, 122. *See also* Islamophobia

Nazi/Nazism
   and fetishism   14, 31, 33, 98, 128
   Fourth Reich   73–4, 76
   'good Nazi' the   148
   Nazisploitation   15, 128
   occultism   74, 149, 153, 177n
   Senior figures in Latin America   39, 71, 73, 78–84
   war crime trials   179n (*see also* Eichmann, Trial of; Hitler, on trial; Nuremberg Trials)
   zombies   149
Niemöller, Martin   118
Novick, Peter   3–4, 8, 39–40
nuclear weapons
   Hiroshima   37, 81, 98
   Manhattan Project   36–7, 64
   nuclear bombing of Berlin   90
   nuclear war   43, 50
Nuremberg Trials   7, 8, 53, 71, 75, 170n

Orwell, George   24–5, 43, 51, 126, 168n, 173n
Ozick, Cynthia   5

Palestine   82, 93, 96, 98, 131, 139, 152
Patai, Daphne   22
Porajmos   8, 164n. *See also* Romani and Sinti
Priest, Christopher   187n
Protocols of the Elders of Zion, The   19–20, 25, 93

Raczymow, Henri   86
Radin, Max   74
realism   2, 9–13, 78, 85–6, 113, 122, 124, 126, 143, 148, 151, 157, 159–61
   magic   158
   traumatic   9–10
Rieder, John   48
Roberts, Andrew   60

Romani and Sinti   8, 37, 154, 155, 164n, 167n
Roosevelt, Franklin D.   43, 89, 101, 103, 106–7, 112
Rosenbaum, Thane   91
Rosenfeld, Alvin H.   1, 4, 7
Rosenfeld, Gavriel D.   23, 35, 38, 55, 65, 74–5, 79, 82, 108, 122, 130
Roth, Philip   17, 101–11, 113, 118, 120, 122, 123, 144
   American Pastoral   102
   Ghost Writer   85–6, 88
   '"I Always Wanted You to Admire My Fasting"; or, Looking at Kafka'   180n
Rothberg, Michael   9–10, 29
Rousset, David   10, 166n
Rovner, Adam   182n
Rowling, J. K.   79, 178n
Rubenstein, Richard   91

Sansom, C. J.   187n
Sarban   14, 30–3, 37
Sargent, Pamela   44
Saville, Guy   45
Saxena, Vandana   157
Sayers, Dorothy   115
Schaub, Michael   109
Schiff, Hilda   159
Schlegel, Friedrich   60
Shaykevitch, Nokhem-Meyer   124
Sheers, Owen   168n
Shirer, William L.   14, 38–9
shund   124–5, 127, 187n
Sicher, Efraim   82
silence   4, 5, 6, 15, 79, 80, 161. *See also* Holocaust and language
   myth of   15, 25–40
Skibell, Joseph   158
Snyder, Timothy   9
Sobibor   8, 56, 73
Solzhenitsyn, Aleksandr   81
Sontag, Susan   57, 160
Speer, Albert   58, 112
Spiegelman, Art   32, 85
Spinrad, Norman   98, 123
Stalin, Joseph   52–4, 64, 71, 81–2, 87, 166n, 179n
Stangl, Franz   73

Steiner, George 6, 16, 72, 79–84, 86, 166n
Stinson, J. G. 118, 121
Superman: War of the Worlds 111
Suvin, Darko 11–13

Taylor, D. J. 184n
Tey, Josephine 113, 115
Thomas, D. M. 2
Thomas, Dylan 133
Tidhar, Lavie 2, 17, 18, 102, 123–32, 144
  'Uganda' 96
  Unholy Land 96–7
trauma 1, 7–8, 29, 91, 93, 95, 98, 101, 104, 108, 122, 132, 156–61. See also Freud, Sigmund
  cultural 73, 100
  trauma fiction 2, 13 (*see also* realism)
Treblinka 9, 73, 117, 148, 191n
Trump, Donald J. 18, 101, 144, 183n
Turtledove, Harry 111
Tuttle, Lisa 183n

United Kingdom 17, 25, 29, 44, 53, 64, 84, 102, 122–3, 129, 143, 156
  as ally to Nazi Germany 20, 45, 101, 108, 111–13, 187n (*see also* Mosley, Oswald)
  broken up 133
  complicit in Genocide 143, 172n
  departure from European Union (*see* Brexit)
  "finest hour" 122
  'go home' vans 138
  Holocaust memory in 4, 19
  occupied by Germany 21–9, 168n
United States 14, 17, 25, 29, 63, 65, 72, 78, 82–4, 89, 94–6, 103, 105–11, 122, 143, 180n. See also Lindburgh, Charles; nuclear weapons, Manhattan Project; Roosevelt, Franklin D.; Trump, Donald J.; Vietnam War
  genocide in 17, 143
  Holocaust memory in 3, 19
  isolationist 102–4
  Pearl Harbour 44, 104, 107
  President Joseph P. Kennedy 53–4
  occupied by Axis Powers 36–9, 42–50
  relations with Native Americans 17, 92–6

van Rjndt, Phillipe 75
Vietnam War 40, 81

Wagner, Wilhelm Richard 136, 141
Walters, Guy 111–13, 120
Walton, Jo 17, 101, 108, 113–23, 144
  'Still Life With Fascists' 117–18
Waxman, Zoë Vania 13
Weil, Ellen R. 151
Weissman, Gary 156
Wells, H. G. 111
Wheatley, Dennis 156
Wiesel, Elie 2–3, 5, 10, 16, 40, 66, 91, 125–6, 147–8, 150, 158, 171n
Wiesenthal, Simon 73, 76
Wilkomirski 165n, 199n–200n
Wisse, Ruth 87
Wolfe, Gary K. 157
Women. See also Frank, Anne
  Holocaust victims 5, 14, 24, 30, 51, 53, 55, 154, 160, 194n
  and Nazi ideology 21, 22, 23
  violence towards 22, 23, 31–3
Wordsworth, William 33–4
Wyndham, John 30–1, 74, 115

Yiddish 90–5, 103, 136–7, 149, 158, 171n. See also Holocaust and language; Jews; *shund*
Yolen Jane 158, 194n
  Briar Rose 157
  Devil's Arithmetic, The 135, 156
  Mapping the Bones 194n
Young, James 132, 164n
Young, Michael 34, 74
Yulsman, Jerry 99, 149

Zafke, Huber 179
Žižek, Slavoj 10
Zugzwang 94. *See also* chess

www.ingramcontent.com/pod-product-compliance
Lightning Source LLC
Chambersburg PA
CBHW052040300426
44117CB00012B/1911